Dykes To Watch Out For
THE SEQUEL

ADDED ATTRACTION! "SERIAL MONOGAMY"—A DOCUMENTARY

The author would like to thank Lyn Oligino, Judith Katz, Sara Van Arsdale, and her publisher, Nancy K. Bereano, for their support and criticism. Also, all her friends in Minneapolis and Burlington, the generous women who consulted with her on various issues, and the many remarkable women she's met on her travels.

Alison Bechdel's cartoons appear regularly in more than forty publications in the United States and Canada.

Cover Design by Tom Devlin

Printed in Canada

Library of Congress Card No. 92-4452

Dykes To Watch Out For
THE SEQUEL

ADDED ATTRACTION! "SERIAL MONOGAMY"—A DOCUMENTARY

by Alison Bechdel

Firebrand
Books

Starring...

FASTER THAN A SPEEDING BULLET (AT MAKING JUDGMENTS)... A WHINE MORE POWERFUL THAN A LOCOMOTIVE'S... ABLE TO LEAP TO DRASTIC CONCLUSIONS IN A SINGLE BOUND... LOOK! SLUMPED IN THE CHAIR! IT'S A NERD! IT'S A PAIN!

IT'S **MO!** OUR PRINCIPLED ANTI-HEROINE FIGHTS A NEVER-ENDING BATTLE FOR TRUTH, JUSTICE, AND OTHER UNAMERICAN WAYS.

BY DAY, MO'S LOVELY CONSORT TOILS QUIETLY FOR THE STATE DEPARTMENT OF HUMAN RIGHTS.

BUT IS ALL AS TRANQUIL AS IT **SEEMS** WITH HARRIET?

WHAT HIDDEN SORROWS, WHAT LOFTY THOUGHTS, WHAT SUBLIME YEARNINGS SEETHE BENEATH HER IMPERTURBABLE SURFACE?

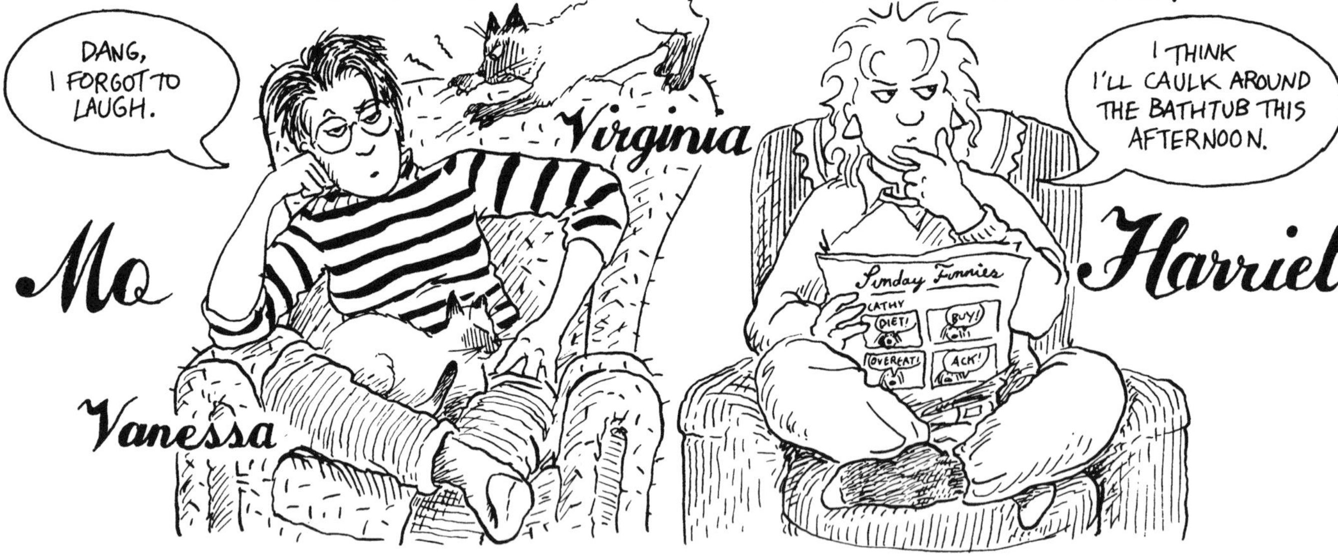
DANG, I FORGOT TO LAUGH.
Virginia
Mo
Vanessa
I THINK I'LL CAULK AROUND THE BATHTUB THIS AFTERNOON.
Harriet
Sunday Funnies
CATHY
DIET!
BUY!
OVEREAT!
ACK!

AH, OUR HOPELESSLY HETEROGENEOUS HOUSEMATES! THE SENSUAL LOIS . . . THE TRANSCENDENTAL SPARROW . . . THE RATIONAL GINGER.

THANKS TO THE DEEP PERSONAL RESPECT WHICH UNDERLIES THEIR IDEOLOGICAL AND STYLISTIC DIFFERENCES, THIS VOLATILE TRIO MANAGES TO LIVE TOGETHER QUITE PEACEFULLY.

ON OCCASION.

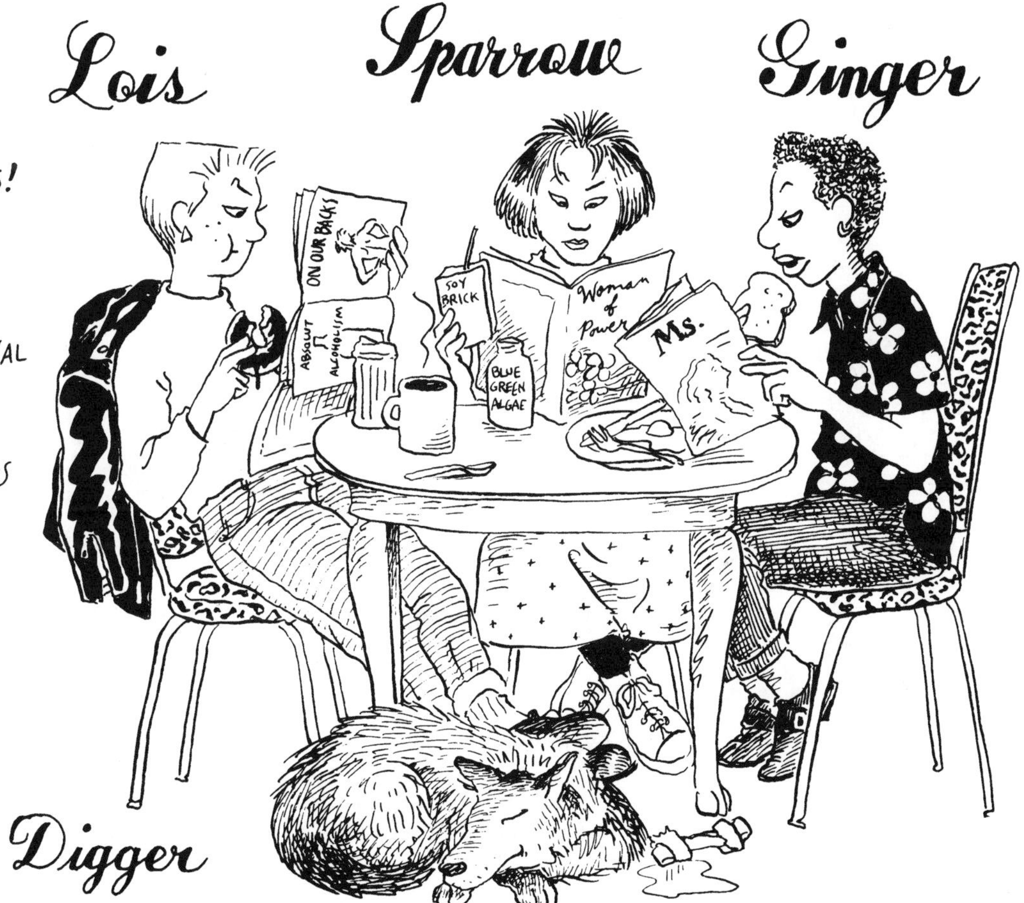
Lois
Sparrow
Ginger
ON OUR BACKS
ABSOLUT
ALCOHOLISM
SOY BRICK
Woman of Power
Ms.
BLUE GREEN ALGAE
Digger

STILL PASSIONATE AFTER ALL THESE YEARS! AS OUR EXEMPLARY COUPLE NEARS THEIR TENTH ANNIVERSARY, IT LOOKS LIKE THEIR SEX LIFE IS ALIVE AND WELL.

WHATEVER. WITH CLARICE BEGINNING HER LAW CAREER AND TONI PLANNING IMMINENT INSEMINATION, THEY SEEM TO BE HURTLING HEADLONG INTO THE BRAVE, NEW WORLD OF LESBIAN NUCLEAR FAMILYHOOD — WATCH OUT, P.T.A.!

With...

Jezanna

THE SAVVY OWNER AND MANAGER OF THAT JUMPING CULTURAL HOT SPOT, MADWIMMIN BOOKS.

Emma

LOIS'S PROVOKINGLY PREOCCUPIED PARAMOUR.

Anya

MO'S THOROUGHLY THANKLESS THERAPIST.

and Introducing...

Yoshiko

LOIS'S QUEER NATION GAL PAL, AND GINGER'S FRESHMAN ENGLISH STUDENT.

YOU CALL THIS STORE ACCESSIBLE? NO WAY CAN A WOMAN IN A WHEELCHAIR REACH THE LESBIAN EROTICA BOOKS!

Thea

MADWIMMIN'S NEW EMPLOYEE

and Malika

I CAN'T WAIT!

GINGER'S PEN PAL!

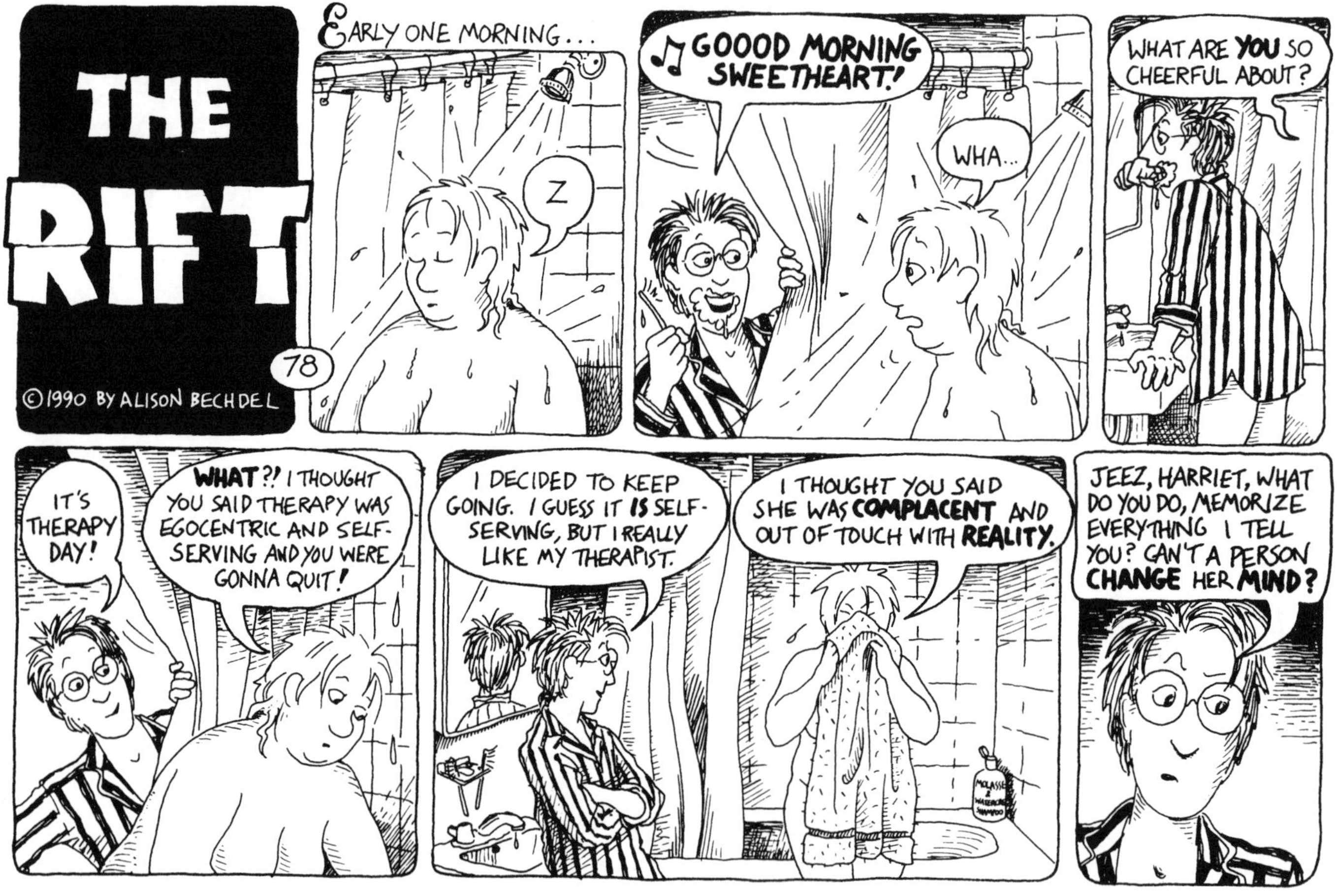
THE RIFT
78
©1990 BY ALISON BECHDEL
EARLY ONE MORNING...
Z
♫ GOOOD MORNING SWEETHEART!
WHA...
WHAT ARE YOU SO CHEERFUL ABOUT?
IT'S THERAPY DAY!
WHAT?! I THOUGHT YOU SAID THERAPY WAS EGOCENTRIC AND SELF-SERVING AND YOU WERE GONNA QUIT!
I DECIDED TO KEEP GOING. I GUESS IT IS SELF-SERVING, BUT I REALLY LIKE MY THERAPIST.
I THOUGHT YOU SAID SHE WAS COMPLACENT AND OUT OF TOUCH WITH REALITY.
JEEZ, HARRIET, WHAT DO YOU DO, MEMORIZE EVERYTHING I TELL YOU? CAN'T A PERSON CHANGE HER MIND?

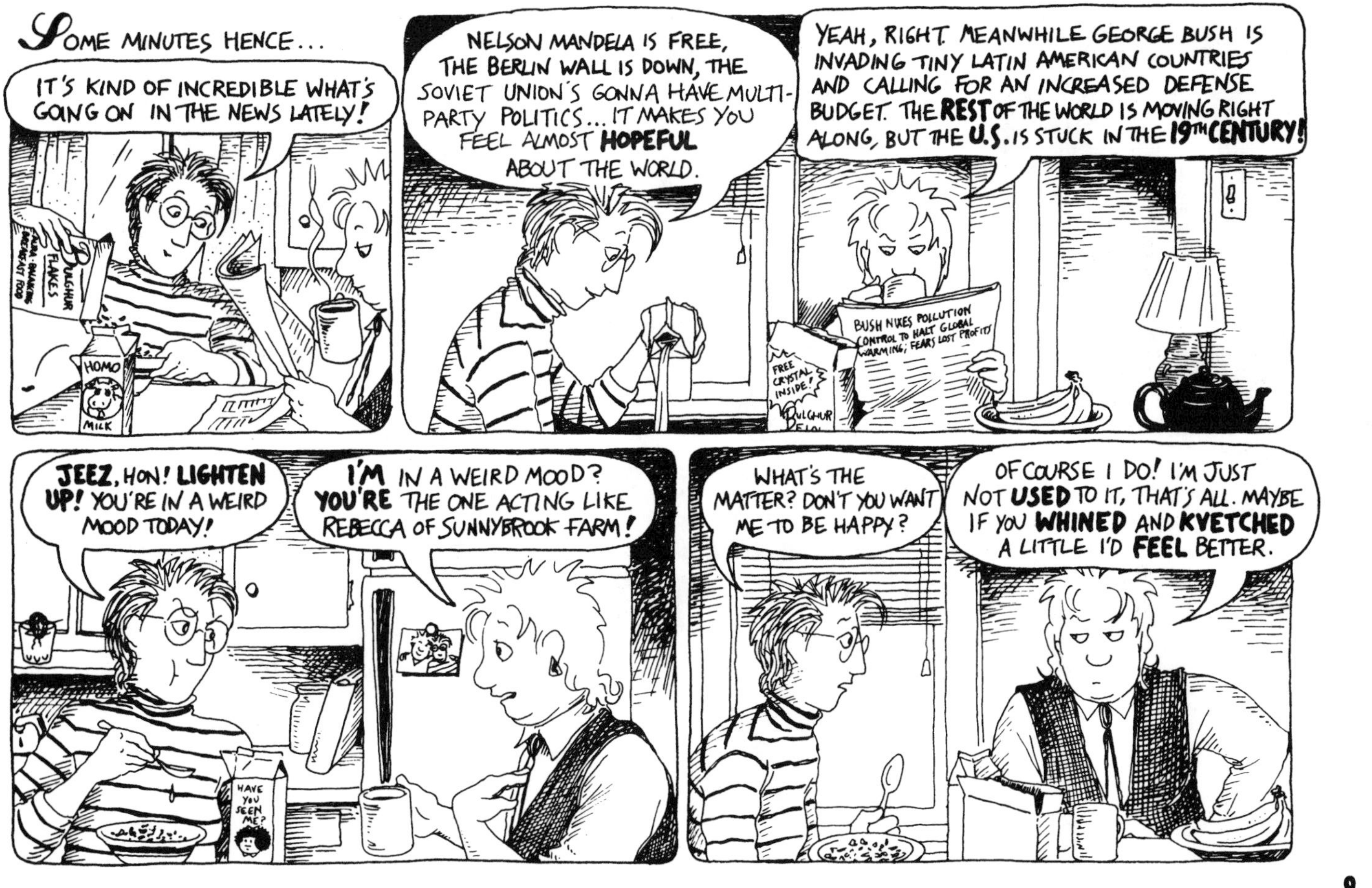
SOME MINUTES HENCE...
IT'S KIND OF INCREDIBLE WHAT'S GOING ON IN THE NEWS LATELY!
BULGHUR FLAKES
HOMO
MILK
NELSON MANDELA IS FREE, THE BERLIN WALL IS DOWN, THE SOVIET UNION'S GONNA HAVE MULTI-PARTY POLITICS... IT MAKES YOU FEEL ALMOST **HOPEFUL** ABOUT THE WORLD.
YEAH, RIGHT. MEANWHILE GEORGE BUSH IS INVADING TINY LATIN AMERICAN COUNTRIES AND CALLING FOR AN INCREASED DEFENSE BUDGET. THE **REST** OF THE WORLD IS MOVING RIGHT ALONG, BUT THE **U.S.** IS STUCK IN THE **19TH CENTURY!**
BUSH NIXES POLLUTION CONTROL TO HALT GLOBAL WARMING; FEARS LOST PROFITS
FREE CRYSTAL INSIDE!
JEEZ, HON! **LIGHTEN UP!** YOU'RE IN A WEIRD MOOD TODAY!
I'M IN A WEIRD MOOD? **YOU'RE** THE ONE ACTING LIKE REBECCA OF SUNNYBROOK FARM!
HAVE YOU SEEN ME?
WHAT'S THE MATTER? DON'T YOU WANT ME TO BE HAPPY?
OF COURSE I DO! I'M JUST NOT **USED** TO IT, THAT'S ALL. MAYBE IF YOU **WHINED** AND **KVETCHED** A LITTLE I'D **FEEL** BETTER.

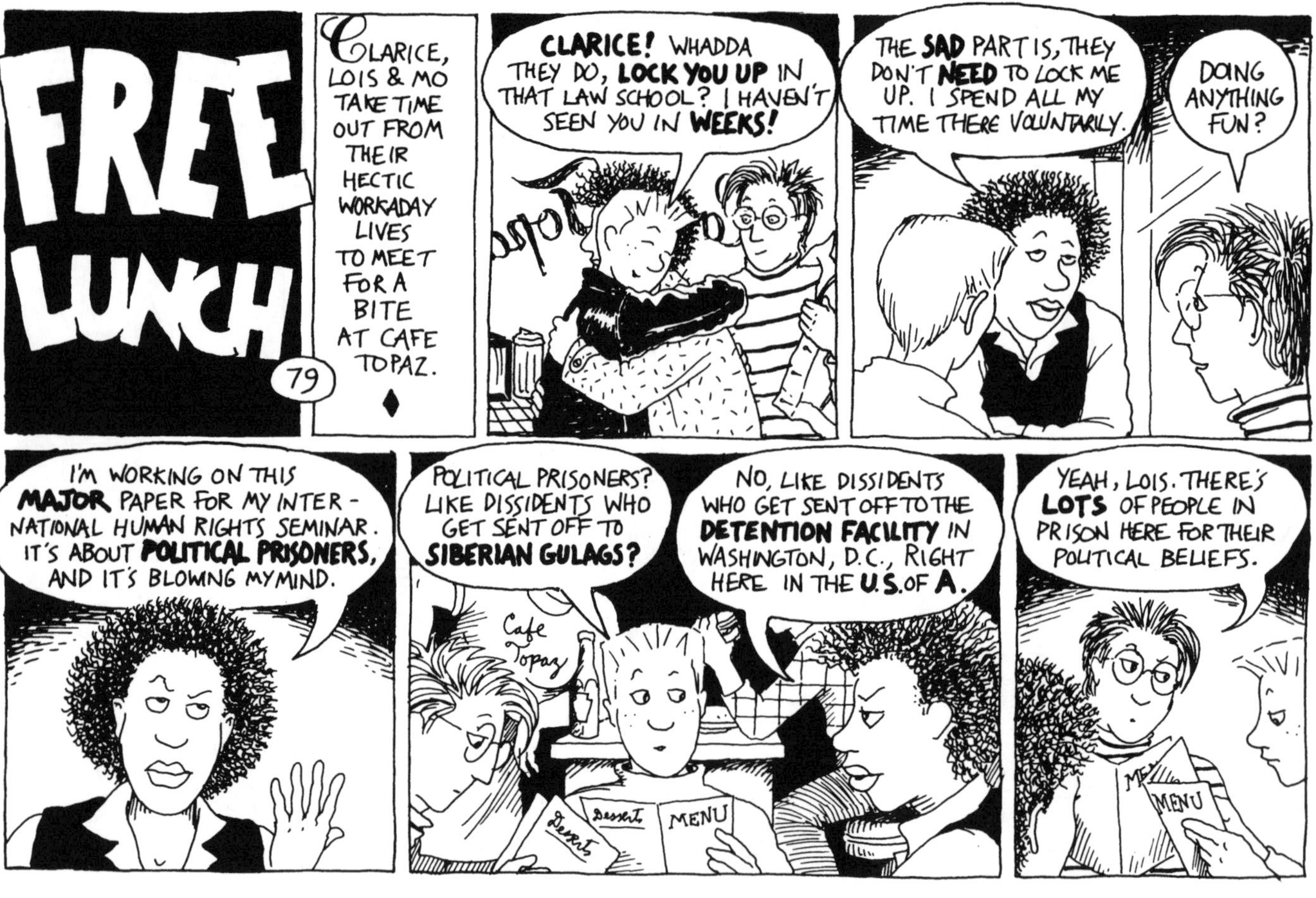
FREE LUNCH
79
CLARICE, LOIS & MO TAKE TIME OUT FROM THEIR HECTIC WORKADAY LIVES TO MEET FOR A BITE AT CAFE TOPAZ.
CLARICE! WHADDA THEY DO, LOCK YOU UP IN THAT LAW SCHOOL? I HAVEN'T SEEN YOU IN WEEKS!
THE SAD PART IS, THEY DON'T NEED TO LOCK ME UP. I SPEND ALL MY TIME THERE VOLUNTARILY.
DOING ANYTHING FUN?
I'M WORKING ON THIS MAJOR PAPER FOR MY INTER-NATIONAL HUMAN RIGHTS SEMINAR. IT'S ABOUT POLITICAL PRISONERS, AND IT'S BLOWING MY MIND.
POLITICAL PRISONERS? LIKE DISSIDENTS WHO GET SENT OFF TO SIBERIAN GULAGS?
Cafe Topaz
NO, LIKE DISSIDENTS WHO GET SENT OFF TO THE DETENTION FACILITY IN WASHINGTON, D.C., RIGHT HERE IN THE U.S. OF A.
Desserts
MENU
YEAH, LOIS. THERE'S LOTS OF PEOPLE IN PRISON HERE FOR THEIR POLITICAL BELIEFS.
MENU

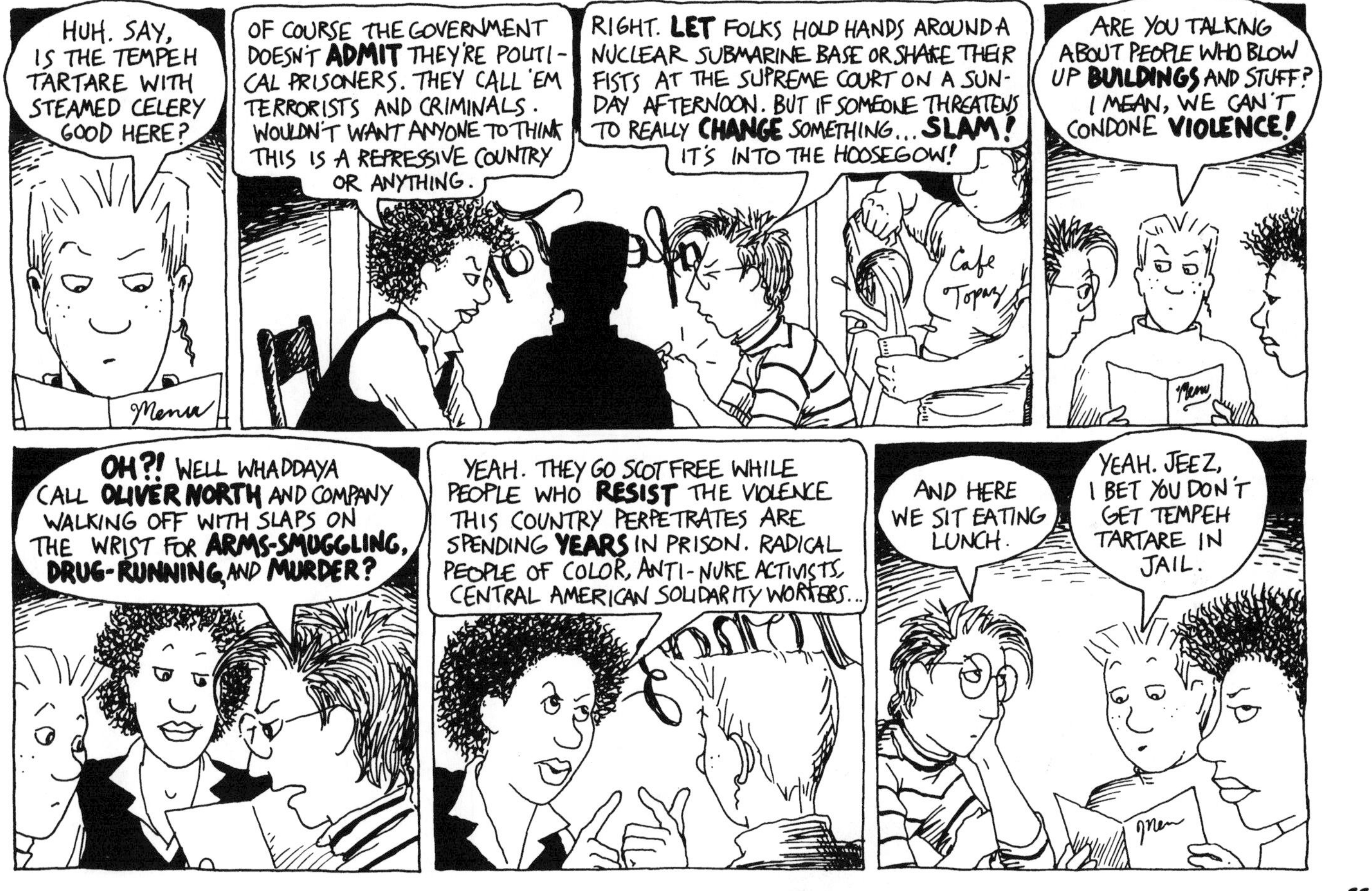

HUH. SAY, IS THE TEMPEH TARTARE WITH STEAMED CELERY GOOD HERE?
Menu
OF COURSE THE GOVERNMENT DOESN'T **ADMIT** THEY'RE POLITI-CAL PRISONERS. THEY CALL 'EM TERRORISTS AND CRIMINALS. WOULDN'T WANT ANYONE TO THINK THIS IS A REPRESSIVE COUNTRY OR ANYTHING.
RIGHT. **LET** FOLKS HOLD HANDS AROUND A NUCLEAR SUBMARINE BASE OR SHAKE THEIR FISTS AT THE SUPREME COURT ON A SUN-DAY AFTERNOON. BUT IF SOMEONE THREATENS TO REALLY **CHANGE** SOMETHING... **SLAM!** IT'S INTO THE HOOSEGOW!
Cafe Topaz
ARE YOU TALKING ABOUT PEOPLE WHO BLOW UP **BUILDINGS** AND STUFF? I MEAN, WE CAN'T CONDONE **VIOLENCE!**
Menu
OH?! WELL WHADDAYA CALL **OLIVER NORTH** AND COMPANY WALKING OFF WITH SLAPS ON THE WRIST FOR **ARMS-SMUGGLING, DRUG-RUNNING**, AND **MURDER?**
YEAH. THEY GO SCOT FREE WHILE PEOPLE WHO **RESIST** THE VIOLENCE THIS COUNTRY PERPETRATES ARE SPENDING **YEARS** IN PRISON. RADICAL PEOPLE OF COLOR, ANTI-NUKE ACTIVISTS, CENTRAL AMERICAN SOLIDARITY WORKERS...
AND HERE WE SIT EATING LUNCH.
YEAH. JEEZ, I BET YOU DON'T GET TEMPEH TARTARE IN JAIL.

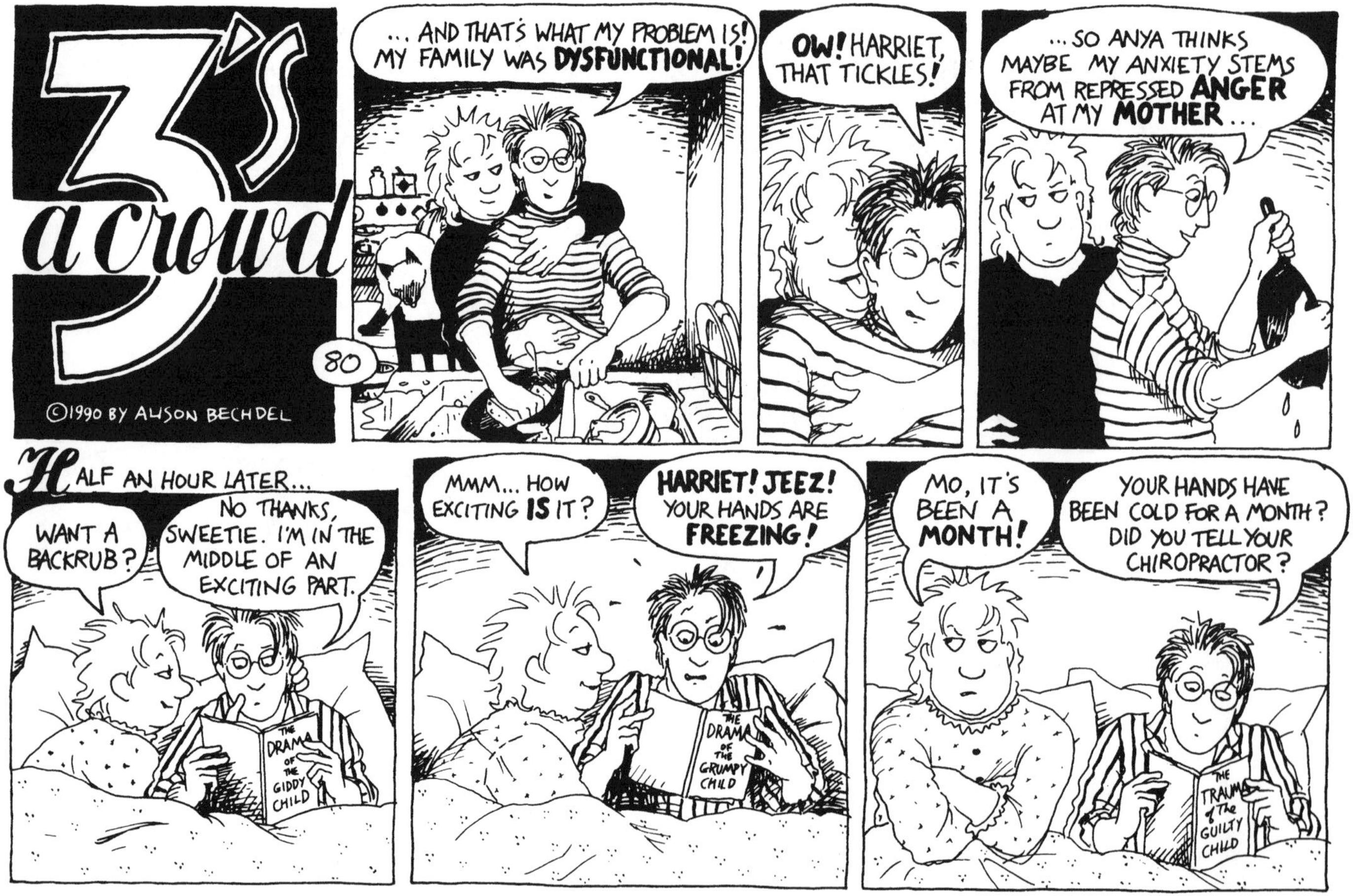
3's a crowd
80
©1990 BY ALISON BECHDEL
... AND THAT'S WHAT MY PROBLEM IS! MY FAMILY WAS DYSFUNCTIONAL!
OW! HARRIET, THAT TICKLES!
... SO ANYA THINKS MAYBE MY ANXIETY STEMS FROM REPRESSED ANGER AT MY MOTHER...
HALF AN HOUR LATER...
WANT A BACKRUB?
NO THANKS, SWEETIE. I'M IN THE MIDDLE OF AN EXCITING PART.
THE DRAMA OF THE GIDDY CHILD
MMM... HOW EXCITING IS IT?
HARRIET! JEEZ! YOUR HANDS ARE FREEZING!
THE DRAMA OF THE GRUMPY CHILD
MO, IT'S BEEN A MONTH!
YOUR HANDS HAVE BEEN COLD FOR A MONTH? DID YOU TELL YOUR CHIROPRACTOR?
THE TRAUMA of The GUILTY CHILD

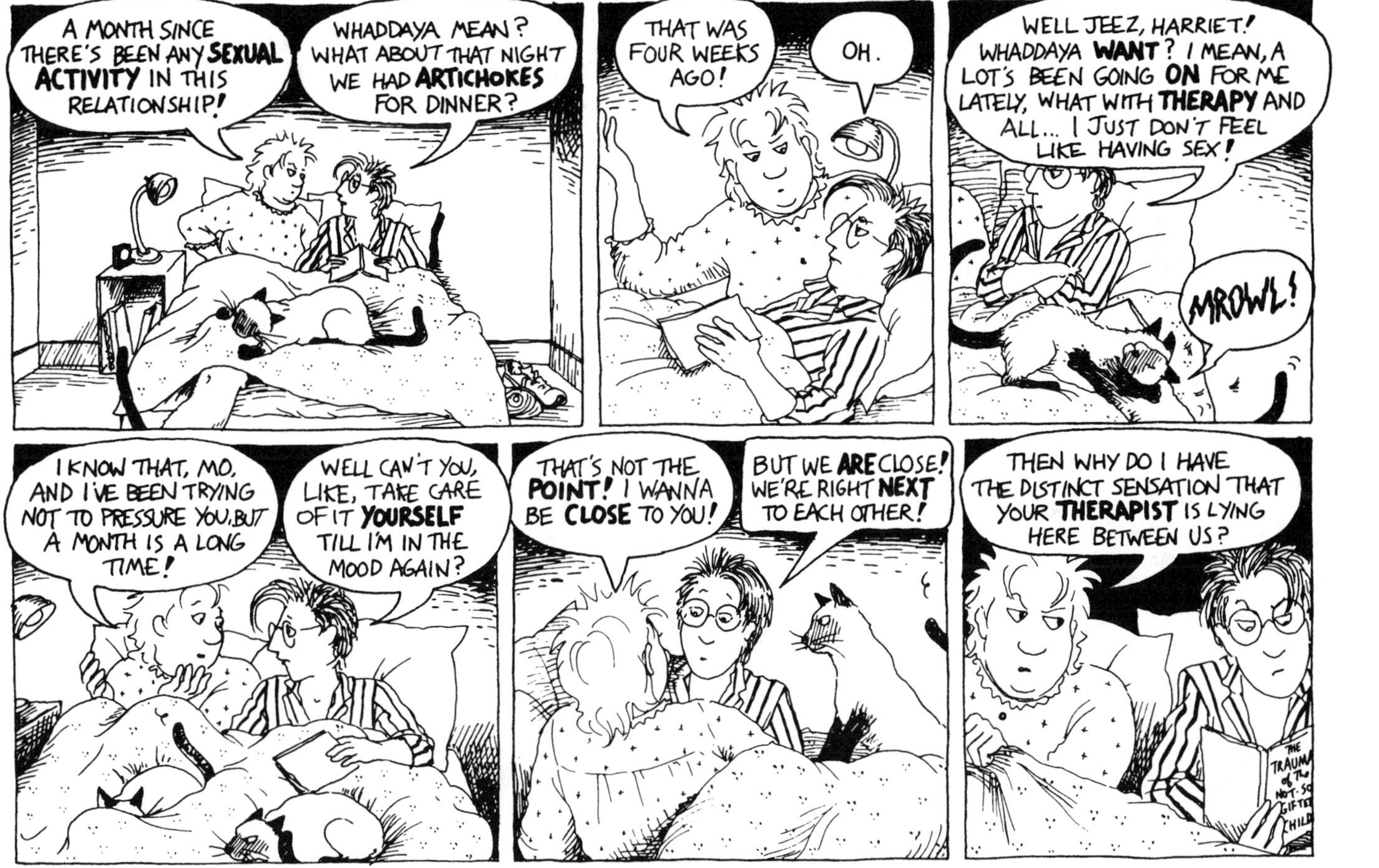
A MONTH SINCE THERE'S BEEN ANY **SEXUAL ACTIVITY** IN THIS RELATIONSHIP!
WHADDAYA MEAN? WHAT ABOUT THAT NIGHT WE HAD **ARTICHOKES** FOR DINNER?
THAT WAS FOUR WEEKS AGO!
OH.
WELL JEEZ, HARRIET! WHADDAYA **WANT**? I MEAN, A LOT'S BEEN GOING **ON** FOR ME LATELY, WHAT WITH **THERAPY** AND ALL... I JUST DON'T FEEL LIKE HAVING SEX!
MROWL!
I KNOW THAT, MO, AND I'VE BEEN TRYING NOT TO PRESSURE YOU. BUT A MONTH IS A LONG TIME!
WELL CAN'T YOU, LIKE, TAKE CARE OF IT **YOURSELF** TILL I'M IN THE MOOD AGAIN?
THAT'S NOT THE **POINT**! I WANNA BE **CLOSE** TO YOU!
BUT WE **ARE** CLOSE! WE'RE RIGHT **NEXT** TO EACH OTHER!
THEN WHY DO I HAVE THE DISTINCT SENSATION THAT YOUR **THERAPIST** IS LYING HERE BETWEEN US?

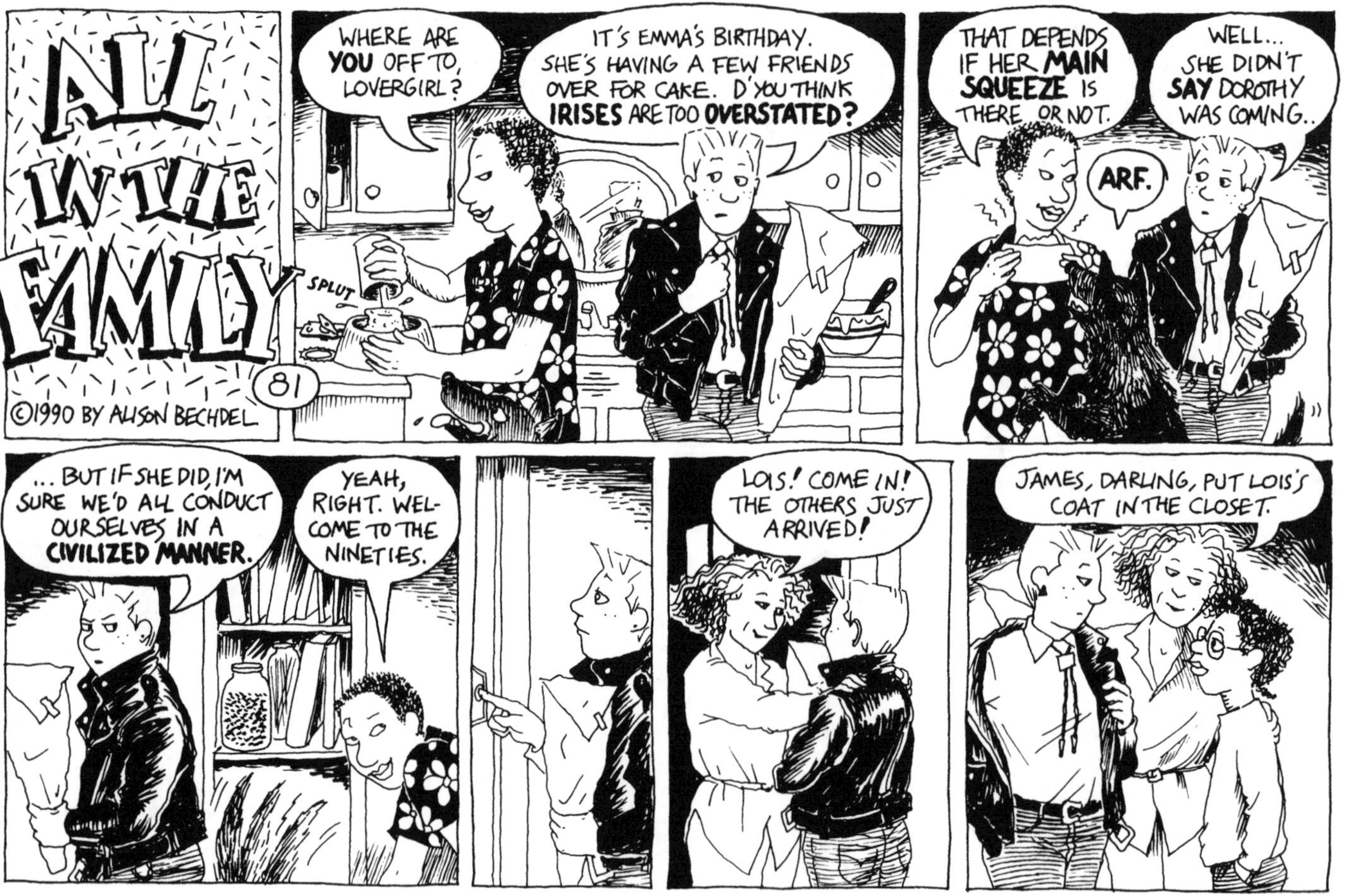
ALL IN THE FAMILY
81
©1990 BY ALISON BECHDEL
WHERE ARE YOU OFF TO, LOVERGIRL?
SPLUT
IT'S EMMA'S BIRTHDAY. SHE'S HAVING A FEW FRIENDS OVER FOR CAKE. D'YOU THINK IRISES ARE TOO OVERSTATED?
THAT DEPENDS IF HER MAIN SQUEEZE IS THERE OR NOT.
ARF.
WELL... SHE DIDN'T SAY DOROTHY WAS COMING..
... BUT IF SHE DID, I'M SURE WE'D ALL CONDUCT OURSELVES IN A CIVILIZED MANNER.
YEAH, RIGHT. WEL-COME TO THE NINETIES.
LOIS! COME IN! THE OTHERS JUST ARRIVED!
JAMES, DARLING, PUT LOIS'S COAT IN THE CLOSET.

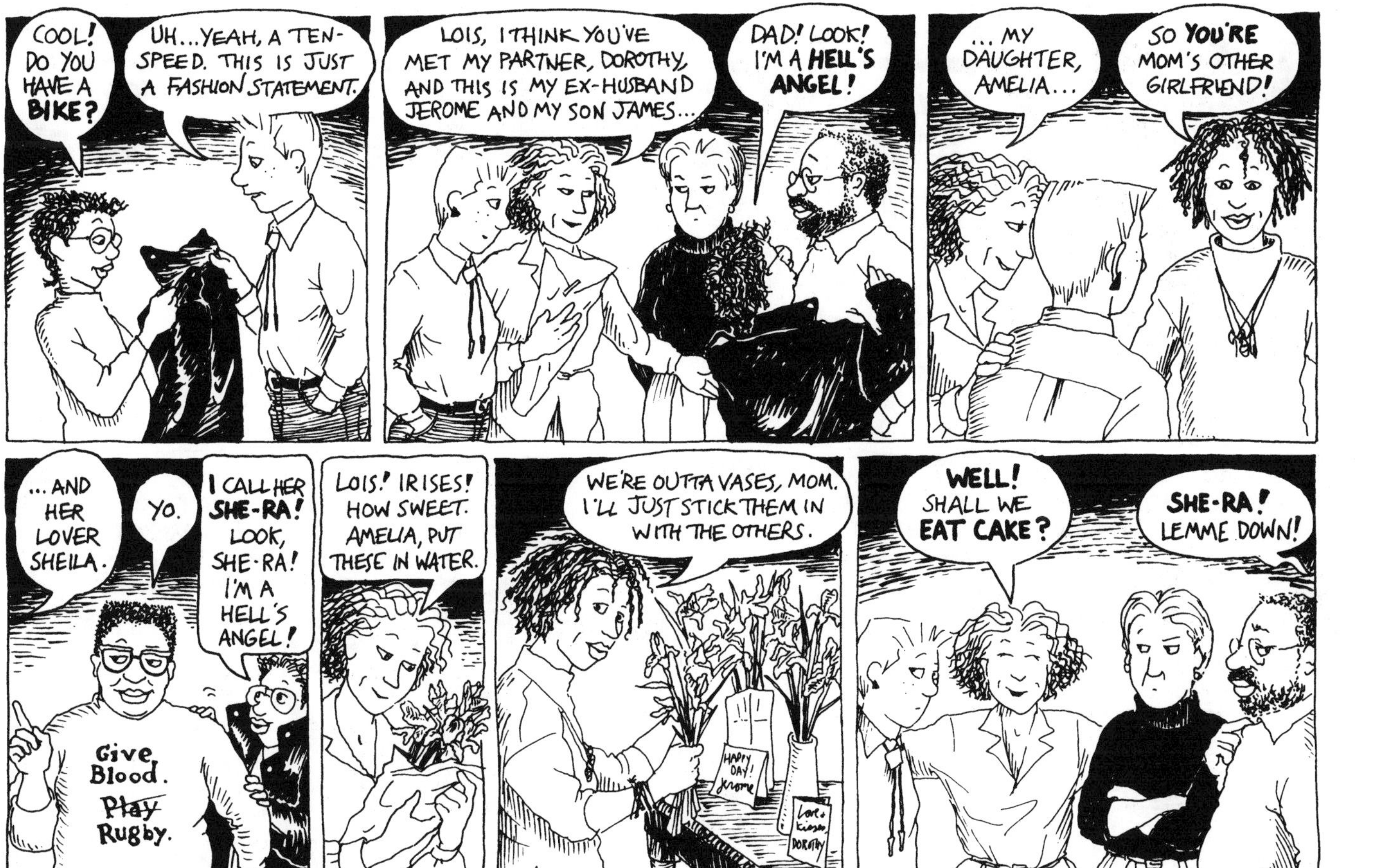
COOL! DO YOU HAVE A BIKE?
UH...YEAH, A TEN-SPEED. THIS IS JUST A FASHION STATEMENT.
LOIS, I THINK YOU'VE MET MY PARTNER, DOROTHY, AND THIS IS MY EX-HUSBAND JEROME AND MY SON JAMES...
DAD! LOOK! I'M A HELL'S ANGEL!
...MY DAUGHTER, AMELIA...
SO YOU'RE MOM'S OTHER GIRLFRIEND!
...AND HER LOVER SHEILA.
YO.
I CALL HER SHE-RA!
LOOK, SHE-RA! I'M A HELL'S ANGEL!
Give Blood.
Play
Rugby.
LOIS! IRISES! HOW SWEET. AMELIA, PUT THESE IN WATER.
WE'RE OUTTA VASES, MOM. I'LL JUST STICK THEM IN WITH THE OTHERS.
HAPPY DAY! Jerome
WELL! SHALL WE EAT CAKE?
SHE-RA! LEMME DOWN!

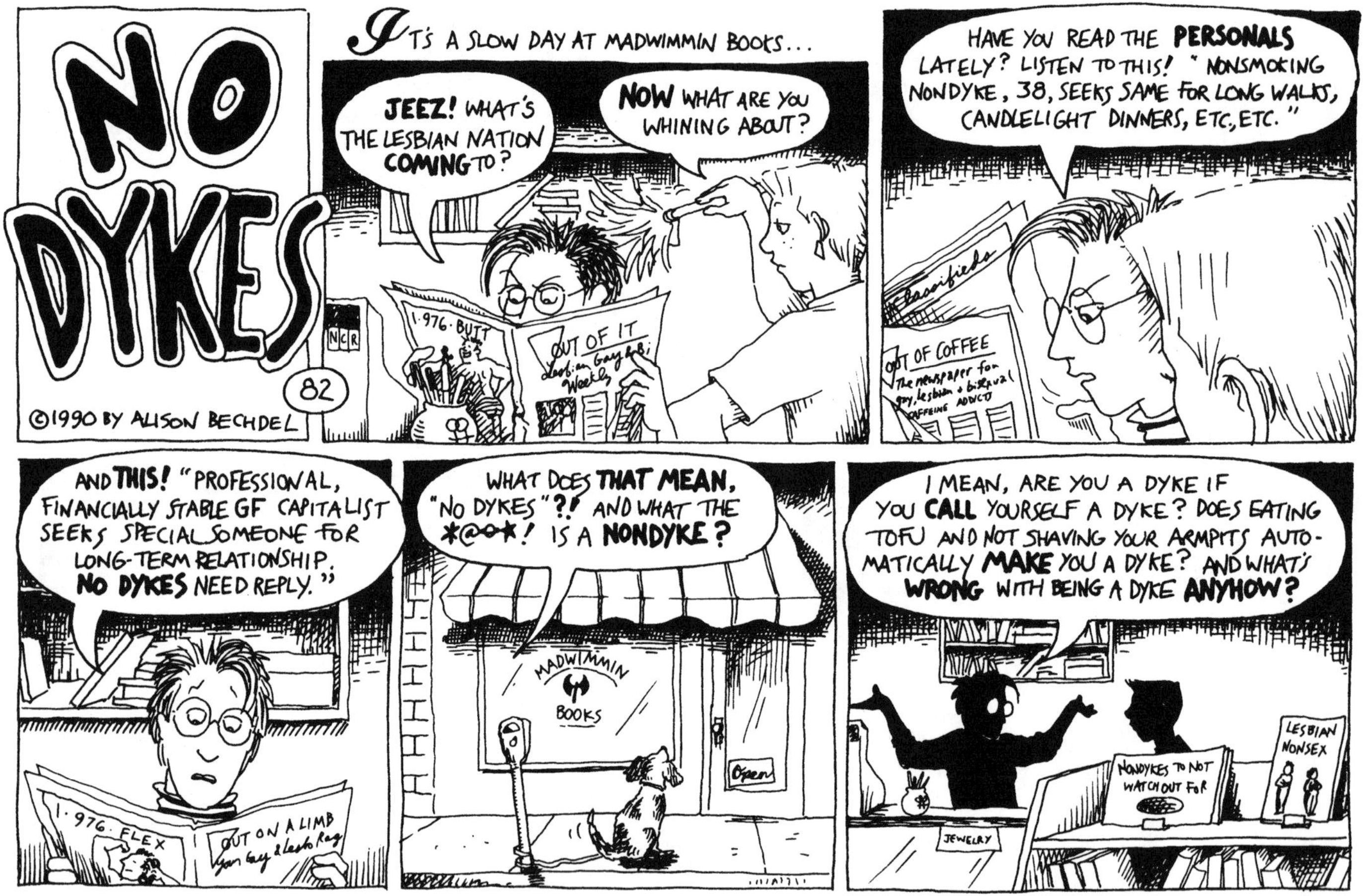
NO DYKES
82
©1990 BY ALISON BECHDEL
IT'S A SLOW DAY AT MADWIMMIN BOOKS...
JEEZ! WHAT'S THE LESBIAN NATION COMING TO?
NOW WHAT ARE YOU WHINING ABOUT?
OUT OF IT
1·976·BUTT
HAVE YOU READ THE PERSONALS LATELY? LISTEN TO THIS! "NONSMOKING NONDYKE, 38, SEEKS SAME FOR LONG WALKS, CANDLELIGHT DINNERS, ETC., ETC."
Classifieds
OUT OF COFFEE
AND THIS! "PROFESSIONAL, FINANCIALLY STABLE GF CAPITALIST SEEKS SPECIAL SOMEONE FOR LONG-TERM RELATIONSHIP. NO DYKES NEED REPLY."
OUT ON A LIMB
1·976·FLEX
WHAT DOES THAT MEAN, "NO DYKES"?! AND WHAT THE *@~*! IS A NONDYKE?
MADWIMMIN BOOKS
Open
I MEAN, ARE YOU A DYKE IF YOU CALL YOURSELF A DYKE? DOES EATING TOFU AND NOT SHAVING YOUR ARMPITS AUTOMATICALLY MAKE YOU A DYKE? AND WHAT'S WRONG WITH BEING A DYKE ANYHOW?
NONDYKES TO NOT WATCH OUT FOR
LESBIAN NONSEX
JEWELRY

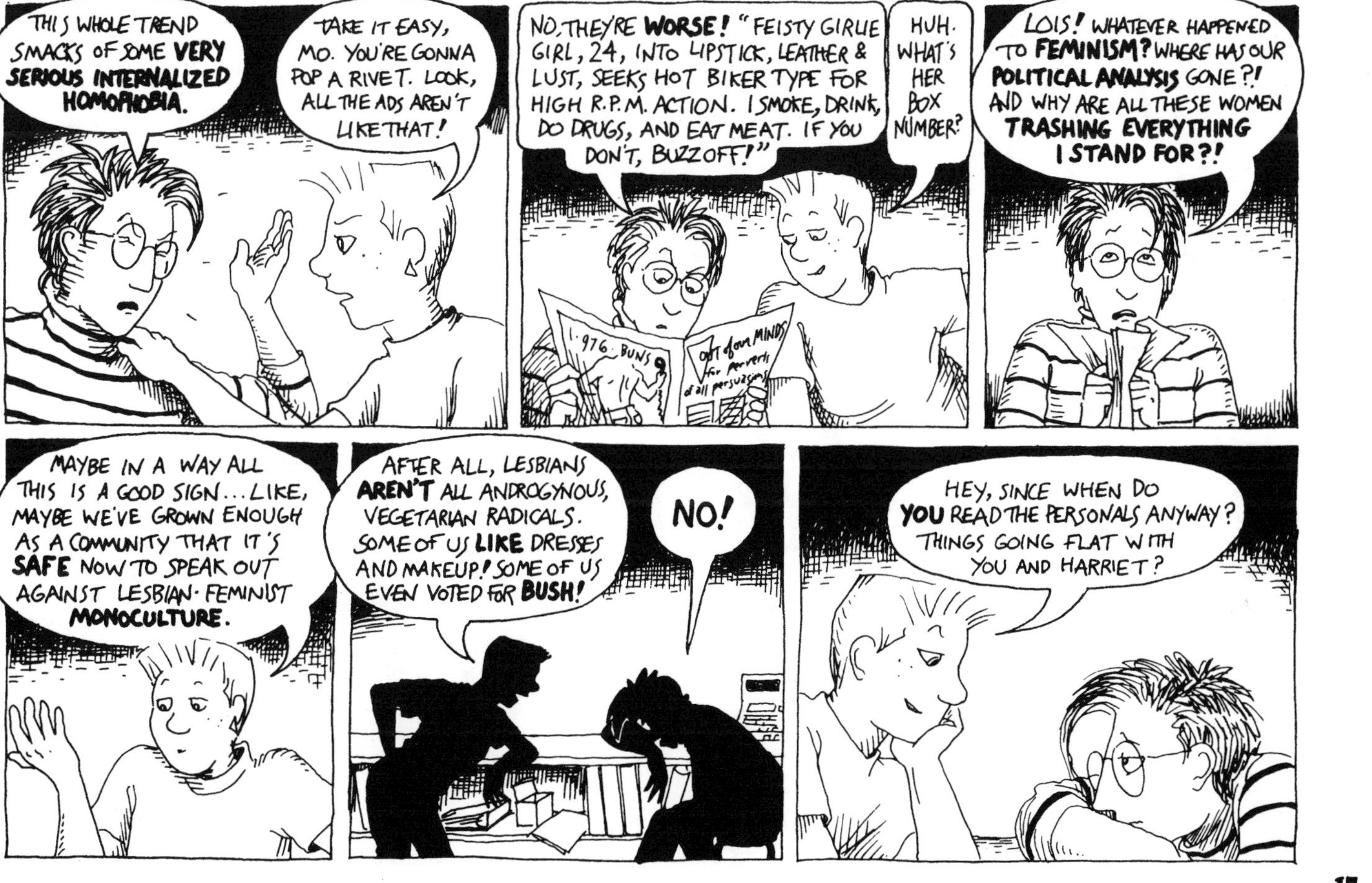
THIS WHOLE TREND SMACKS OF SOME **VERY SERIOUS INTERNALIZED HOMOPHOBIA.**
TAKE IT EASY, MO. YOU'RE GONNA POP A RIVET. LOOK, ALL THE ADS AREN'T LIKE THAT!
NO, THEY'RE **WORSE!** "FEISTY GIRLIE GIRL, 24, INTO LIPSTICK, LEATHER & LUST, SEEKS HOT BIKER TYPE FOR HIGH R.P.M. ACTION. I SMOKE, DRINK, DO DRUGS, AND EAT MEAT. IF YOU DON'T, BUZZ OFF!"
HUH. WHAT'S HER BOX NUMBER?
LOIS! WHATEVER HAPPENED TO **FEMINISM?** WHERE HAS OUR **POLITICAL ANALYSIS** GONE?! AND WHY ARE ALL THESE WOMEN **TRASHING EVERYTHING I STAND FOR?!**
MAYBE IN A WAY ALL THIS IS A GOOD SIGN... LIKE, MAYBE WE'VE GROWN ENOUGH AS A COMMUNITY THAT IT'S **SAFE** NOW TO SPEAK OUT AGAINST LESBIAN-FEMINIST **MONOCULTURE.**
AFTER ALL, LESBIANS **AREN'T** ALL ANDROGYNOUS, VEGETARIAN RADICALS. SOME OF US **LIKE** DRESSES AND MAKEUP! SOME OF US EVEN VOTED FOR **BUSH!**
NO!
HEY, SINCE WHEN DO **YOU** READ THE PERSONALS ANYWAY? THINGS GOING FLAT WITH YOU AND HARRIET?

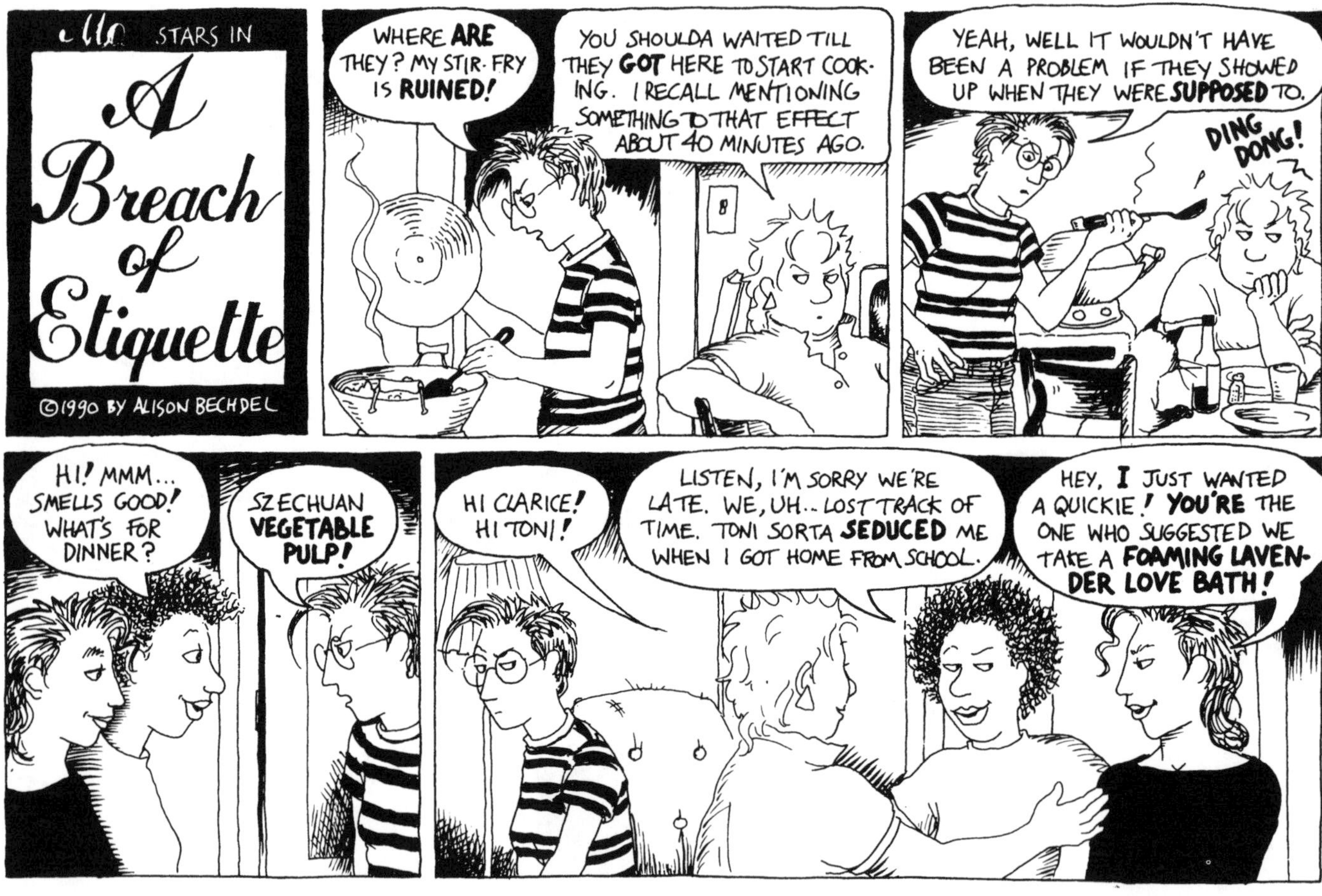
STARS IN
A Breach of Etiquette
©1990 BY ALISON BECHDEL
WHERE ARE THEY? MY STIR-FRY IS RUINED!
YOU SHOULDA WAITED TILL THEY GOT HERE TO START COOKING. I RECALL MENTIONING SOMETHING TO THAT EFFECT ABOUT 40 MINUTES AGO.
YEAH, WELL IT WOULDN'T HAVE BEEN A PROBLEM IF THEY SHOWED UP WHEN THEY WERE SUPPOSED TO.
DING DONG!
HI! MMM... SMELLS GOOD! WHAT'S FOR DINNER?
SZECHUAN VEGETABLE PULP!
HI CLARICE! HI TONI!
LISTEN, I'M SORRY WE'RE LATE. WE, UH.. LOST TRACK OF TIME. TONI SORTA SEDUCED ME WHEN I GOT HOME FROM SCHOOL.
HEY, I JUST WANTED A QUICKIE! YOU'RE THE ONE WHO SUGGESTED WE TAKE A FOAMING LAVENDER LOVE BATH!

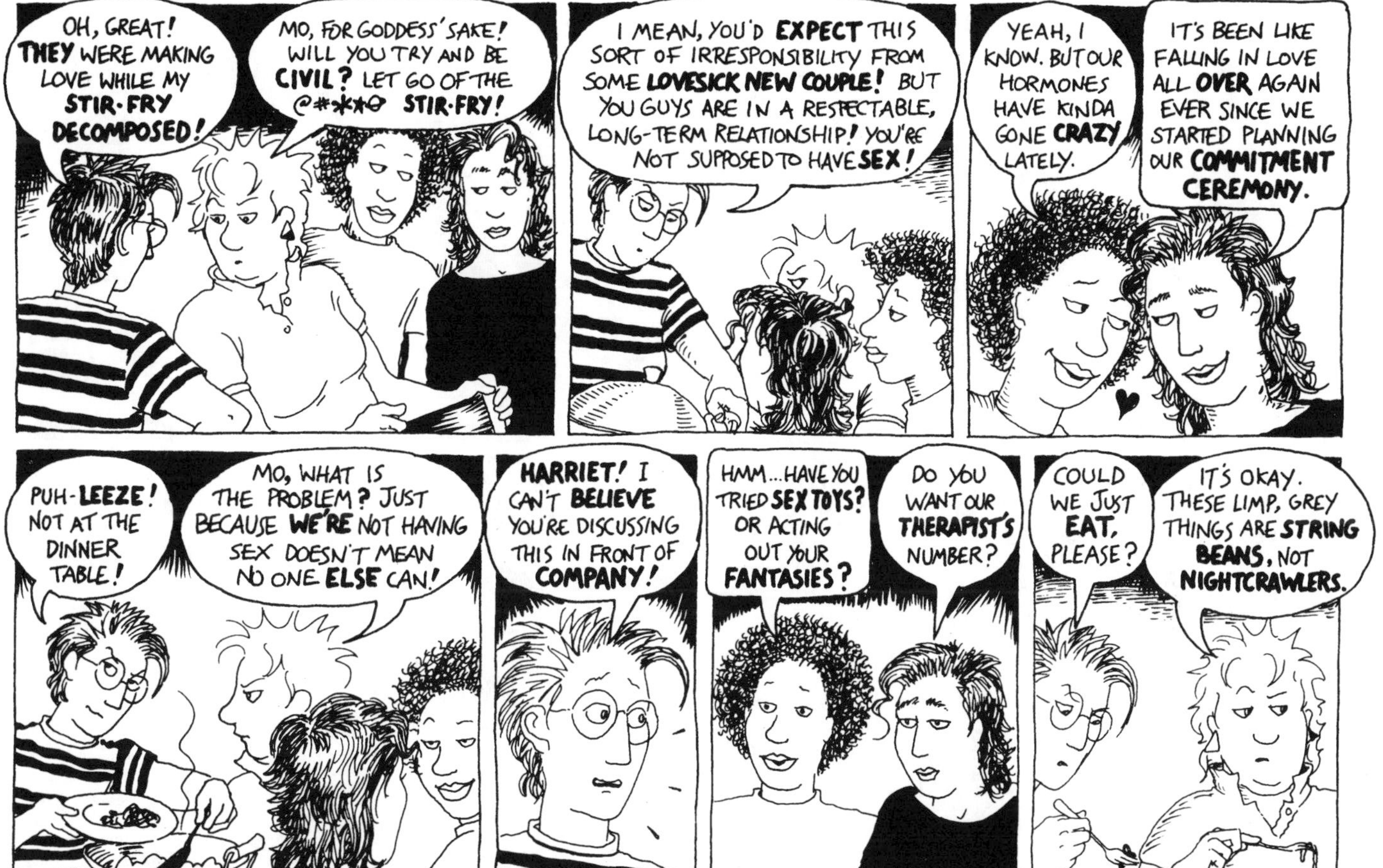
OH, GREAT! THEY WERE MAKING LOVE WHILE MY STIR-FRY DECOMPOSED!
MO, FOR GODDESS' SAKE! WILL YOU TRY AND BE CIVIL? LET GO OF THE @#*** STIR-FRY!
I MEAN, YOU'D EXPECT THIS SORT OF IRRESPONSIBILITY FROM SOME LOVESICK NEW COUPLE! BUT YOU GUYS ARE IN A RESPECTABLE, LONG-TERM RELATIONSHIP! YOU'RE NOT SUPPOSED TO HAVE SEX!
YEAH, I KNOW. BUT OUR HORMONES HAVE KINDA GONE CRAZY LATELY.
IT'S BEEN LIKE FALLING IN LOVE ALL OVER AGAIN EVER SINCE WE STARTED PLANNING OUR COMMITMENT CEREMONY.
PUH-LEEZE! NOT AT THE DINNER TABLE!
MO, WHAT IS THE PROBLEM? JUST BECAUSE WE'RE NOT HAVING SEX DOESN'T MEAN NO ONE ELSE CAN!
HARRIET! I CAN'T BELIEVE YOU'RE DISCUSSING THIS IN FRONT OF COMPANY!
HMM... HAVE YOU TRIED SEX TOYS? OR ACTING OUT YOUR FANTASIES?
DO YOU WANT OUR THERAPIST'S NUMBER?
COULD WE JUST EAT, PLEASE?
IT'S OKAY. THESE LIMP, GREY THINGS ARE STRING BEANS, NOT NIGHTCRAWLERS.

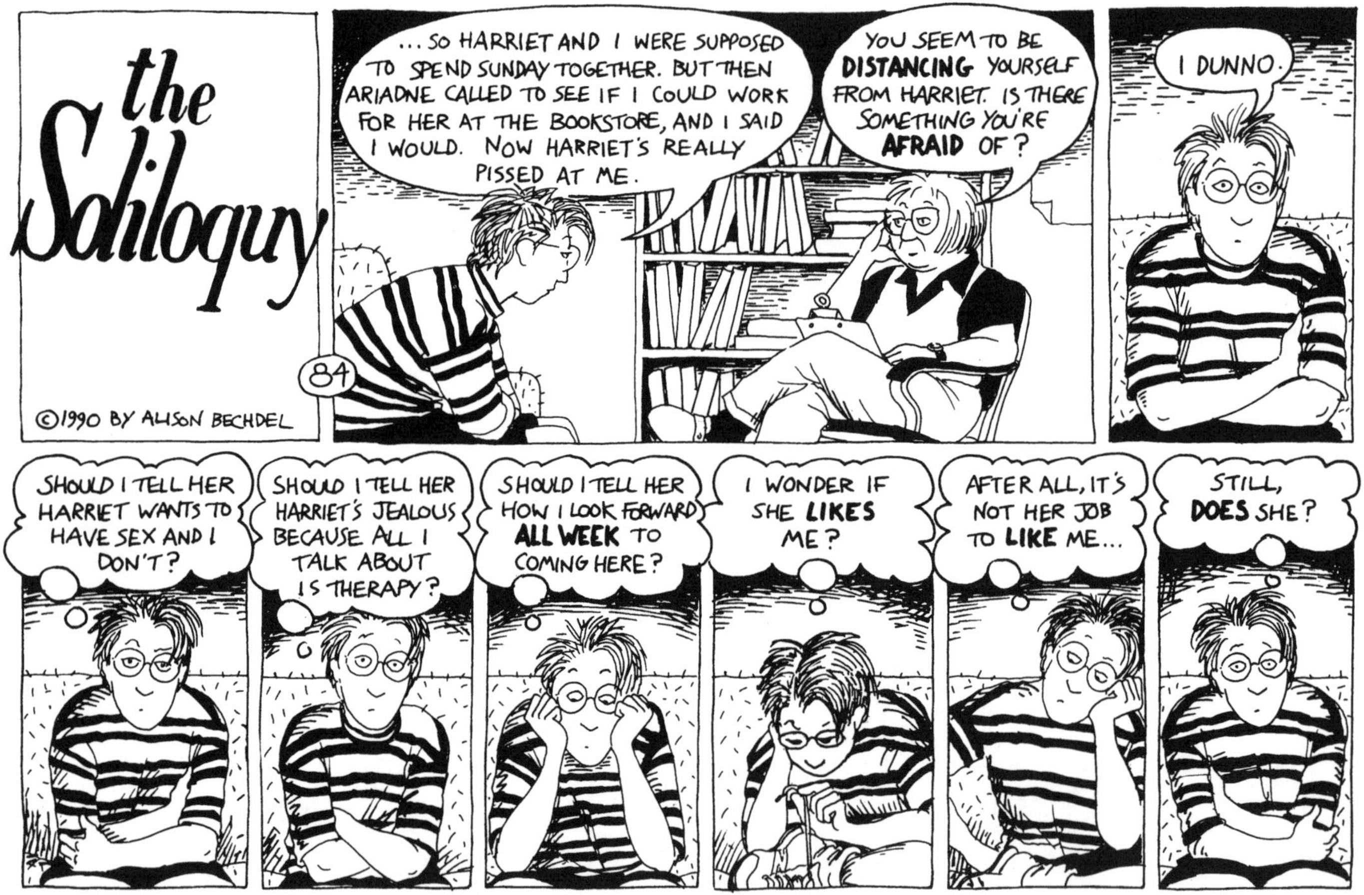
the Soliloquy
84
©1990 BY ALISON BECHDEL
... SO HARRIET AND I WERE SUPPOSED TO SPEND SUNDAY TOGETHER. BUT THEN ARIADNE CALLED TO SEE IF I COULD WORK FOR HER AT THE BOOKSTORE, AND I SAID I WOULD. NOW HARRIET'S REALLY PISSED AT ME.
YOU SEEM TO BE **DISTANCING** YOURSELF FROM HARRIET. IS THERE SOMETHING YOU'RE **AFRAID** OF?
I DUNNO.
SHOULD I TELL HER HARRIET WANTS TO HAVE SEX AND I DON'T?
SHOULD I TELL HER HARRIET'S JEALOUS BECAUSE ALL I TALK ABOUT IS THERAPY?
SHOULD I TELL HER HOW I LOOK FORWARD **ALL WEEK** TO COMING HERE?
I WONDER IF SHE **LIKES** ME?
AFTER ALL, IT'S NOT HER JOB TO **LIKE** ME...
STILL, **DOES** SHE?

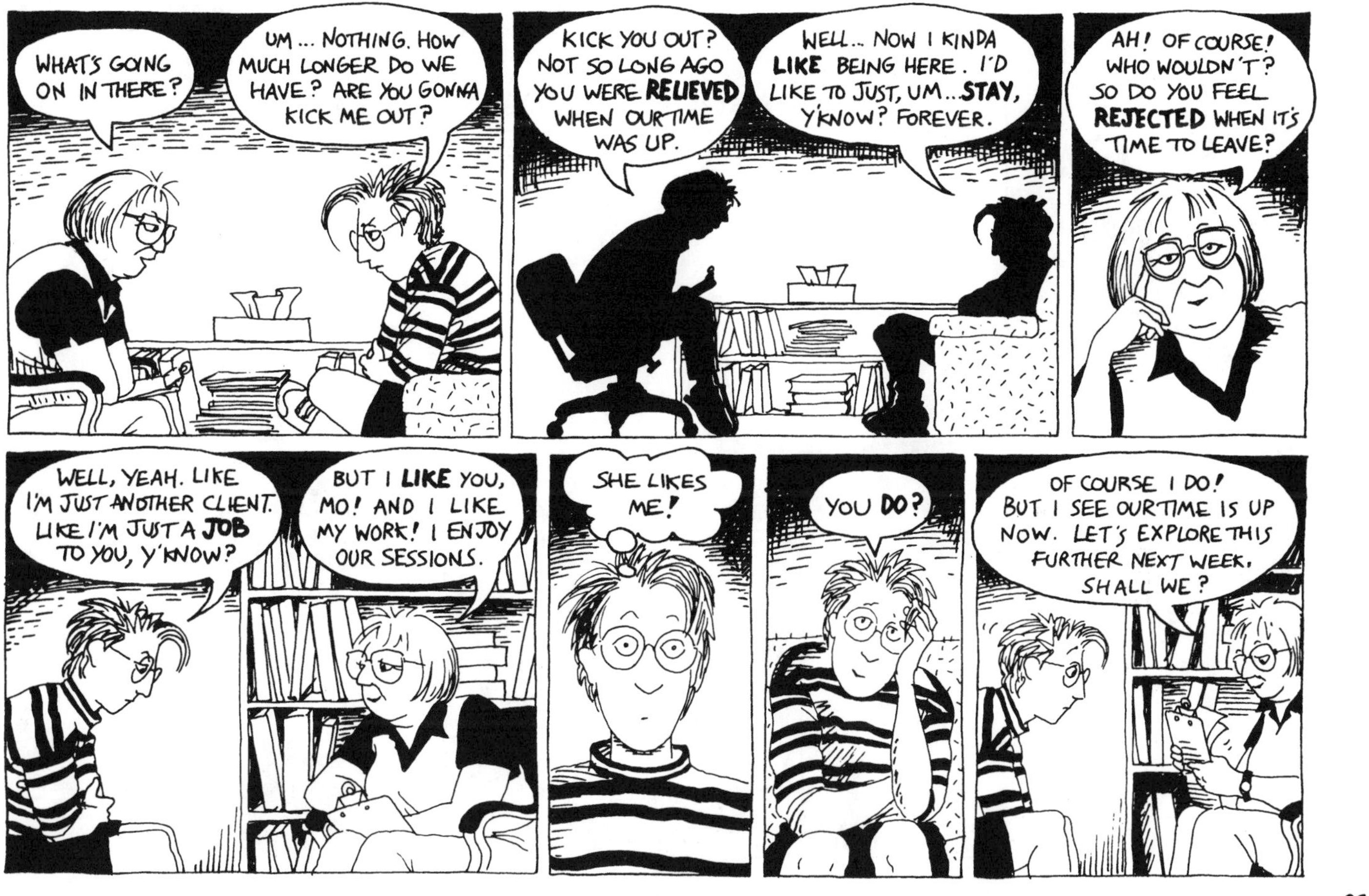
WHAT'S GOING ON IN THERE?
UM ... NOTHING. HOW MUCH LONGER DO WE HAVE? ARE YOU GONNA KICK ME OUT?
KICK YOU OUT? NOT SO LONG AGO YOU WERE **RELIEVED** WHEN OUR TIME WAS UP.
WELL... NOW I KINDA **LIKE** BEING HERE. I'D LIKE TO JUST, UM... **STAY,** Y'KNOW? FOREVER.
AH! OF COURSE! WHO WOULDN'T? SO DO YOU FEEL **REJECTED** WHEN IT'S TIME TO LEAVE?
WELL, YEAH. LIKE I'M JUST ANOTHER CLIENT. LIKE I'M JUST A **JOB** TO YOU, Y'KNOW?
BUT I **LIKE** YOU, MO! AND I LIKE MY WORK! I ENJOY OUR SESSIONS.
SHE LIKES ME!
YOU **DO**?
OF COURSE I DO! BUT I SEE OUR TIME IS UP NOW. LET'S EXPLORE THIS FURTHER NEXT WEEK, SHALL WE?

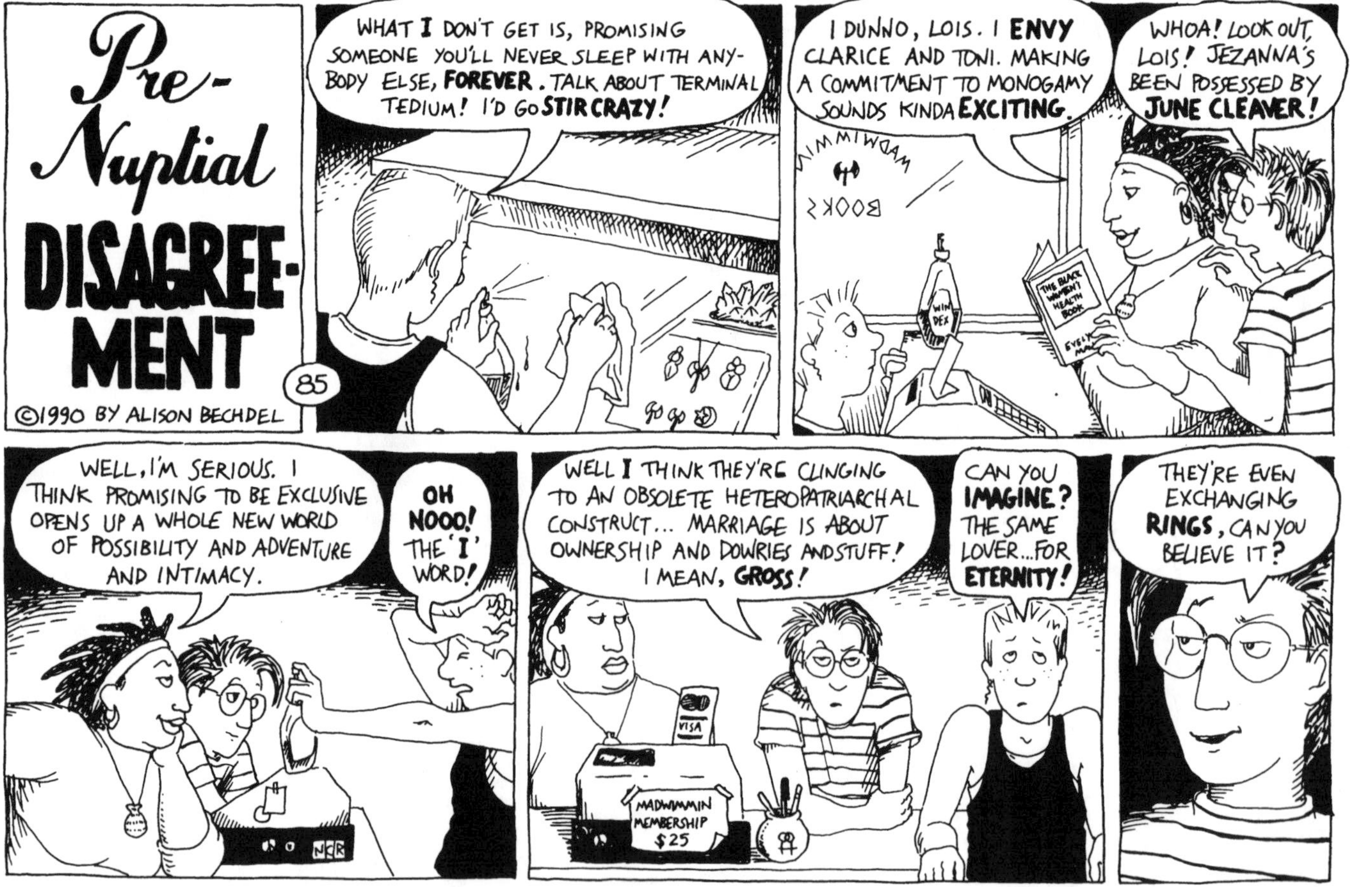
Pre-Nuptial
DISAGREE-MENT
85
©1990 BY ALISON BECHDEL
WHAT I DON'T GET IS, PROMISING SOMEONE YOU'LL NEVER SLEEP WITH ANYBODY ELSE, FOREVER. TALK ABOUT TERMINAL TEDIUM! I'D GO STIR CRAZY!
I DUNNO, LOIS. I ENVY CLARICE AND TONI. MAKING A COMMITMENT TO MONOGAMY SOUNDS KINDA EXCITING.
WHOA! LOOK OUT, LOIS! JEZANNA'S BEEN POSSESSED BY JUNE CLEAVER!
WIN DEX
THE BLACK WOMEN'S HEALTH BOOK
WELL, I'M SERIOUS. I THINK PROMISING TO BE EXCLUSIVE OPENS UP A WHOLE NEW WORLD OF POSSIBILITY AND ADVENTURE AND INTIMACY.
OH NOOO! THE 'I' WORD!
NCR
WELL I THINK THEY'RE CLINGING TO AN OBSOLETE HETEROPATRIARCHAL CONSTRUCT... MARRIAGE IS ABOUT OWNERSHIP AND DOWRIES AND STUFF! I MEAN, GROSS!
CAN YOU IMAGINE? THE SAME LOVER...FOR ETERNITY!
VISA
MADWIMMIN MEMBERSHIP $25
THEY'RE EVEN EXCHANGING RINGS, CAN YOU BELIEVE IT?

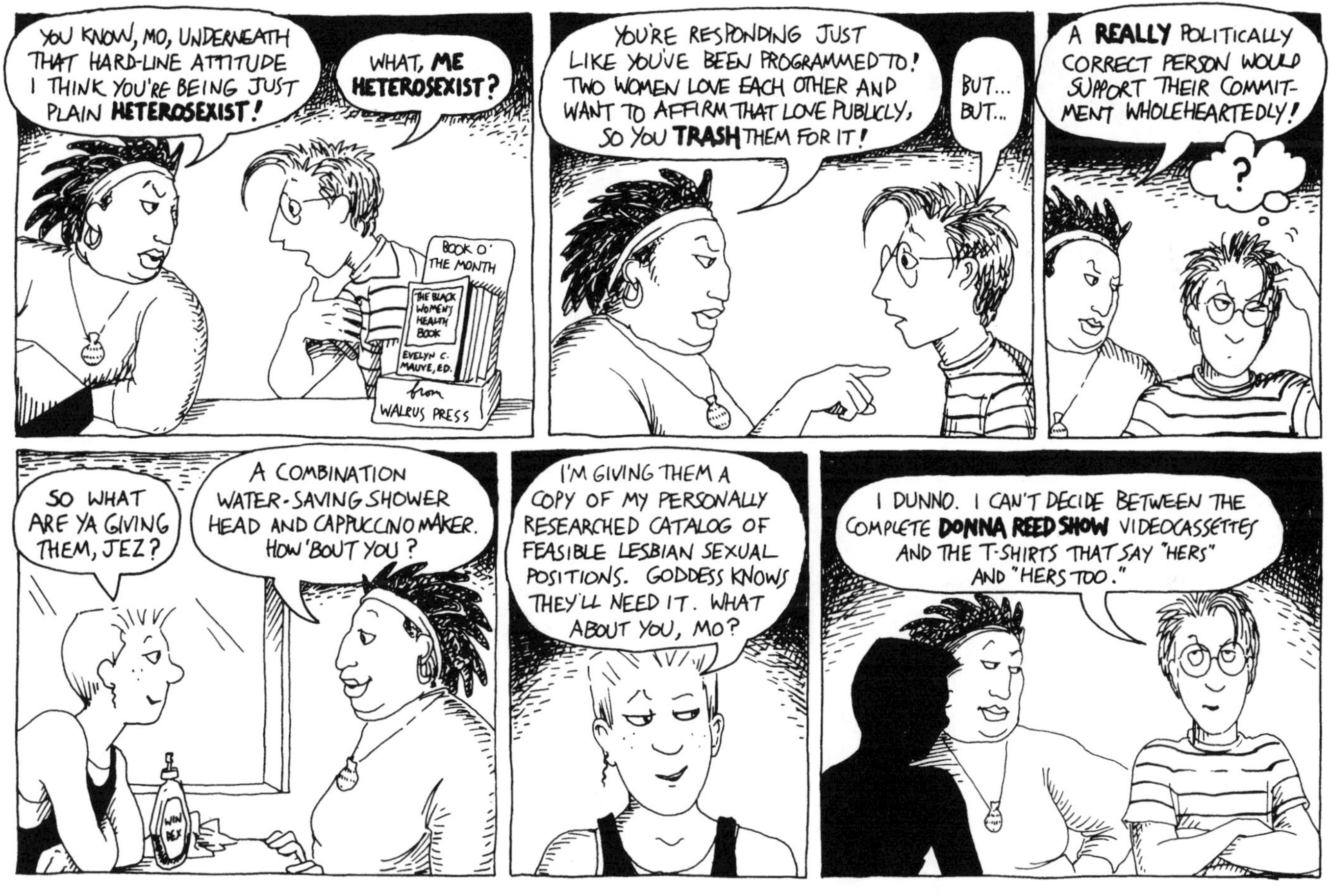
YOU KNOW, MO, UNDERNEATH THAT HARD-LINE ATTITUDE I THINK YOU'RE BEING JUST PLAIN HETEROSEXIST!
WHAT, ME HETEROSEXIST?
BOOK O' THE MONTH
THE BLACK WOMEN'S HEALTH BOOK
EVELYN C. MAUVE, ED.
from
WALRUS PRESS
YOU'RE RESPONDING JUST LIKE YOU'VE BEEN PROGRAMMED TO! TWO WOMEN LOVE EACH OTHER AND WANT TO AFFIRM THAT LOVE PUBLICLY, SO YOU TRASH THEM FOR IT!
BUT... BUT...
A REALLY POLITICALLY CORRECT PERSON WOULD SUPPORT THEIR COMMITMENT WHOLEHEARTEDLY!
?
SO WHAT ARE YA GIVING THEM, JEZ?
A COMBINATION WATER-SAVING SHOWER HEAD AND CAPPUCCINO MAKER. HOW 'BOUT YOU?
I'M GIVING THEM A COPY OF MY PERSONALLY RESEARCHED CATALOG OF FEASIBLE LESBIAN SEXUAL POSITIONS. GODDESS KNOWS THEY'LL NEED IT. WHAT ABOUT YOU, MO?
I DUNNO. I CAN'T DECIDE BETWEEN THE COMPLETE DONNA REED SHOW VIDEOCASSETTES AND THE T-SHIRTS THAT SAY "HERS" AND "HERS TOO."

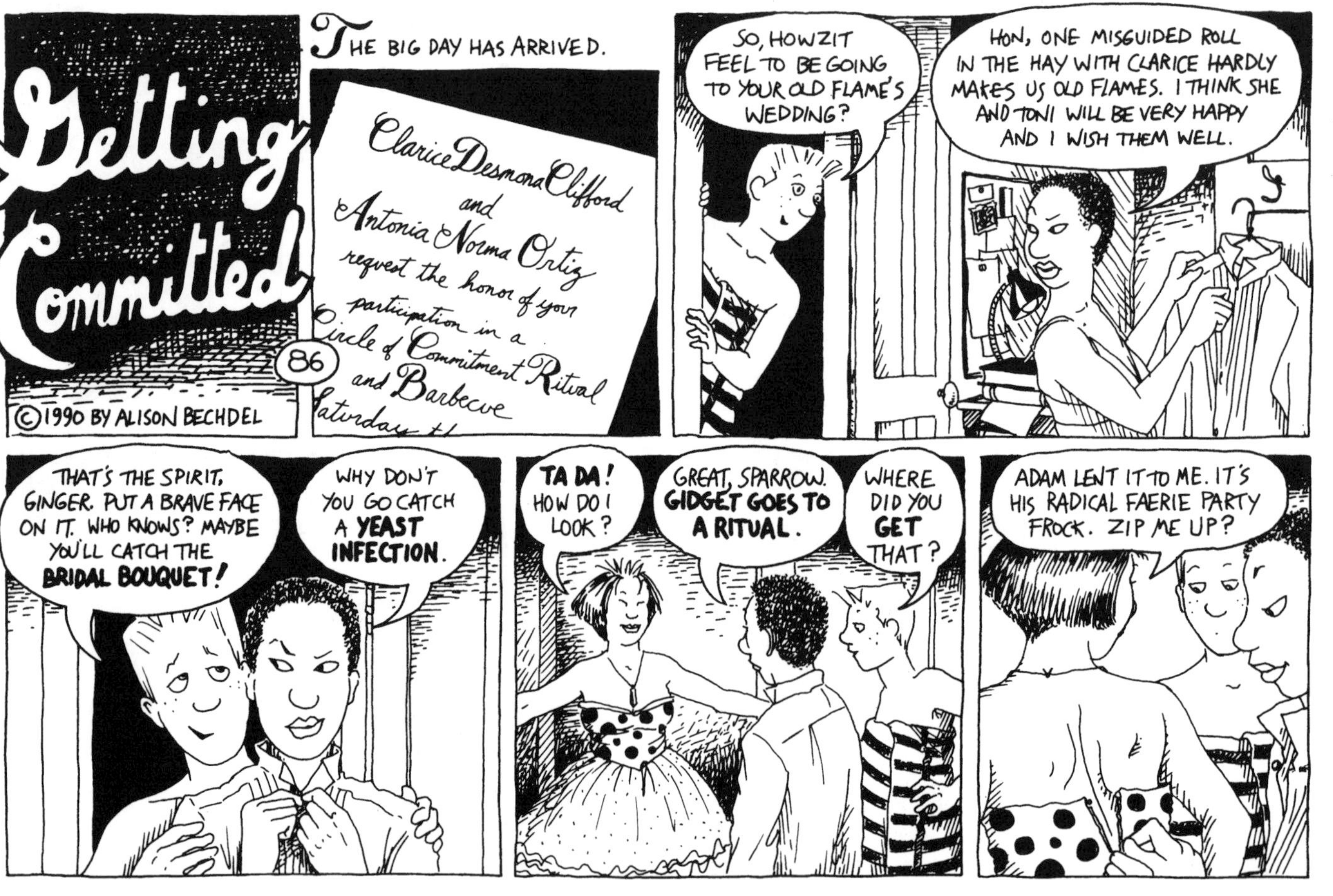
Getting Committed
86
©1990 BY ALISON BECHDEL
THE BIG DAY HAS ARRIVED.
Clarice Desmona Clifford and Antonia Norma Ortiz request the honor of your participation in a Circle of Commitment Ritual and Barbecue
SO, HOWZIT FEEL TO BE GOING TO YOUR OLD FLAME'S WEDDING?
HON, ONE MISGUIDED ROLL IN THE HAY WITH CLARICE HARDLY MAKES US OLD FLAMES. I THINK SHE AND TONI WILL BE VERY HAPPY AND I WISH THEM WELL.
THAT'S THE SPIRIT, GINGER. PUT A BRAVE FACE ON IT. WHO KNOWS? MAYBE YOU'LL CATCH THE **BRIDAL BOUQUET**!
WHY DON'T YOU GO CATCH A **YEAST INFECTION**.
TA DA! HOW DO I LOOK?
GREAT, SPARROW. **GIDGET GOES TO A RITUAL**.
WHERE DID YOU **GET** THAT?
ADAM LENT IT TO ME. IT'S HIS RADICAL FAERIE PARTY FROCK. ZIP ME UP?

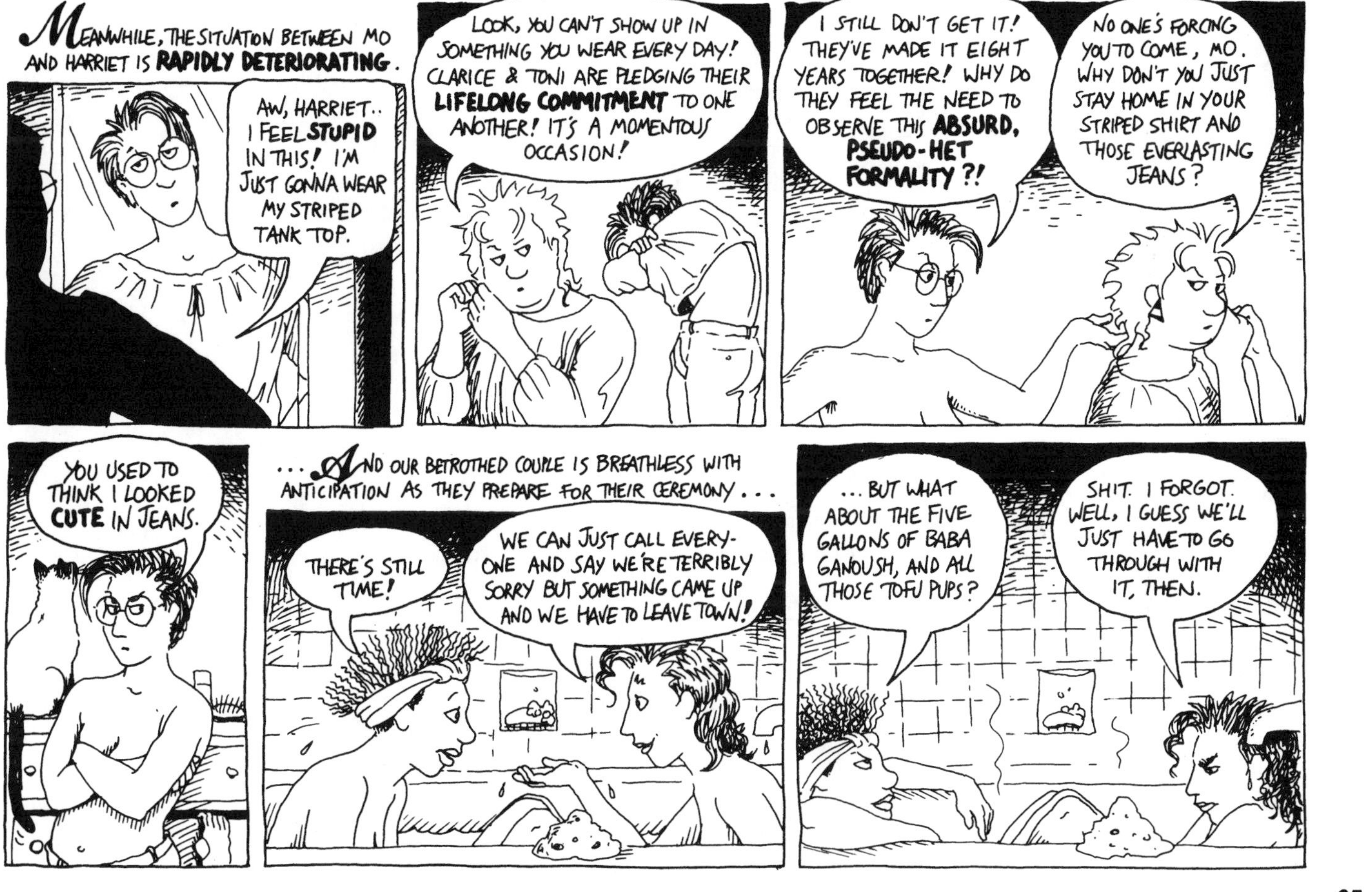
MEANWHILE, THE SITUATION BETWEEN MO AND HARRIET IS RAPIDLY DETERIORATING.
AW, HARRIET.. I FEEL STUPID IN THIS! I'M JUST GONNA WEAR MY STRIPED TANK TOP.
LOOK, YOU CAN'T SHOW UP IN SOMETHING YOU WEAR EVERY DAY! CLARICE & TONI ARE PLEDGING THEIR LIFELONG COMMITMENT TO ONE ANOTHER! IT'S A MOMENTOUS OCCASION!
I STILL DON'T GET IT! THEY'VE MADE IT EIGHT YEARS TOGETHER! WHY DO THEY FEEL THE NEED TO OBSERVE THIS ABSURD, PSEUDO-HET FORMALITY ?!
NO ONE'S FORCING YOU TO COME, MO. WHY DON'T YOU JUST STAY HOME IN YOUR STRIPED SHIRT AND THOSE EVERLASTING JEANS?
YOU USED TO THINK I LOOKED CUTE IN JEANS.
...AND OUR BETROTHED COUPLE IS BREATHLESS WITH ANTICIPATION AS THEY PREPARE FOR THEIR CEREMONY...
THERE'S STILL TIME!
WE CAN JUST CALL EVERY-ONE AND SAY WE'RE TERRIBLY SORRY BUT SOMETHING CAME UP AND WE HAVE TO LEAVE TOWN!
...BUT WHAT ABOUT THE FIVE GALLONS OF BABA GANOUSH, AND ALL THOSE TOFU PUPS?
SHIT. I FORGOT. WELL, I GUESS WE'LL JUST HAVE TO GO THROUGH WITH IT, THEN.

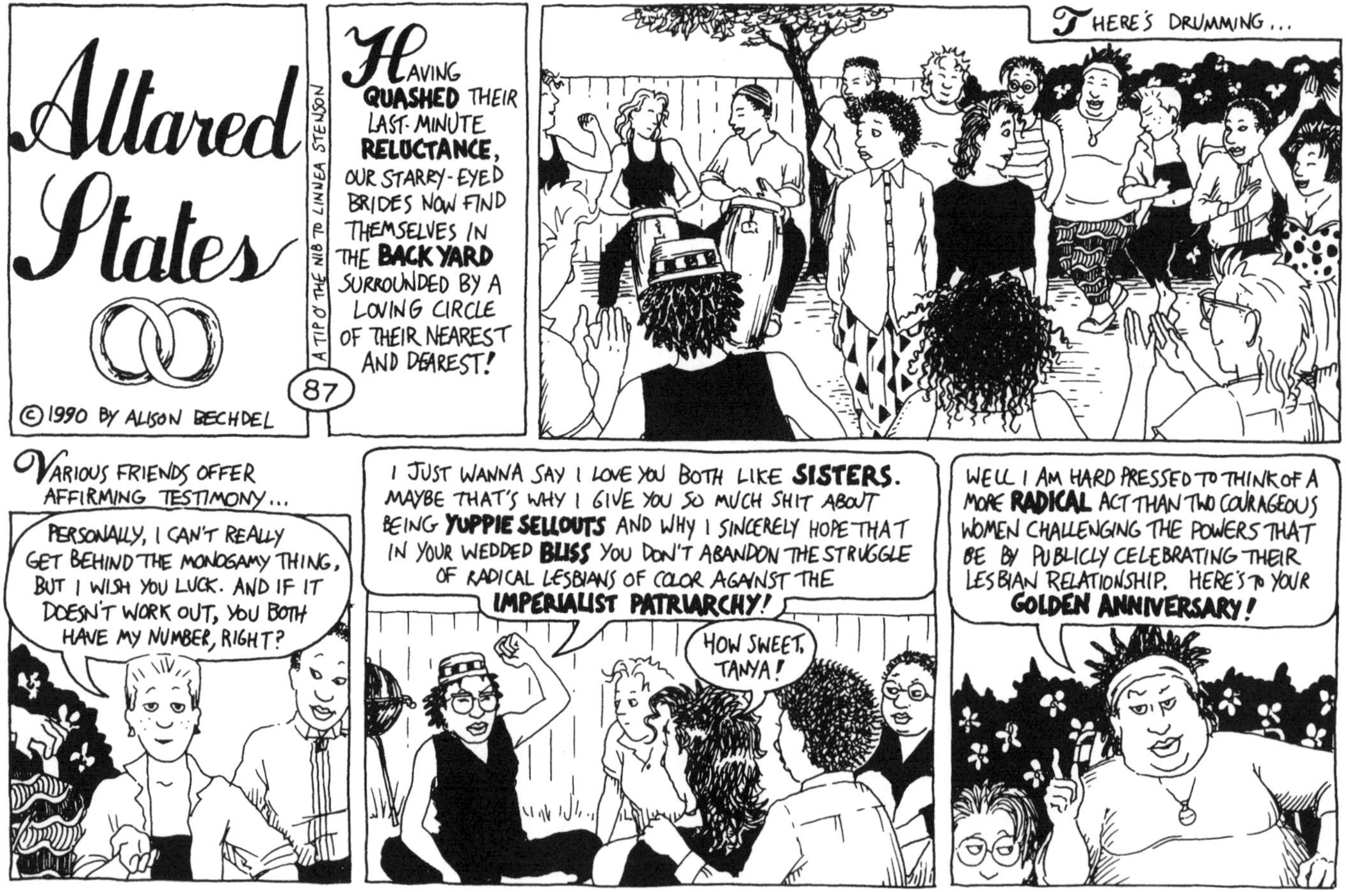
Altared States
87
A TIP O' THE NIB TO LINNEA STENSON
© 1990 BY ALISON BECHDEL
HAVING QUASHED THEIR LAST-MINUTE RELUCTANCE, OUR STARRY-EYED BRIDES NOW FIND THEMSELVES IN THE BACK YARD SURROUNDED BY A LOVING CIRCLE OF THEIR NEAREST AND DEAREST!
THERE'S DRUMMING...
VARIOUS FRIENDS OFFER AFFIRMING TESTIMONY...
PERSONALLY, I CAN'T REALLY GET BEHIND THE MONOGAMY THING, BUT I WISH YOU LUCK. AND IF IT DOESN'T WORK OUT, YOU BOTH HAVE MY NUMBER, RIGHT?
I JUST WANNA SAY I LOVE YOU BOTH LIKE SISTERS. MAYBE THAT'S WHY I GIVE YOU SO MUCH SHIT ABOUT BEING YUPPIE SELLOUTS AND WHY I SINCERELY HOPE THAT IN YOUR WEDDED BLISS YOU DON'T ABANDON THE STRUGGLE OF RADICAL LESBIANS OF COLOR AGAINST THE IMPERIALIST PATRIARCHY!
HOW SWEET, TANYA!
WELL I AM HARD PRESSED TO THINK OF A MORE RADICAL ACT THAN TWO COURAGEOUS WOMEN CHALLENGING THE POWERS THAT BE BY PUBLICLY CELEBRATING THEIR LESBIAN RELATIONSHIP. HERE'S TO YOUR GOLDEN ANNIVERSARY!

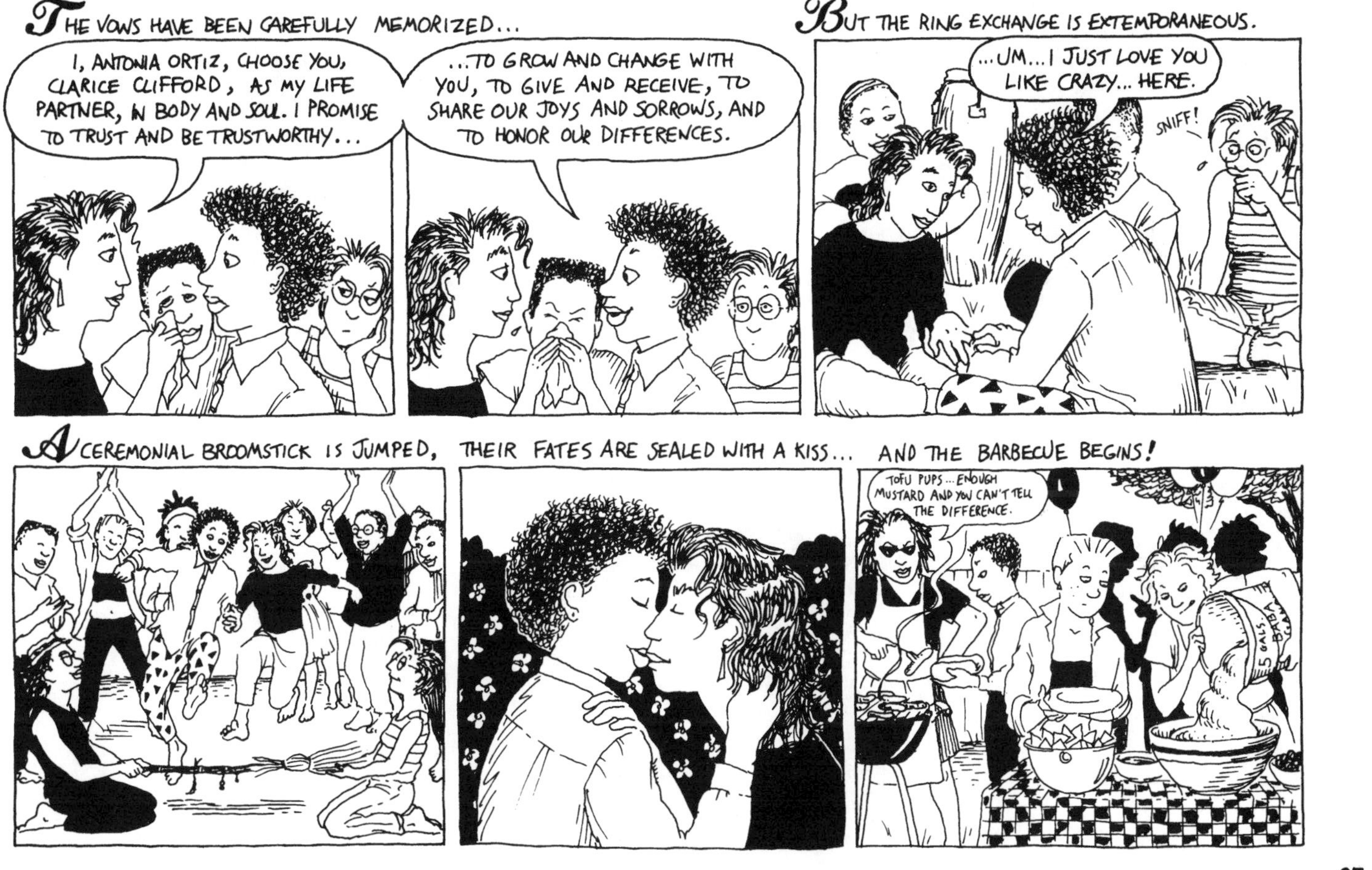
THE VOWS HAVE BEEN CAREFULLY MEMORIZED...
I, ANTONIA ORTIZ, CHOOSE YOU, CLARICE CLIFFORD, AS MY LIFE PARTNER, IN BODY AND SOUL. I PROMISE TO TRUST AND BE TRUSTWORTHY...
...TO GROW AND CHANGE WITH YOU, TO GIVE AND RECEIVE, TO SHARE OUR JOYS AND SORROWS, AND TO HONOR OUR DIFFERENCES.
BUT THE RING EXCHANGE IS EXTEMPORANEOUS.
...UM...I JUST LOVE YOU LIKE CRAZY... HERE.
SNIFF!
A CEREMONIAL BROOMSTICK IS JUMPED,
THEIR FATES ARE SEALED WITH A KISS...
AND THE BARBECUE BEGINS!
TOFU PUPS...ENOUGH MUSTARD AND YOU CAN'T TELL THE DIFFERENCE.

The Honey-mooners

88

©1990 BY ALISON BECHDEL

AFTER THE LAST REVELERS DEPART, OUR NEWLYWEDS UNPLUG THE PHONE AND RETIRE TO THEIR MATRIMONIAL FUTON IN SEARCH OF NEW HEIGHTS IN **CONJUGAL RAPTURE.**

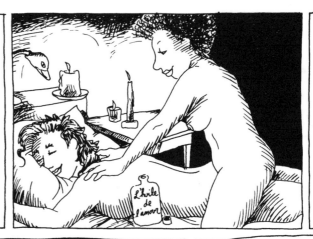

MEANWHILE... INSPIRED BY CLARICE & TONI'S ROMANTIC VOW OF COMMITMENT, MO & HARRIET ARE DETERMINED TO **FAN** THE **FALTERING FLAMES** OF THEIR OWN LACKLUSTER LOVE LIFE!

YOU HAD **ONIONS** ON YOUR TOFU PUP, DIDN'T YOU?

ALL RIGHT, ALL RIGHT. I'LL BRUSH MY TEETH AGAIN.

COULD WE, LIKE, SLOW DOWN? YOU ALWAYS GO RIGHT FOR MY BREASTS. HOW COME YOU NEVER KISS MY **HANDS** OR ANYTHING ANYMORE?

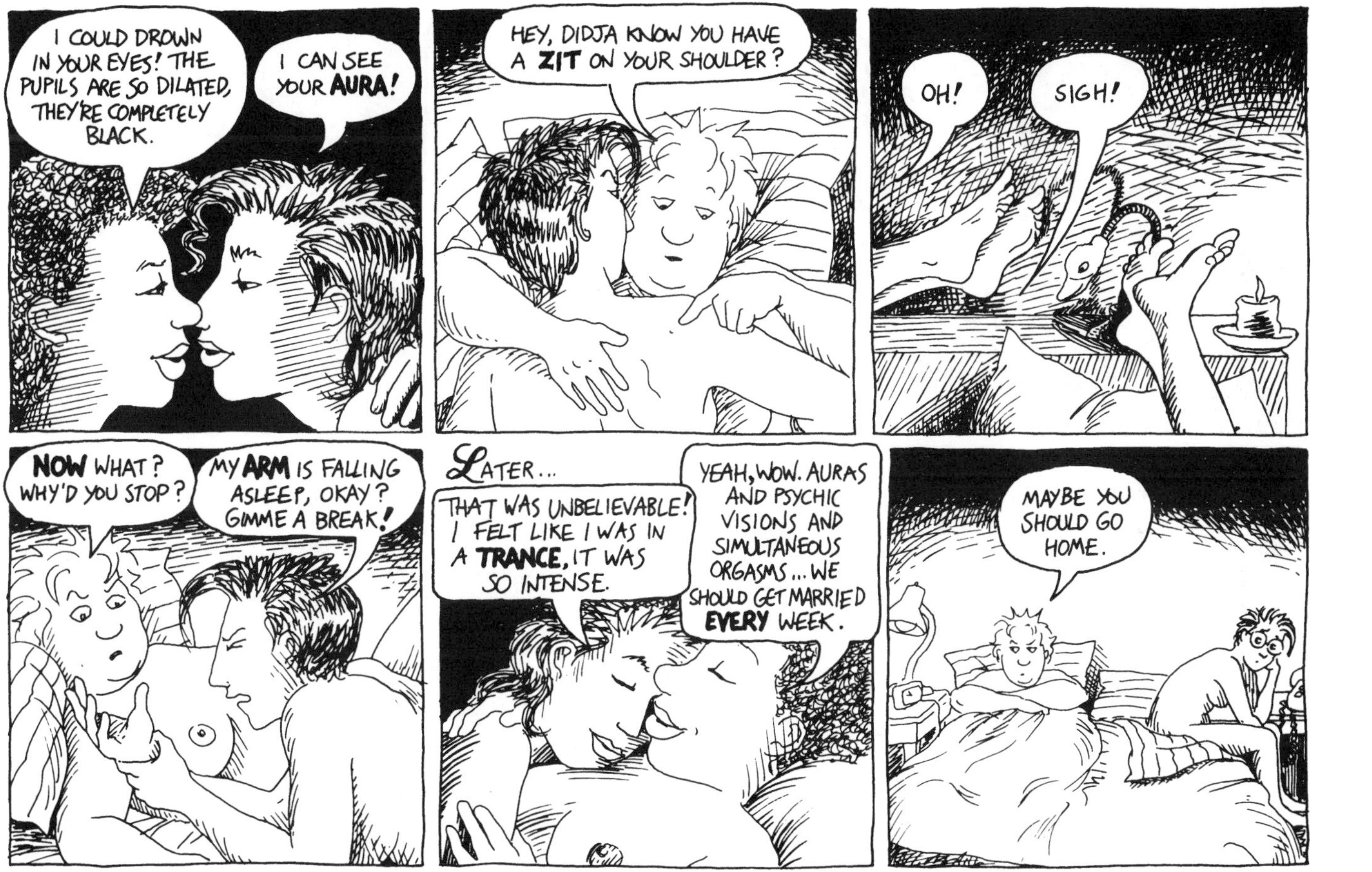
I COULD DROWN IN YOUR EYES! THE PUPILS ARE SO DILATED, THEY'RE COMPLETELY BLACK.
I CAN SEE YOUR **AURA**!
HEY, DIDJA KNOW YOU HAVE A **ZIT** ON YOUR SHOULDER?
OH!
SIGH!
NOW WHAT? WHY'D YOU STOP?
MY **ARM** IS FALLING ASLEEP, OKAY? GIMME A BREAK!
LATER...
THAT WAS UNBELIEVABLE! I FELT LIKE I WAS IN A **TRANCE**, IT WAS SO INTENSE.
YEAH, WOW. AURAS AND PSYCHIC VISIONS AND SIMULTANEOUS ORGASMS... WE SHOULD GET MARRIED **EVERY** WEEK.
MAYBE YOU SHOULD GO HOME.

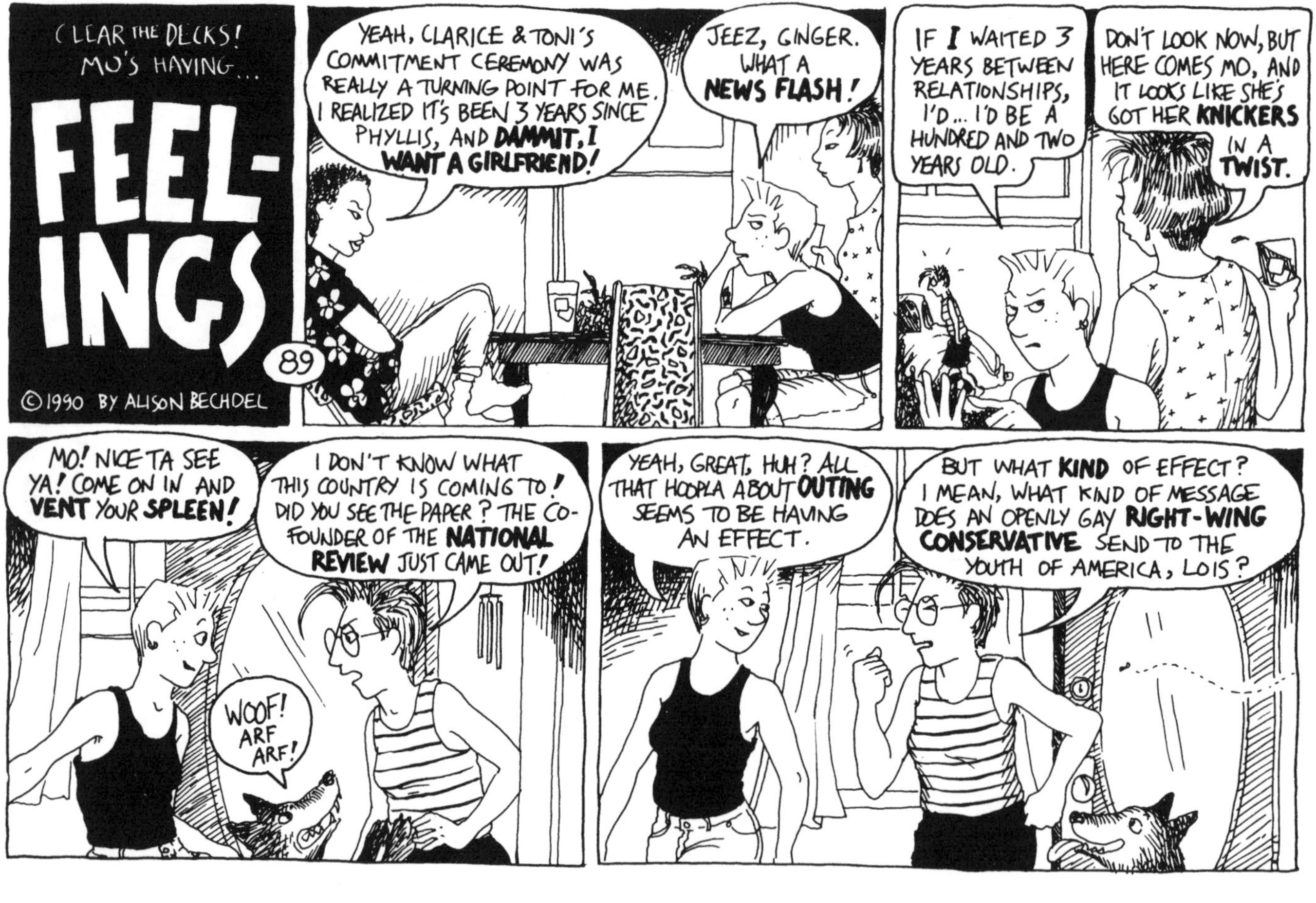
CLEAR THE DECKS! MO'S HAVING...
FEEL-INGS
89
©1990 BY ALISON BECHDEL
YEAH, CLARICE & TONI'S COMMITMENT CEREMONY WAS REALLY A TURNING POINT FOR ME. I REALIZED IT'S BEEN 3 YEARS SINCE PHYLLIS, AND DAMMIT, I WANT A GIRLFRIEND!
JEEZ, GINGER. WHAT A NEWS FLASH!
IF I WAITED 3 YEARS BETWEEN RELATIONSHIPS, I'D... I'D BE A HUNDRED AND TWO YEARS OLD.
DON'T LOOK NOW, BUT HERE COMES MO, AND IT LOOKS LIKE SHE'S GOT HER KNICKERS IN A TWIST.
MO! NICE TA SEE YA! COME ON IN AND VENT YOUR SPLEEN!
I DON'T KNOW WHAT THIS COUNTRY IS COMING TO! DID YOU SEE THE PAPER? THE CO-FOUNDER OF THE NATIONAL REVIEW JUST CAME OUT!
WOOF! ARF ARF!
YEAH, GREAT, HUH? ALL THAT HOOPLA ABOUT OUTING SEEMS TO BE HAVING AN EFFECT.
BUT WHAT KIND OF EFFECT? I MEAN, WHAT KIND OF MESSAGE DOES AN OPENLY GAY RIGHT-WING CONSERVATIVE SEND TO THE YOUTH OF AMERICA, LOIS?

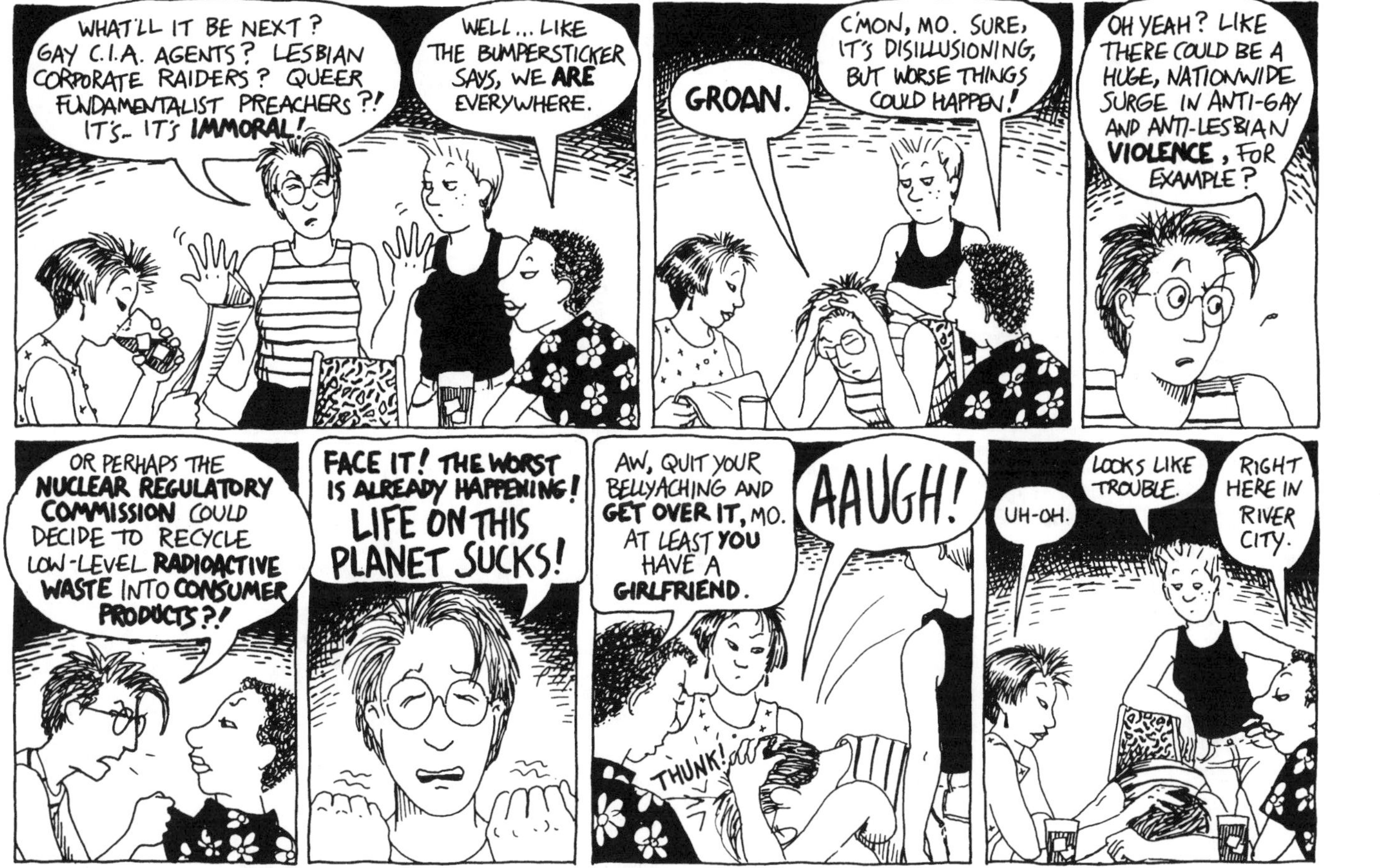
WHAT'LL IT BE NEXT? GAY C.I.A. AGENTS? LESBIAN CORPORATE RAIDERS? QUEER FUNDAMENTALIST PREACHERS?! IT'S.. IT'S IMMORAL!
WELL... LIKE THE BUMPERSTICKER SAYS, WE ARE EVERYWHERE.
GROAN.
C'MON, MO. SURE, IT'S DISILLUSIONING, BUT WORSE THINGS COULD HAPPEN!
OH YEAH? LIKE THERE COULD BE A HUGE, NATIONWIDE SURGE IN ANTI-GAY AND ANTI-LESBIAN VIOLENCE, FOR EXAMPLE?
OR PERHAPS THE NUCLEAR REGULATORY COMMISSION COULD DECIDE TO RECYCLE LOW-LEVEL RADIOACTIVE WASTE INTO CONSUMER PRODUCTS?!
FACE IT! THE WORST IS ALREADY HAPPENING! LIFE ON THIS PLANET SUCKS!
AW, QUIT YOUR BELLYACHING AND GET OVER IT, MO. AT LEAST YOU HAVE A GIRLFRIEND.
AAUGH!
THUNK!
UH-OH.
LOOKS LIKE TROUBLE.
RIGHT HERE IN RIVER CITY.

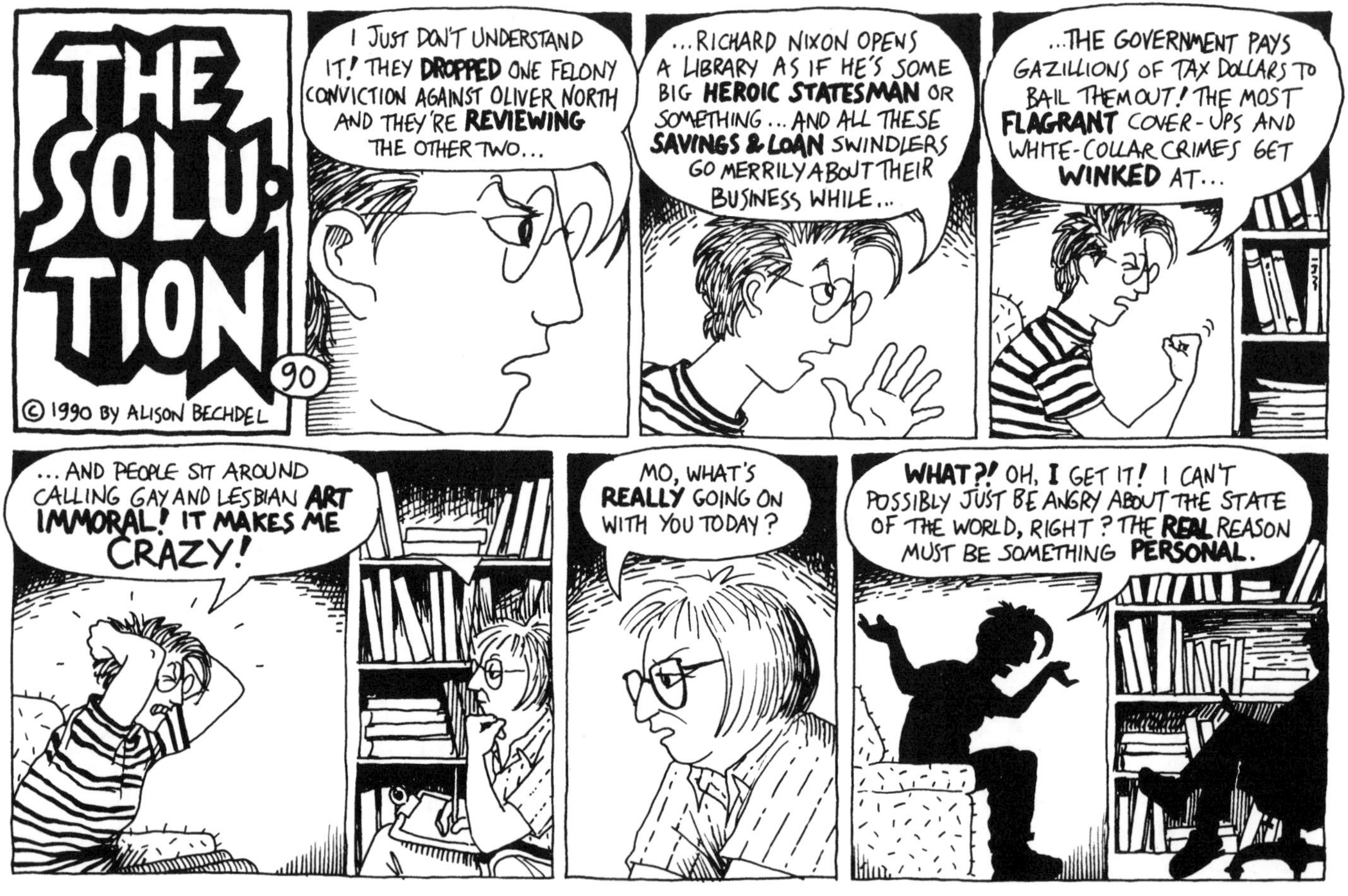
THE SOLU-TION
90
© 1990 BY ALISON BECHDEL
I JUST DON'T UNDERSTAND IT! THEY DROPPED ONE FELONY CONVICTION AGAINST OLIVER NORTH AND THEY'RE REVIEWING THE OTHER TWO...
...RICHARD NIXON OPENS A LIBRARY AS IF HE'S SOME BIG HEROIC STATESMAN OR SOMETHING... AND ALL THESE SAVINGS & LOAN SWINDLERS GO MERRILY ABOUT THEIR BUSINESS WHILE...
...THE GOVERNMENT PAYS GAZILLIONS OF TAX DOLLARS TO BAIL THEM OUT! THE MOST FLAGRANT COVER-UPS AND WHITE-COLLAR CRIMES GET WINKED AT...
...AND PEOPLE SIT AROUND CALLING GAY AND LESBIAN ART IMMORAL! IT MAKES ME CRAZY!
MO, WHAT'S REALLY GOING ON WITH YOU TODAY?
WHAT?! OH, I GET IT! I CAN'T POSSIBLY JUST BE ANGRY ABOUT THE STATE OF THE WORLD, RIGHT? THE REAL REASON MUST BE SOMETHING PERSONAL.

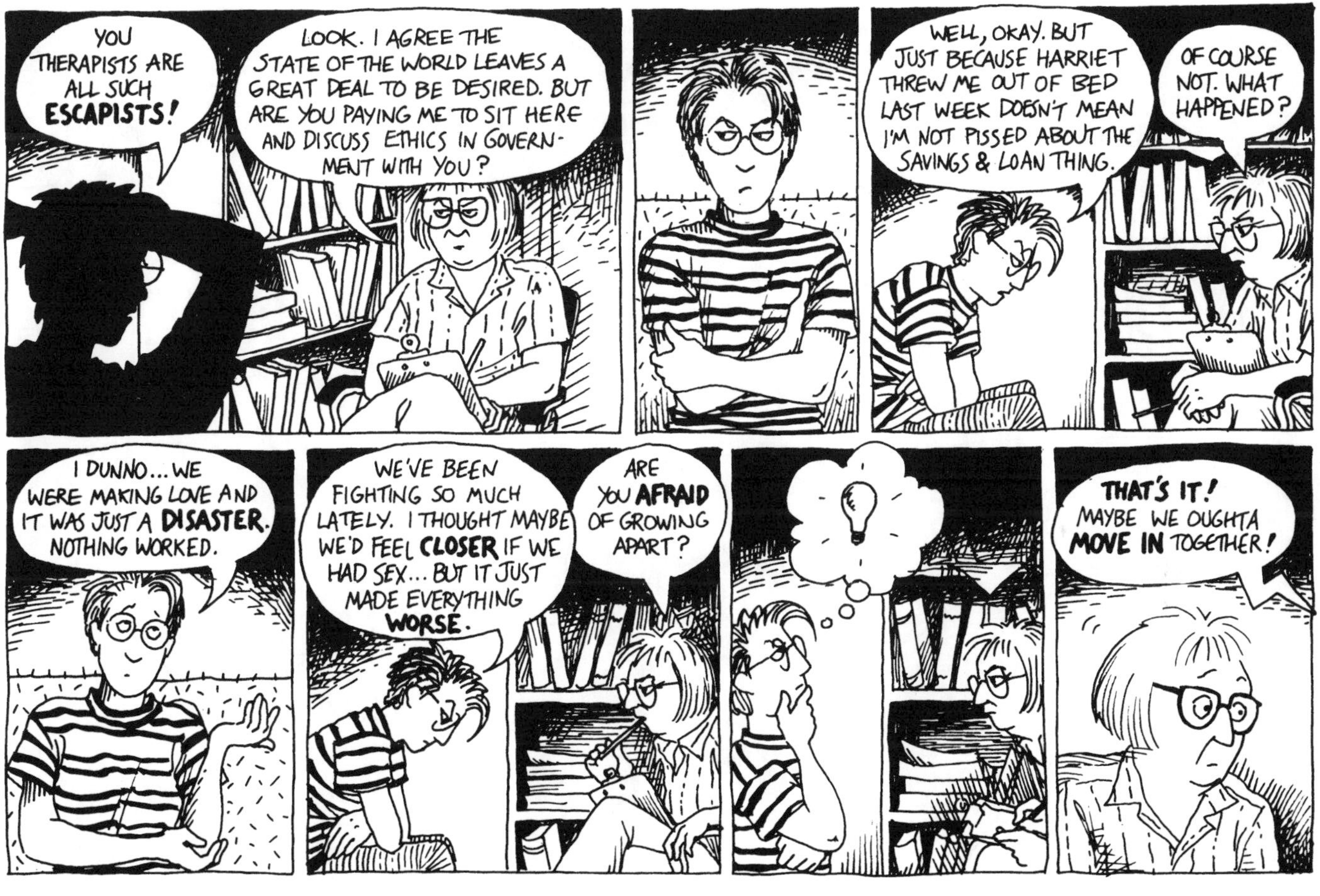
YOU THERAPISTS ARE ALL SUCH **ESCAPISTS**!
LOOK. I AGREE THE STATE OF THE WORLD LEAVES A GREAT DEAL TO BE DESIRED. BUT ARE YOU PAYING ME TO SIT HERE AND DISCUSS ETHICS IN GOVERNMENT WITH YOU?
WELL, OKAY. BUT JUST BECAUSE HARRIET THREW ME OUT OF BED LAST WEEK DOESN'T MEAN I'M NOT PISSED ABOUT THE SAVINGS & LOAN THING.
OF COURSE NOT. WHAT HAPPENED?
I DUNNO... WE WERE MAKING LOVE AND IT WAS JUST A **DISASTER**. NOTHING WORKED.
WE'VE BEEN FIGHTING SO MUCH LATELY. I THOUGHT MAYBE WE'D FEEL **CLOSER** IF WE HAD SEX... BUT IT JUST MADE EVERYTHING **WORSE**.
ARE YOU **AFRAID** OF GROWING APART?
THAT'S IT! MAYBE WE OUGHTA **MOVE IN** TOGETHER!

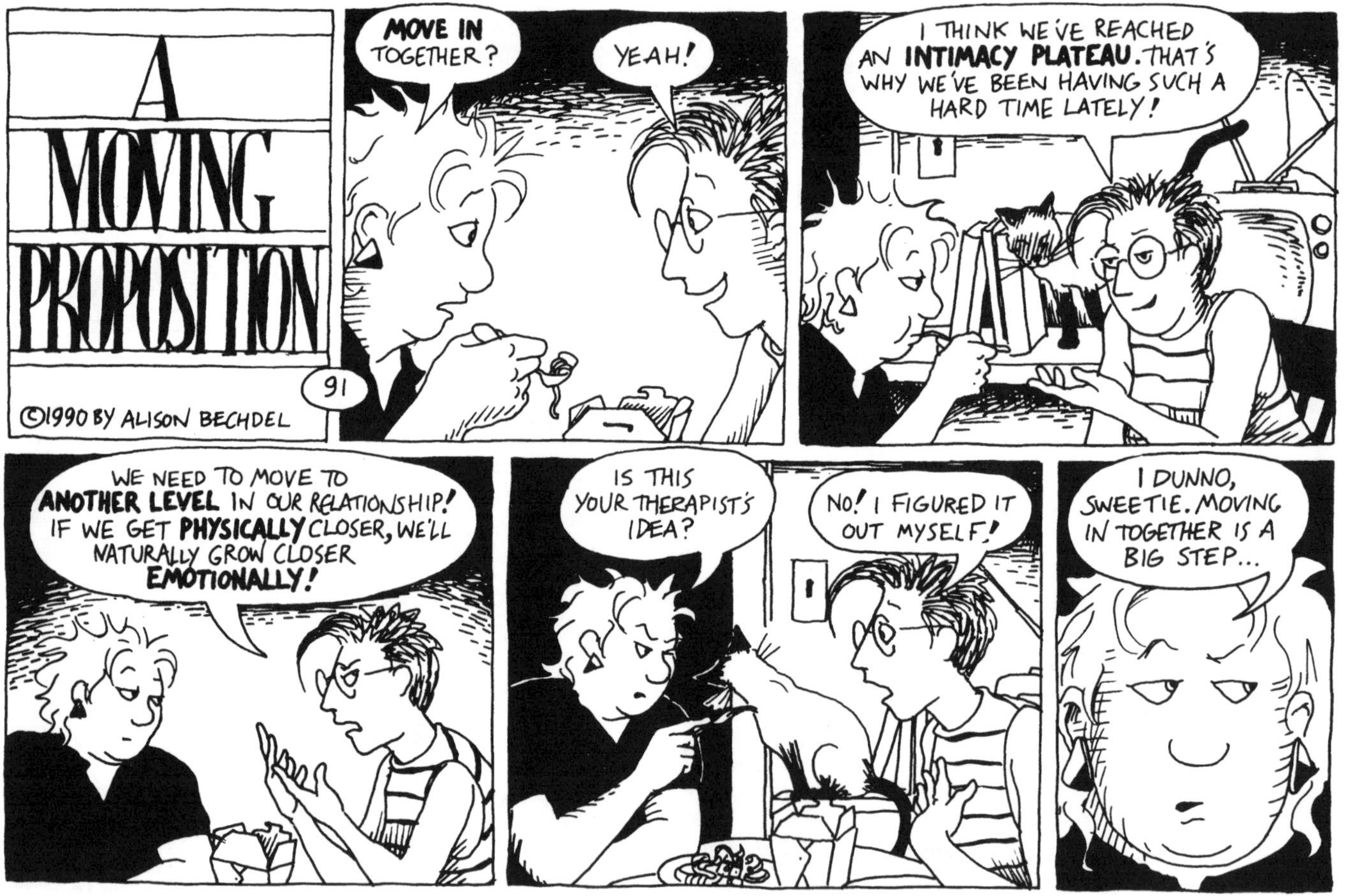
A MOVING PROPOSITION
91
©1990 BY ALISON BECHDEL
MOVE IN TOGETHER?
YEAH!
I THINK WE'VE REACHED AN **INTIMACY PLATEAU**. THAT'S WHY WE'VE BEEN HAVING SUCH A HARD TIME LATELY!
WE NEED TO MOVE TO **ANOTHER LEVEL** IN OUR RELATIONSHIP! IF WE GET **PHYSICALLY** CLOSER, WE'LL NATURALLY GROW CLOSER **EMOTIONALLY**!
IS THIS YOUR THERAPIST'S IDEA?
NO! I FIGURED IT OUT MYSELF!
I DUNNO, SWEETIE. MOVING IN TOGETHER IS A BIG STEP...

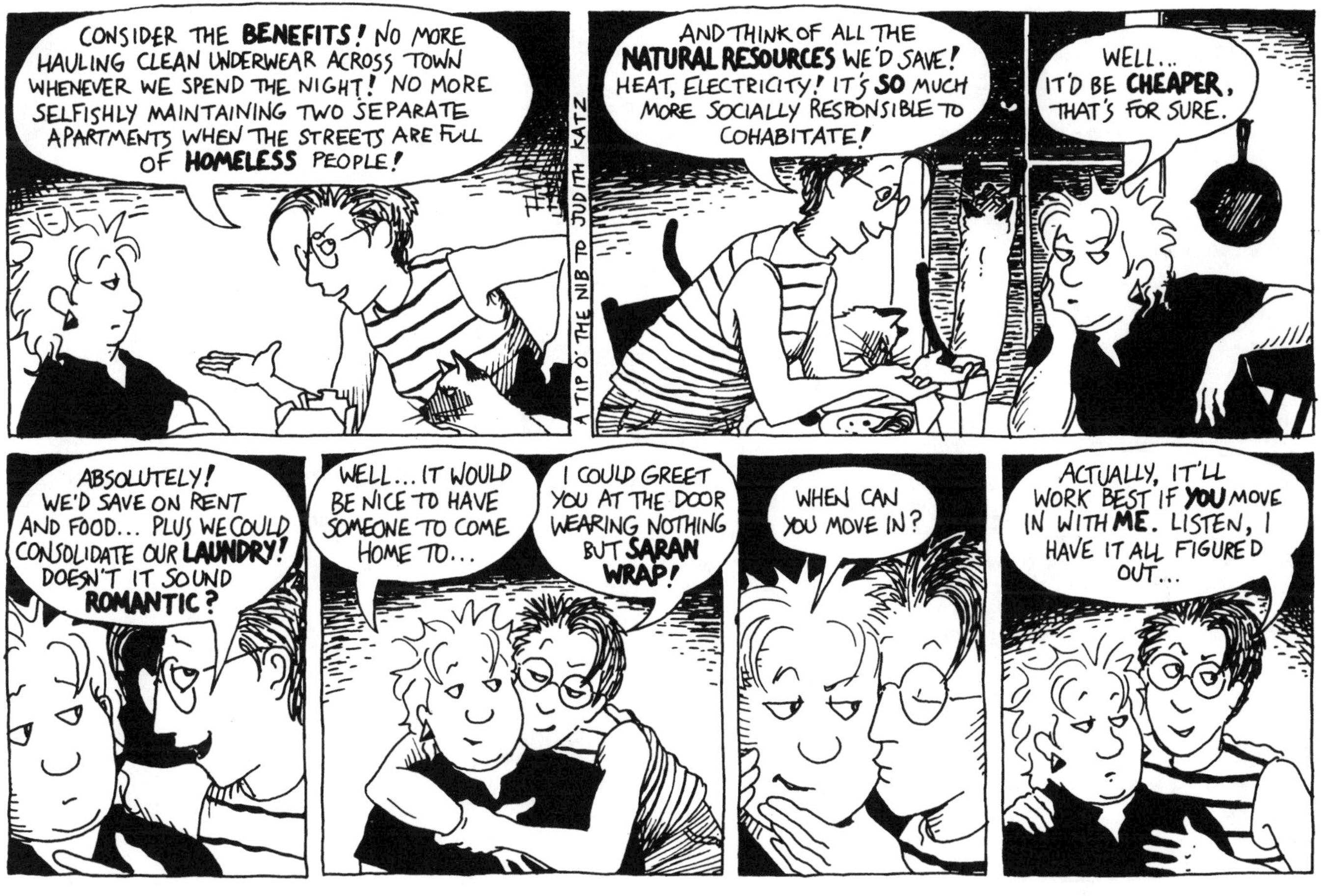
CONSIDER THE **BENEFITS**! NO MORE HAULING CLEAN UNDERWEAR ACROSS TOWN WHENEVER WE SPEND THE NIGHT! NO MORE SELFISHLY MAINTAINING TWO SEPARATE APARTMENTS WHEN THE STREETS ARE FULL OF **HOMELESS** PEOPLE!
A TIP O' THE NIB TO JUDITH KATZ
AND THINK OF ALL THE **NATURAL RESOURCES** WE'D SAVE! HEAT, ELECTRICITY! IT'S **SO** MUCH MORE SOCIALLY RESPONSIBLE TO COHABITATE!
WELL... IT'D BE **CHEAPER**, THAT'S FOR SURE.
ABSOLUTELY! WE'D SAVE ON RENT AND FOOD... PLUS WE COULD CONSOLIDATE OUR **LAUNDRY**! DOESN'T IT SOUND **ROMANTIC**?
WELL... IT WOULD BE NICE TO HAVE SOMEONE TO COME HOME TO...
I COULD GREET YOU AT THE DOOR WEARING NOTHING BUT **SARAN WRAP**!
WHEN CAN YOU MOVE IN?
ACTUALLY, IT'LL WORK BEST IF **YOU** MOVE IN WITH **ME**. LISTEN, I HAVE IT ALL FIGURED OUT...

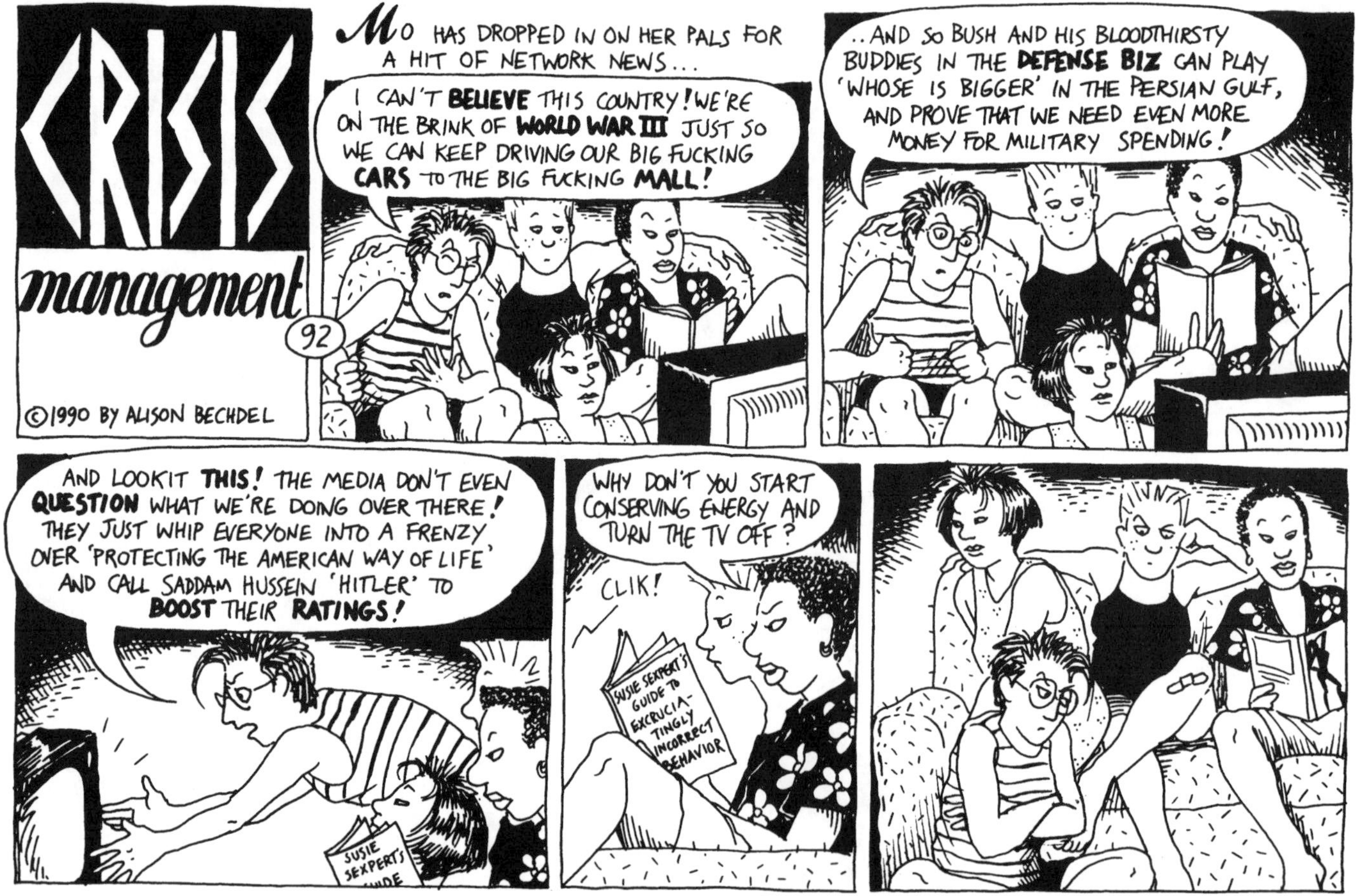
CRISIS management
92
©1990 BY ALISON BECHDEL
MO HAS DROPPED IN ON HER PALS FOR A HIT OF NETWORK NEWS...
I CAN'T BELIEVE THIS COUNTRY! WE'RE ON THE BRINK OF WORLD WAR III JUST SO WE CAN KEEP DRIVING OUR BIG FUCKING CARS TO THE BIG FUCKING MALL!
..AND SO BUSH AND HIS BLOODTHIRSTY BUDDIES IN THE DEFENSE BIZ CAN PLAY 'WHOSE IS BIGGER' IN THE PERSIAN GULF, AND PROVE THAT WE NEED EVEN MORE MONEY FOR MILITARY SPENDING!
AND LOOKIT THIS! THE MEDIA DON'T EVEN QUESTION WHAT WE'RE DOING OVER THERE! THEY JUST WHIP EVERYONE INTO A FRENZY OVER 'PROTECTING THE AMERICAN WAY OF LIFE' AND CALL SADDAM HUSSEIN 'HITLER' TO BOOST THEIR RATINGS!
SUSIE SEXPERT'S
WHY DON'T YOU START CONSERVING ENERGY AND TURN THE TV OFF?
CLIK!
SUSIE SEXPERT'S GUIDE TO EXCRUCIATINGLY INCORRECT BEHAVIOR

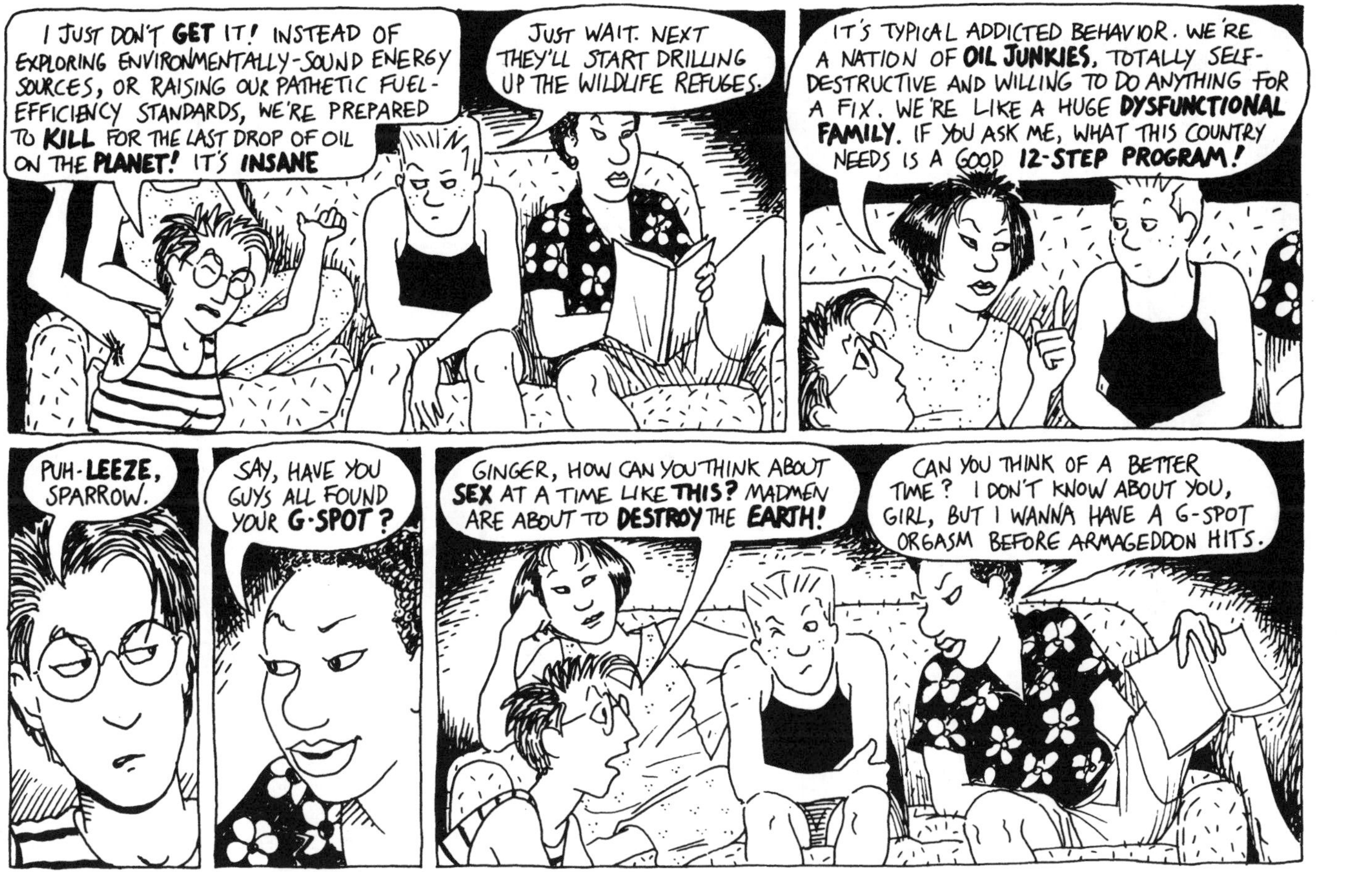

I JUST DON'T **GET** IT! INSTEAD OF EXPLORING ENVIRONMENTALLY-SOUND ENERGY SOURCES, OR RAISING OUR PATHETIC FUEL-EFFICIENCY STANDARDS, WE'RE PREPARED TO **KILL** FOR THE LAST DROP OF OIL ON THE **PLANET!** IT'S **INSANE**
JUST WAIT. NEXT THEY'LL START DRILLING UP THE WILDLIFE REFUGES.
IT'S TYPICAL ADDICTED BEHAVIOR. WE'RE A NATION OF **OIL JUNKIES**, TOTALLY SELF-DESTRUCTIVE AND WILLING TO DO ANYTHING FOR A FIX. WE'RE LIKE A HUGE **DYSFUNCTIONAL FAMILY**. IF YOU ASK ME, WHAT THIS COUNTRY NEEDS IS A GOOD **12-STEP PROGRAM!**
PUH-**LEEZE**, SPARROW.
SAY, HAVE YOU GUYS ALL FOUND YOUR **G-SPOT?**
GINGER, HOW CAN YOU THINK ABOUT **SEX** AT A TIME LIKE **THIS?** MADMEN ARE ABOUT TO **DESTROY** THE **EARTH!**
CAN YOU THINK OF A BETTER TIME? I DON'T KNOW ABOUT YOU, GIRL, BUT I WANNA HAVE A G-SPOT ORGASM BEFORE ARMAGEDDON HITS.

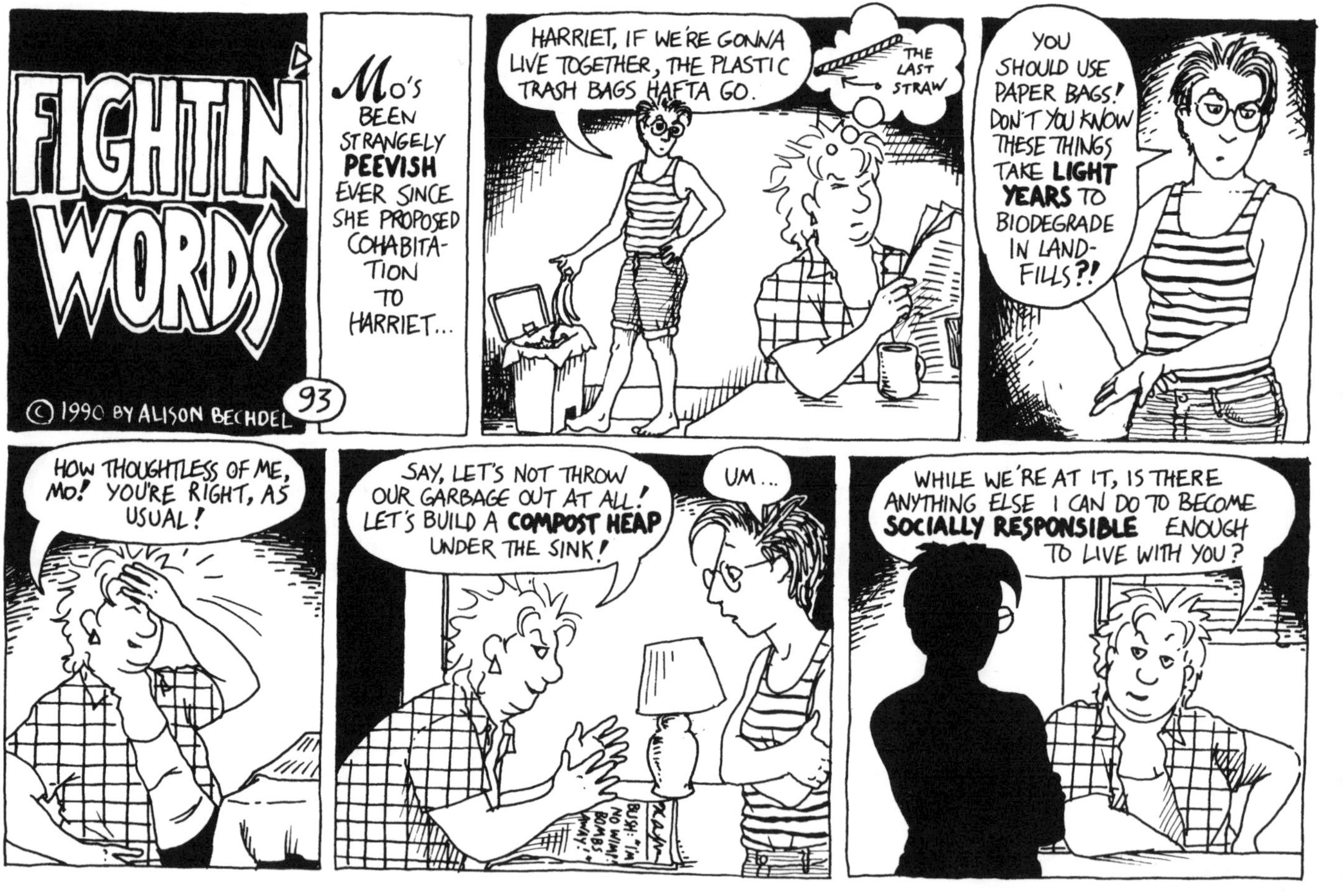
FIGHTIN' WORDS
© 1990 BY ALISON BECHDEL
93
MO'S BEEN STRANGELY PEEVISH EVER SINCE SHE PROPOSED COHABITATION TO HARRIET...
HARRIET, IF WE'RE GONNA LIVE TOGETHER, THE PLASTIC TRASH BAGS HAFTA GO.
THE LAST STRAW
YOU SHOULD USE PAPER BAGS! DON'T YOU KNOW THESE THINGS TAKE LIGHT YEARS TO BIODEGRADE IN LANDFILLS?!
HOW THOUGHTLESS OF ME, MO! YOU'RE RIGHT, AS USUAL!
SAY, LET'S NOT THROW OUR GARBAGE OUT AT ALL! LET'S BUILD A COMPOST HEAP UNDER THE SINK!
UM...
BUSH: "I'M NO WIMP! BOMBS AWAY!"
WHILE WE'RE AT IT, IS THERE ANYTHING ELSE I CAN DO TO BECOME SOCIALLY RESPONSIBLE ENOUGH TO LIVE WITH YOU?

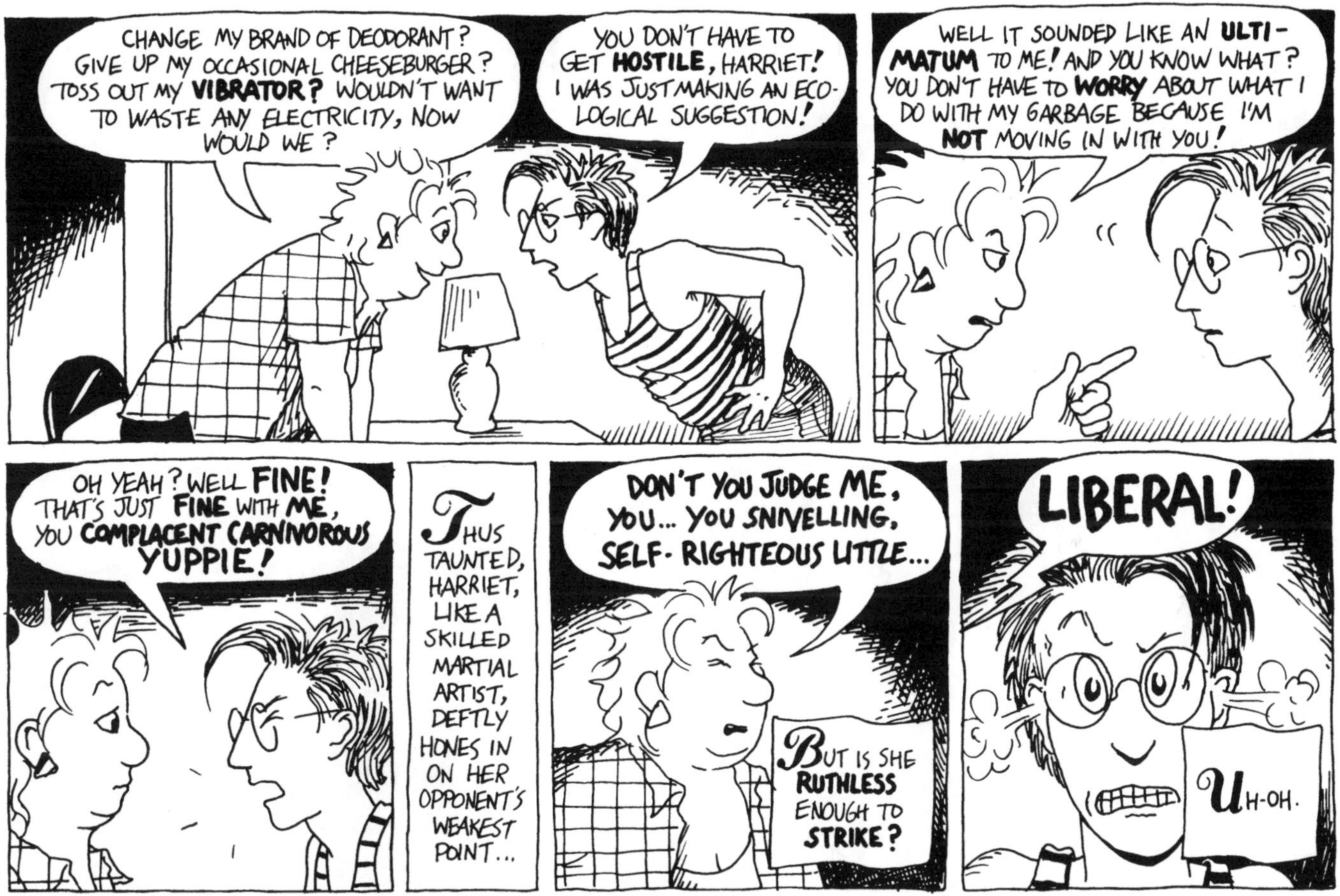
CHANGE MY BRAND OF DEODORANT? GIVE UP MY OCCASIONAL CHEESEBURGER? TOSS OUT MY VIBRATOR? WOULDN'T WANT TO WASTE ANY ELECTRICITY, NOW WOULD WE?
YOU DON'T HAVE TO GET HOSTILE, HARRIET! I WAS JUST MAKING AN ECOLOGICAL SUGGESTION!
WELL IT SOUNDED LIKE AN ULTIMATUM TO ME! AND YOU KNOW WHAT? YOU DON'T HAVE TO WORRY ABOUT WHAT I DO WITH MY GARBAGE BECAUSE I'M NOT MOVING IN WITH YOU!
OH YEAH? WELL FINE! THAT'S JUST FINE WITH ME, YOU COMPLACENT CARNIVOROUS YUPPIE!
THUS TAUNTED, HARRIET, LIKE A SKILLED MARTIAL ARTIST, DEFTLY HONES IN ON HER OPPONENT'S WEAKEST POINT...
DON'T YOU JUDGE ME, YOU... YOU SNIVELLING, SELF-RIGHTEOUS LITTLE...
BUT IS SHE RUTHLESS ENOUGH TO STRIKE?
LIBERAL!
UH-OH.

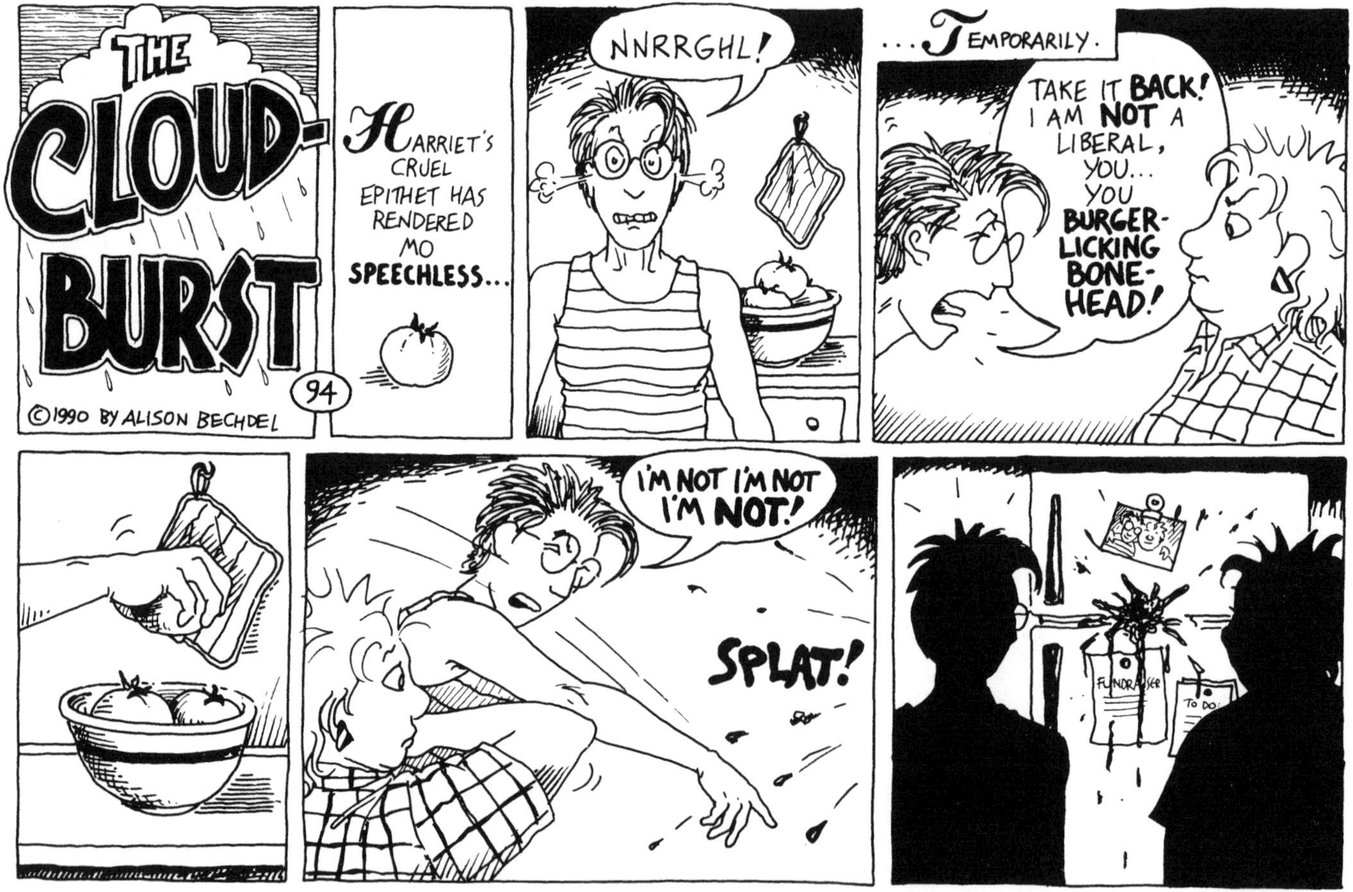
THE CLOUD-BURST
94
©1990 BY ALISON BECHDEL
HARRIET'S CRUEL EPITHET HAS RENDERED MO SPEECHLESS...
NNRRGHL!
...TEMPORARILY.
TAKE IT BACK! I AM NOT A LIBERAL, YOU... YOU BURGER-LICKING BONE-HEAD!
I'M NOT I'M NOT I'M NOT!
SPLAT!
FUNDRAISER
TO DO:

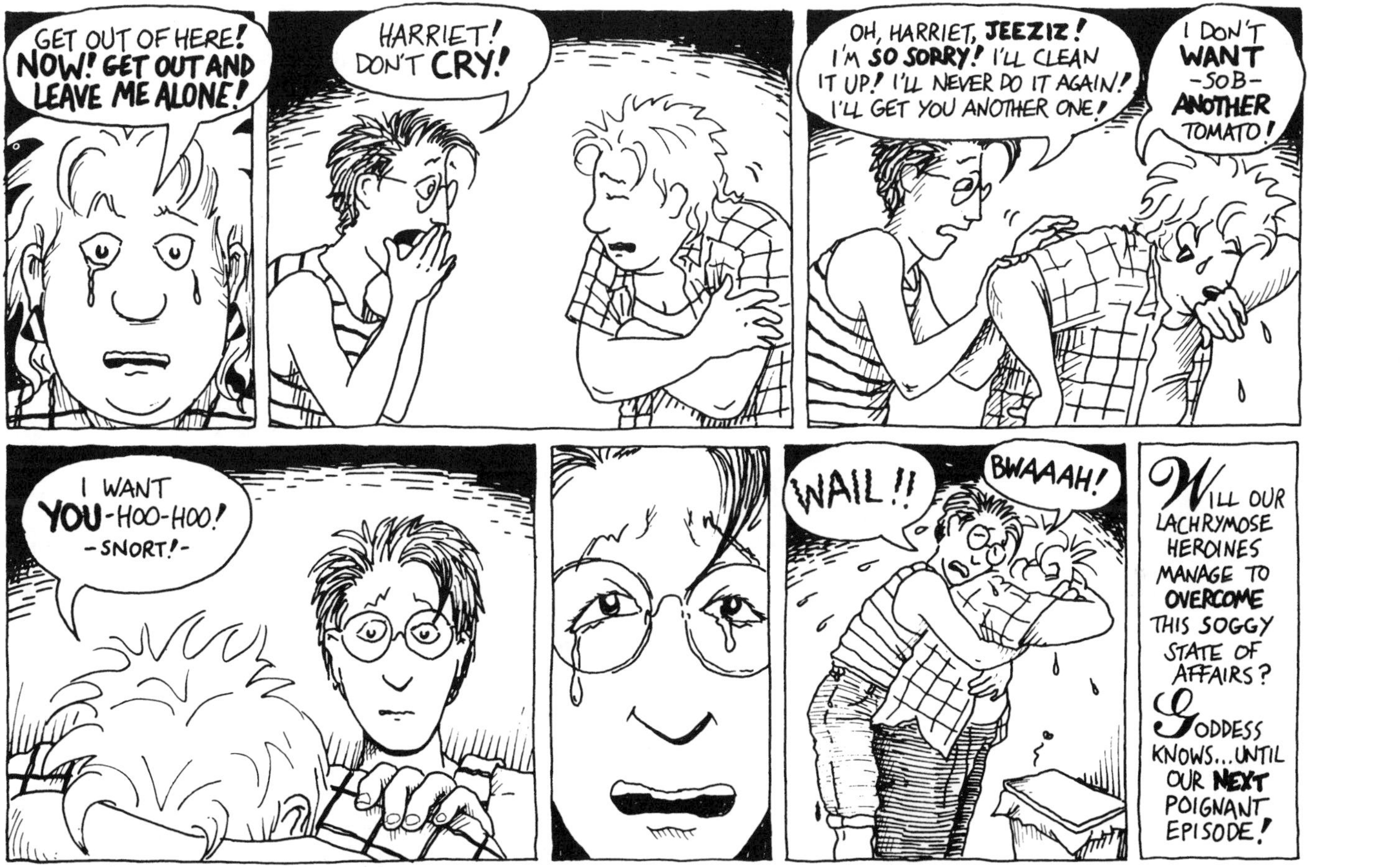
GET OUT OF HERE! NOW! GET OUT AND LEAVE ME ALONE!
HARRIET! DON'T CRY!
OH, HARRIET, JEEZIZ! I'M SO SORRY! I'LL CLEAN IT UP! I'LL NEVER DO IT AGAIN! I'LL GET YOU ANOTHER ONE!
I DON'T WANT -SOB- ANOTHER TOMATO!
I WANT YOU-HOO-HOO! -SNORT!-
WAIL!!
BWAAAH!
WILL OUR LACHRYMOSE HEROINES MANAGE TO OVERCOME THIS SOGGY STATE OF AFFAIRS? GODDESS KNOWS... UNTIL OUR NEXT POIGNANT EPISODE!

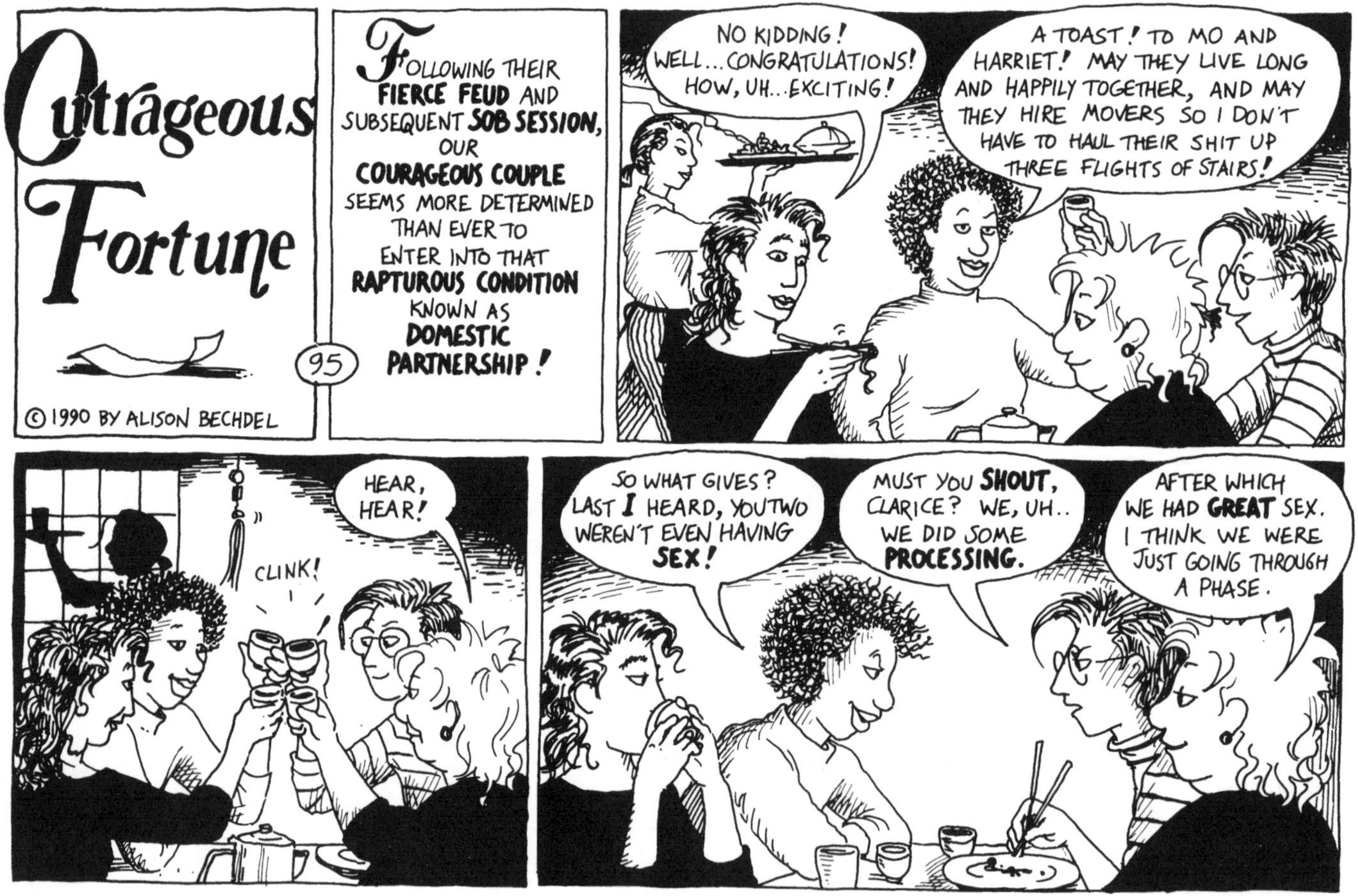
Outrageous Fortune
95
© 1990 BY ALISON BECHDEL
FOLLOWING THEIR FIERCE FEUD AND SUBSEQUENT SOB SESSION, OUR COURAGEOUS COUPLE SEEMS MORE DETERMINED THAN EVER TO ENTER INTO THAT RAPTUROUS CONDITION KNOWN AS DOMESTIC PARTNERSHIP!
NO KIDDING! WELL... CONGRATULATIONS! HOW, UH... EXCITING!
A TOAST! TO MO AND HARRIET! MAY THEY LIVE LONG AND HAPPILY TOGETHER, AND MAY THEY HIRE MOVERS SO I DON'T HAVE TO HAUL THEIR SHIT UP THREE FLIGHTS OF STAIRS!
HEAR, HEAR!
CLINK!
SO WHAT GIVES? LAST I HEARD, YOU TWO WEREN'T EVEN HAVING SEX!
MUST YOU SHOUT, CLARICE? WE, UH.. WE DID SOME PROCESSING.
AFTER WHICH WE HAD GREAT SEX. I THINK WE WERE JUST GOING THROUGH A PHASE.

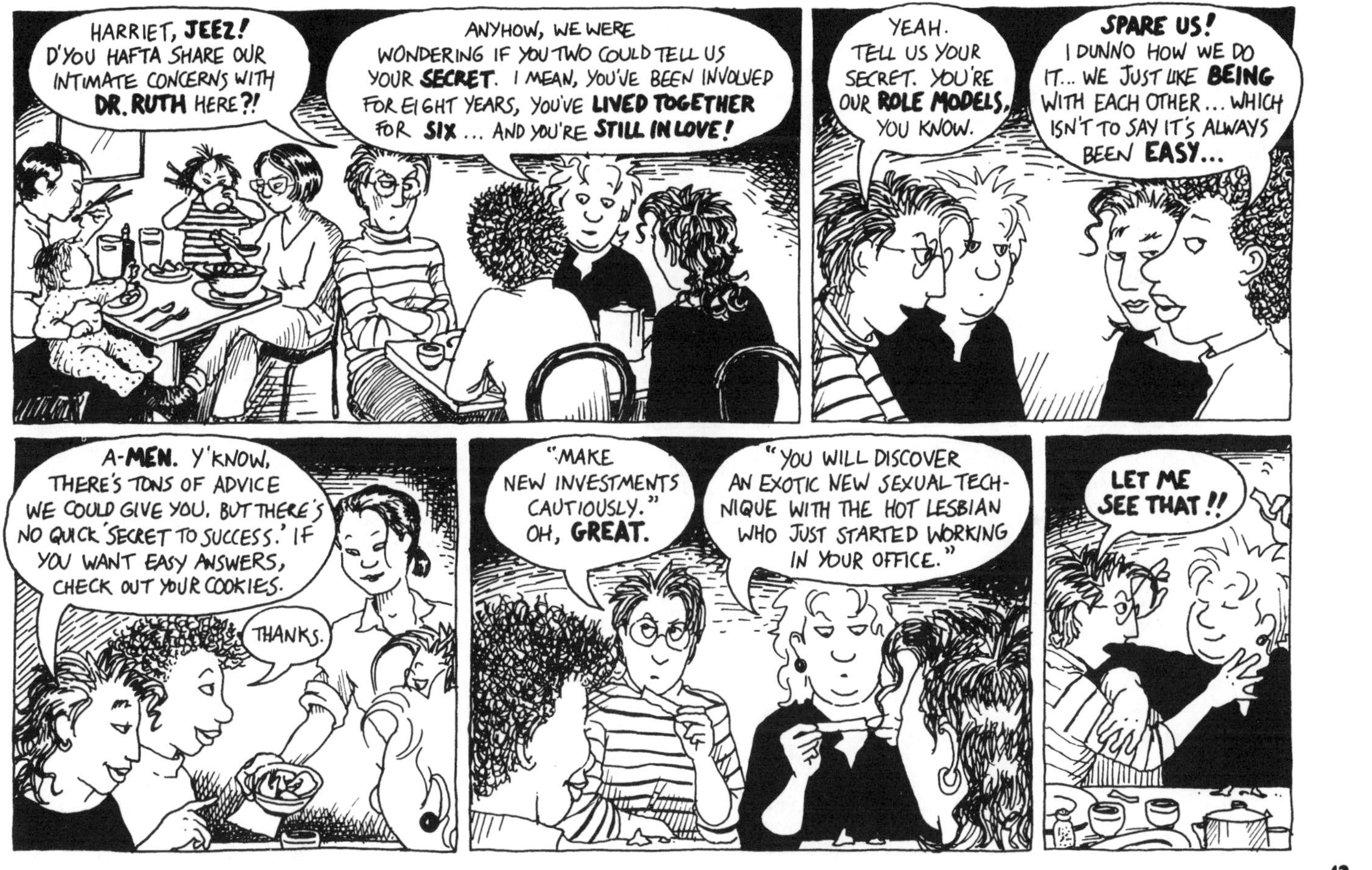
HARRIET, JEEZ! D'YOU HAFTA SHARE OUR INTIMATE CONCERNS WITH DR. RUTH HERE?!
ANYHOW, WE WERE WONDERING IF YOU TWO COULD TELL US YOUR SECRET. I MEAN, YOU'VE BEEN INVOLVED FOR EIGHT YEARS, YOU'VE LIVED TOGETHER FOR SIX ... AND YOU'RE STILL IN LOVE!
YEAH. TELL US YOUR SECRET. YOU'RE OUR ROLE MODELS, YOU KNOW.
SPARE US! I DUNNO HOW WE DO IT... WE JUST LIKE BEING WITH EACH OTHER... WHICH ISN'T TO SAY IT'S ALWAYS BEEN EASY...
A-MEN. Y'KNOW, THERE'S TONS OF ADVICE WE COULD GIVE YOU, BUT THERE'S NO QUICK 'SECRET TO SUCCESS.' IF YOU WANT EASY ANSWERS, CHECK OUT YOUR COOKIES.
THANKS.
"MAKE NEW INVESTMENTS CAUTIOUSLY." OH, GREAT.
"YOU WILL DISCOVER AN EXOTIC NEW SEXUAL TECHNIQUE WITH THE HOT LESBIAN WHO JUST STARTED WORKING IN YOUR OFFICE."
LET ME SEE THAT!!

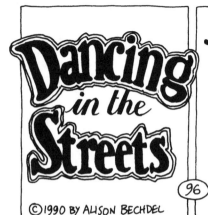

Dancing in the Streets

96

©1990 BY ALISON BECHDEL

A CRISP AUTUMN AFTERNOON FINDS OUR HEROINES **OUTDOORS**, VIGOROUSLY EXERCISING THEIR FIRST AMENDMENT RIGHTS.

HELL NO! WE WON'T GO! WE WON'T FIGHT FOR AMOCO!

U.S. OUT

NO BLOOD FOR OIL

SO LIKE, WHERE'D ALL THESE BEAUTIFUL WOMEN COME FROM?

WHAT BEAUTIFUL WOMEN?

DON'T ASK **HER**, GINGER. SHE ONLY HAS EYES FOR **HARRIET** NOW THAT THEY'RE MOVING IN TOGETHER.

IS THERE SOMETHING **WRONG** WITH THAT?

NOT AT ALL! SOME OF MY **BEST FRIENDS** ARE MONOTONOUS!

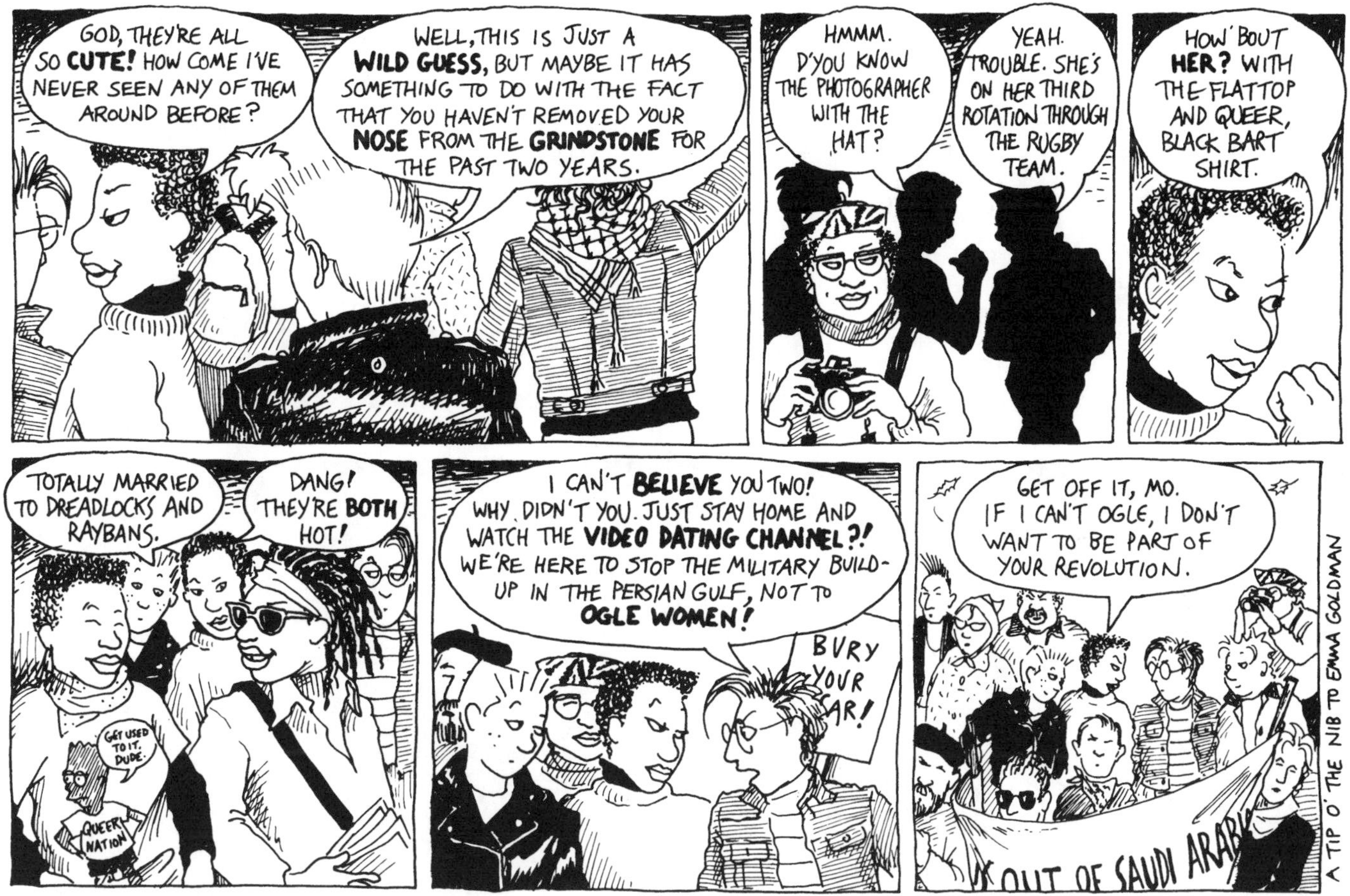
GOD, THEY'RE ALL SO **CUTE!** HOW COME I'VE NEVER SEEN ANY OF THEM AROUND BEFORE?
WELL, THIS IS JUST A **WILD GUESS,** BUT MAYBE IT HAS SOMETHING TO DO WITH THE FACT THAT YOU HAVEN'T REMOVED YOUR **NOSE** FROM THE **GRINDSTONE** FOR THE PAST TWO YEARS.
HMMM. D'YOU KNOW THE PHOTOGRAPHER WITH THE HAT?
YEAH. TROUBLE. SHE'S ON HER THIRD ROTATION THROUGH THE RUGBY TEAM.
HOW 'BOUT **HER?** WITH THE FLATTOP AND QUEER, BLACK BART SHIRT.
TOTALLY MARRIED TO DREADLOCKS AND RAYBANS.
DANG! THEY'RE **BOTH** HOT!
GET USED TO IT, DUDE.
QUEER NATION
I CAN'T **BELIEVE** YOU TWO! WHY DIDN'T YOU JUST STAY HOME AND WATCH THE **VIDEO DATING CHANNEL?!** WE'RE HERE TO STOP THE MILITARY BUILD-UP IN THE PERSIAN GULF, NOT TO **OGLE WOMEN!**
BURY YOUR CAR!
GET OFF IT, MO. IF I CAN'T OGLE, I DON'T WANT TO BE PART OF YOUR REVOLUTION.
S OUT OF SAUDI ARAB
A TIP O' THE NIB TO EMMA GOLDMAN

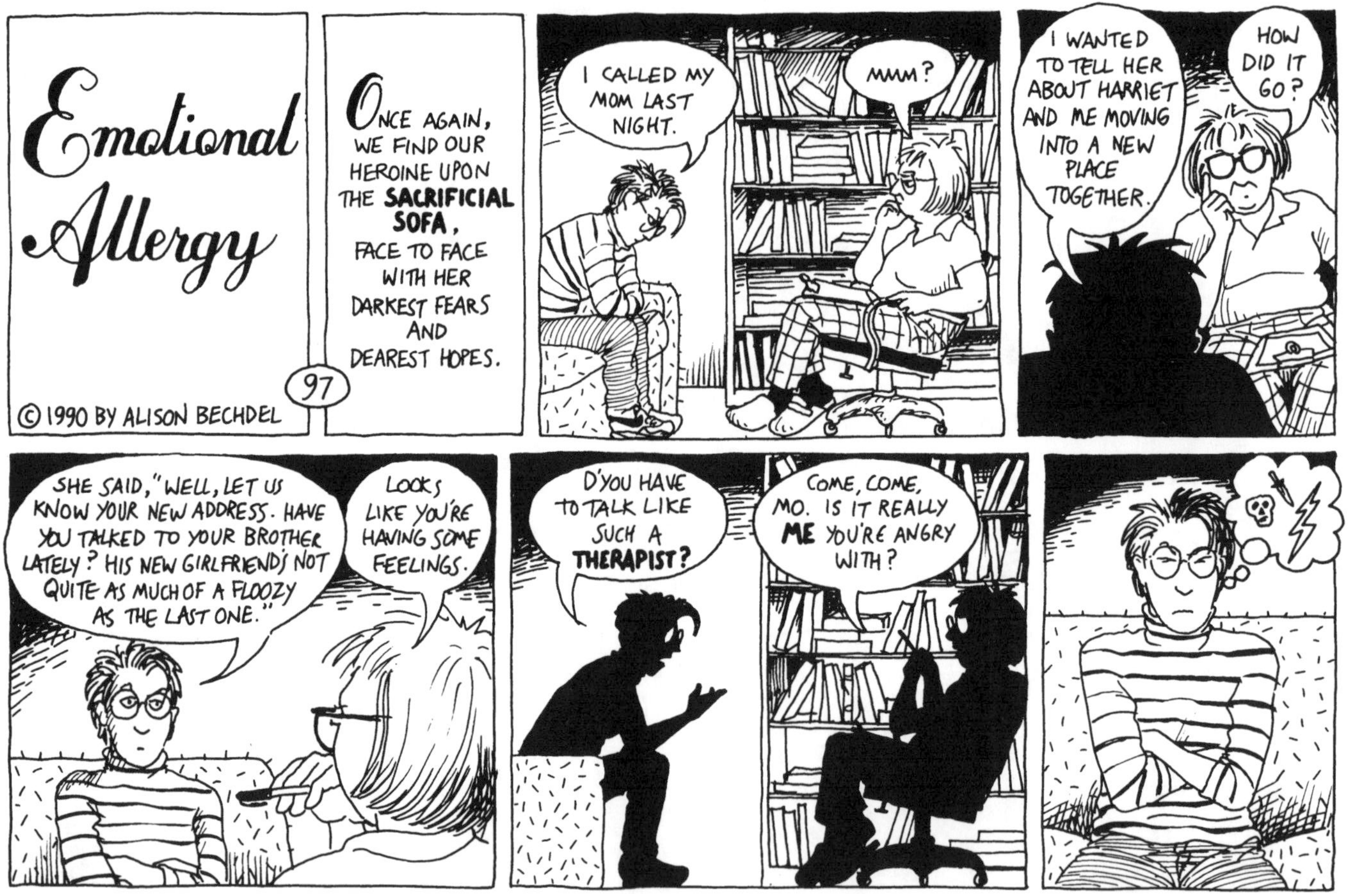
Emotional Allergy
© 1990 BY ALISON BECHDEL
97
ONCE AGAIN, WE FIND OUR HEROINE UPON THE **SACRIFICIAL SOFA**, FACE TO FACE WITH HER DARKEST FEARS AND DEAREST HOPES.
I CALLED MY MOM LAST NIGHT.
MMM?
I WANTED TO TELL HER ABOUT HARRIET AND ME MOVING INTO A NEW PLACE TOGETHER.
HOW DID IT GO?
SHE SAID, "WELL, LET US KNOW YOUR NEW ADDRESS. HAVE YOU TALKED TO YOUR BROTHER LATELY? HIS NEW GIRLFRIEND'S NOT QUITE AS MUCH OF A FLOOZY AS THE LAST ONE."
LOOKS LIKE YOU'RE HAVING SOME FEELINGS.
D'YOU HAVE TO TALK LIKE SUCH A **THERAPIST**?
COME, COME, MO. IS IT REALLY **ME** YOU'RE ANGRY WITH?

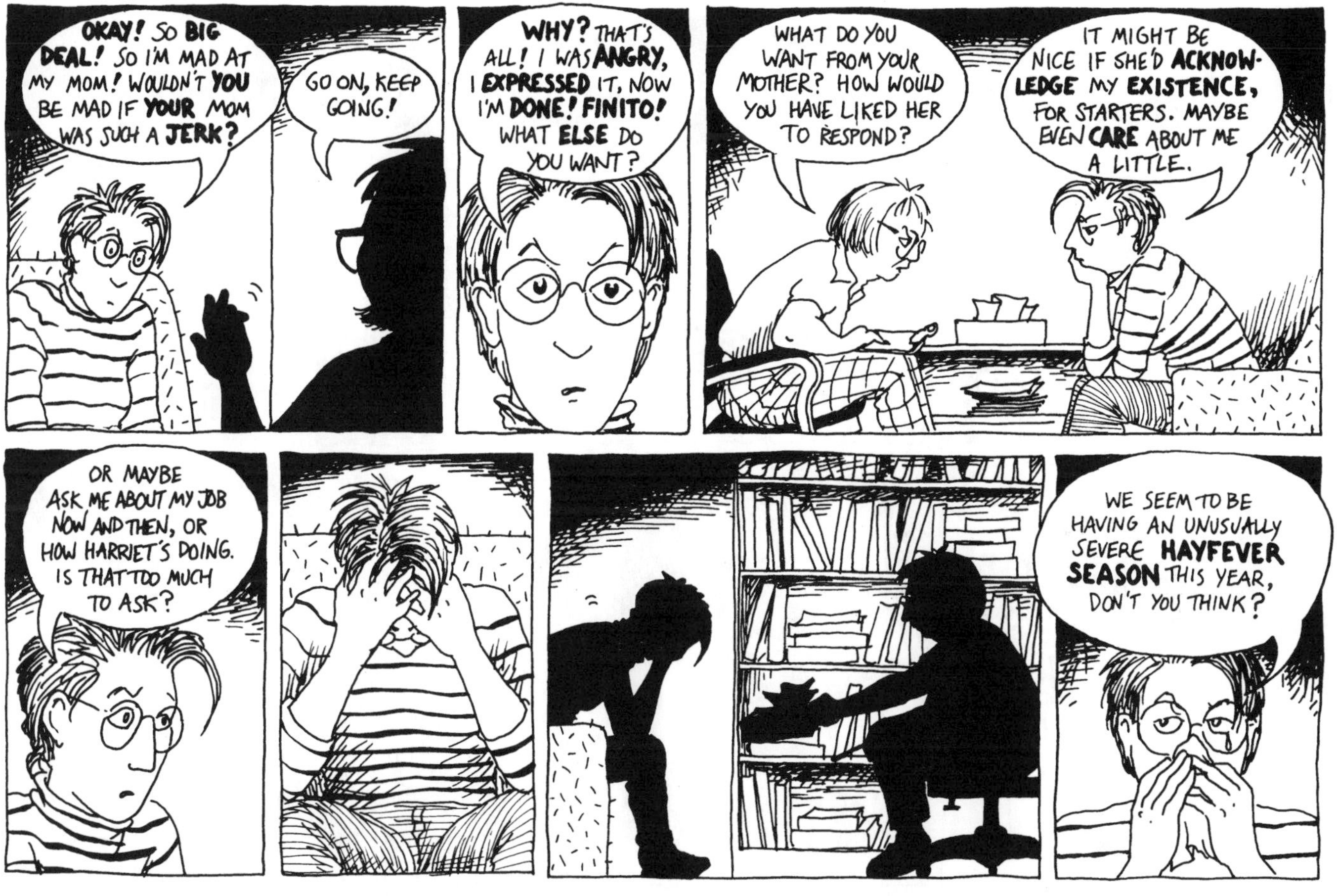
OKAY! SO BIG DEAL! SO I'M MAD AT MY MOM! WOULDN'T YOU BE MAD IF YOUR MOM WAS SUCH A JERK?
GO ON, KEEP GOING!
WHY? THAT'S ALL! I WAS ANGRY, I EXPRESSED IT, NOW I'M DONE! FINITO! WHAT ELSE DO YOU WANT?
WHAT DO YOU WANT FROM YOUR MOTHER? HOW WOULD YOU HAVE LIKED HER TO RESPOND?
IT MIGHT BE NICE IF SHE'D ACKNOWLEDGE MY EXISTENCE, FOR STARTERS. MAYBE EVEN CARE ABOUT ME A LITTLE.
OR MAYBE ASK ME ABOUT MY JOB NOW AND THEN, OR HOW HARRIET'S DOING. IS THAT TOO MUCH TO ASK?
WE SEEM TO BE HAVING AN UNUSUALLY SEVERE HAYFEVER SEASON THIS YEAR, DON'T YOU THINK?

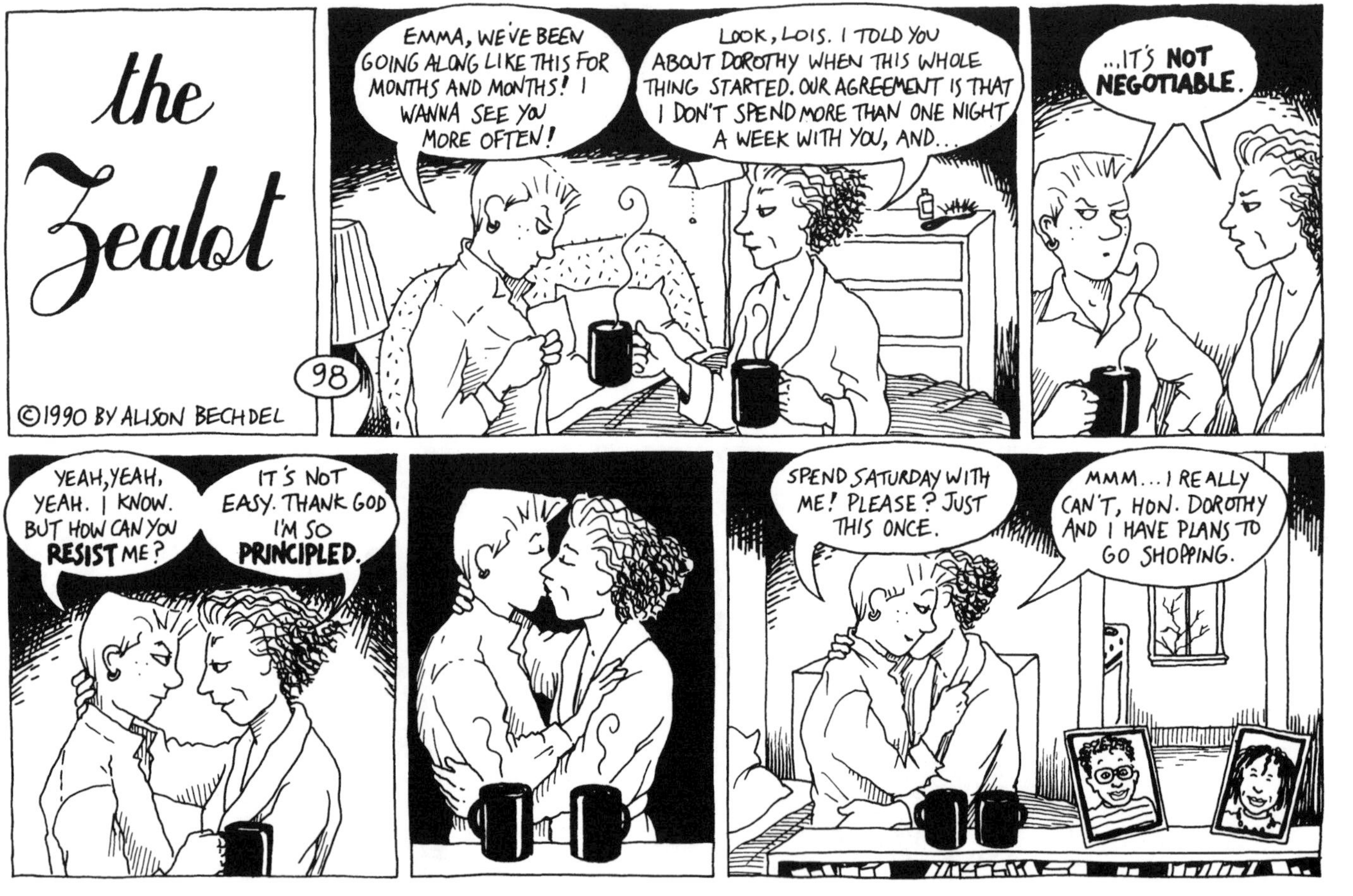
the Zealot
98
©1990 BY ALISON BECHDEL
EMMA, WE'VE BEEN GOING ALONG LIKE THIS FOR MONTHS AND MONTHS! I WANNA SEE YOU MORE OFTEN!
LOOK, LOIS. I TOLD YOU ABOUT DOROTHY WHEN THIS WHOLE THING STARTED. OUR AGREEMENT IS THAT I DON'T SPEND MORE THAN ONE NIGHT A WEEK WITH YOU, AND...
...IT'S **NOT NEGOTIABLE**.
YEAH, YEAH, YEAH. I KNOW. BUT HOW CAN YOU **RESIST** ME?
IT'S NOT EASY. THANK GOD I'M SO **PRINCIPLED**.
SPEND SATURDAY WITH ME! PLEASE? JUST THIS ONCE.
MMM... I REALLY CAN'T, HON. DOROTHY AND I HAVE PLANS TO GO SHOPPING.

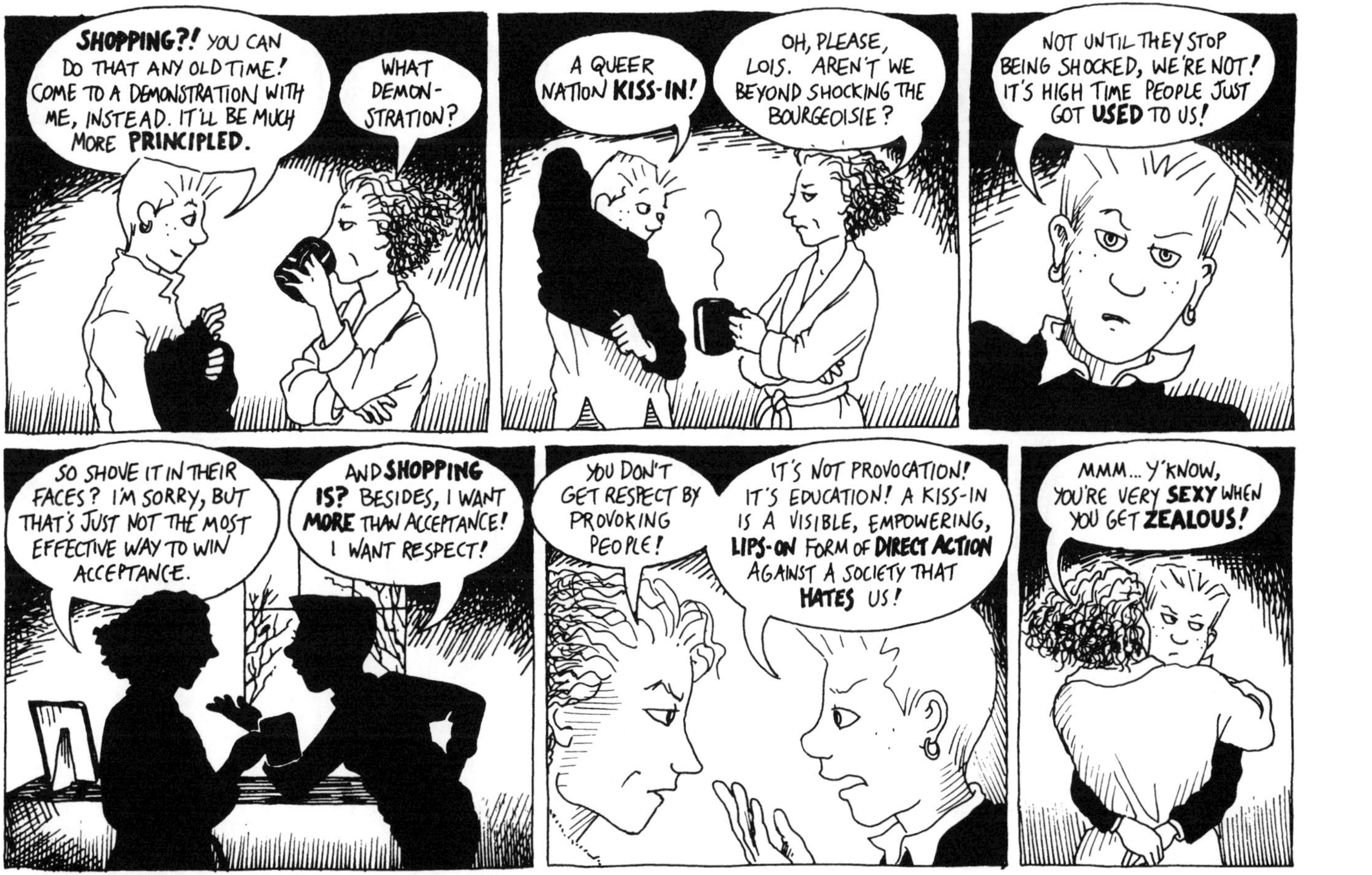
SHOPPING?! YOU CAN DO THAT ANY OLD TIME! COME TO A DEMONSTRATION WITH ME, INSTEAD. IT'LL BE MUCH MORE PRINCIPLED.
WHAT DEMON-STRATION?
A QUEER NATION KISS-IN!
OH, PLEASE, LOIS. AREN'T WE BEYOND SHOCKING THE BOURGEOISIE?
NOT UNTIL THEY STOP BEING SHOCKED, WE'RE NOT! IT'S HIGH TIME PEOPLE JUST GOT USED TO US!
SO SHOVE IT IN THEIR FACES? I'M SORRY, BUT THAT'S JUST NOT THE MOST EFFECTIVE WAY TO WIN ACCEPTANCE.
AND SHOPPING IS? BESIDES, I WANT MORE THAN ACCEPTANCE! I WANT RESPECT!
YOU DON'T GET RESPECT BY PROVOKING PEOPLE!
IT'S NOT PROVOCATION! IT'S EDUCATION! A KISS-IN IS A VISIBLE, EMPOWERING, LIPS-ON FORM OF DIRECT ACTION AGAINST A SOCIETY THAT HATES US!
MMM... Y'KNOW, YOU'RE VERY SEXY WHEN YOU GET ZEALOUS!

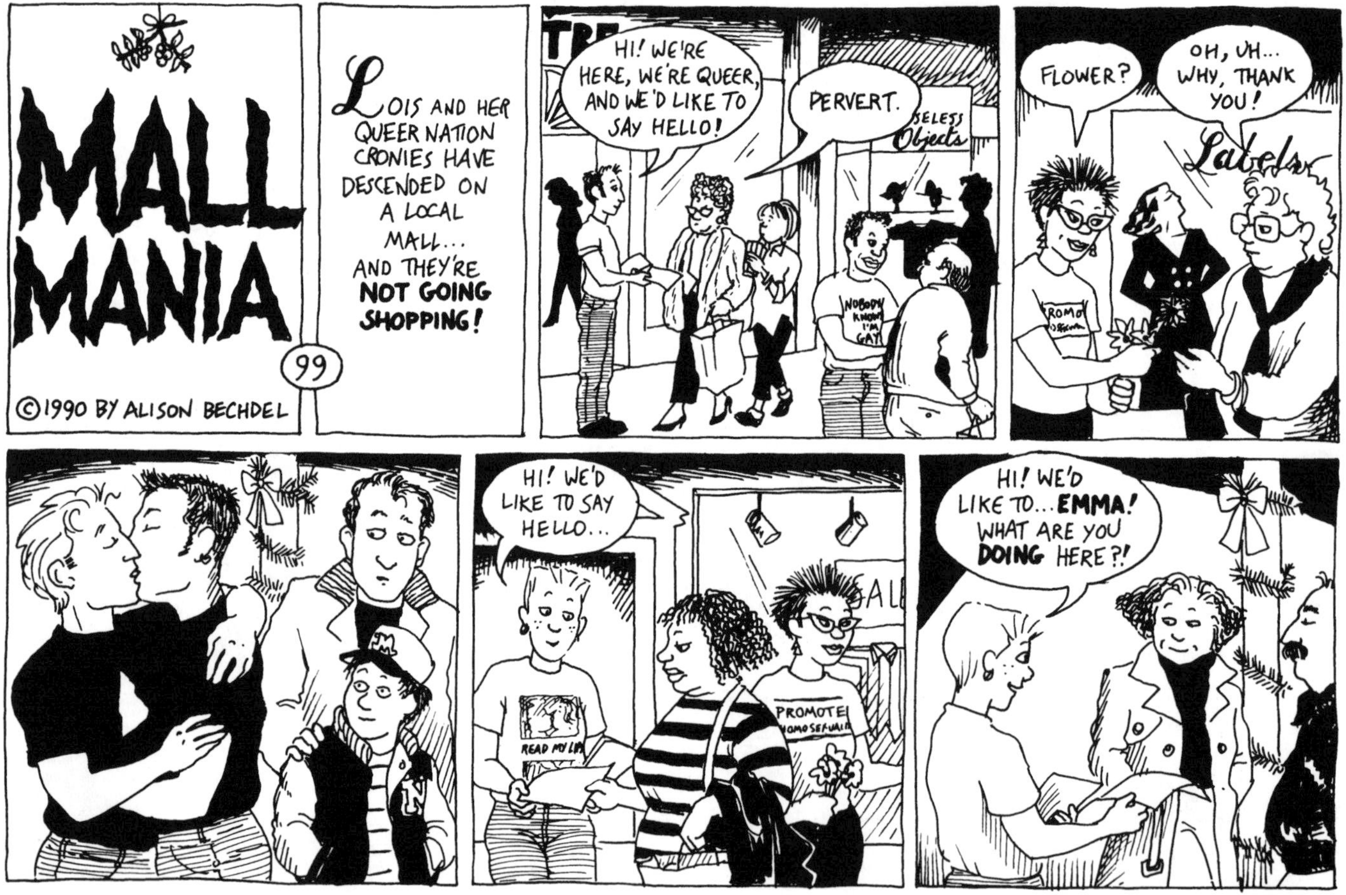
MALL MANIA
99
©1990 BY ALISON BECHDEL
LOIS AND HER QUEER NATION CRONIES HAVE DESCENDED ON A LOCAL MALL... AND THEY'RE NOT GOING SHOPPING!
HI! WE'RE HERE, WE'RE QUEER, AND WE'D LIKE TO SAY HELLO!
PERVERT.
SELESS Objects
NOBODY KNOWS I'M GAY
FLOWER?
OH, UH... WHY, THANK YOU!
Labels
HI! WE'D LIKE TO SAY HELLO...
READ MY LIPS
PROMOTE HOMOSEXUALITY
HI! WE'D LIKE TO... EMMA! WHAT ARE YOU DOING HERE?!

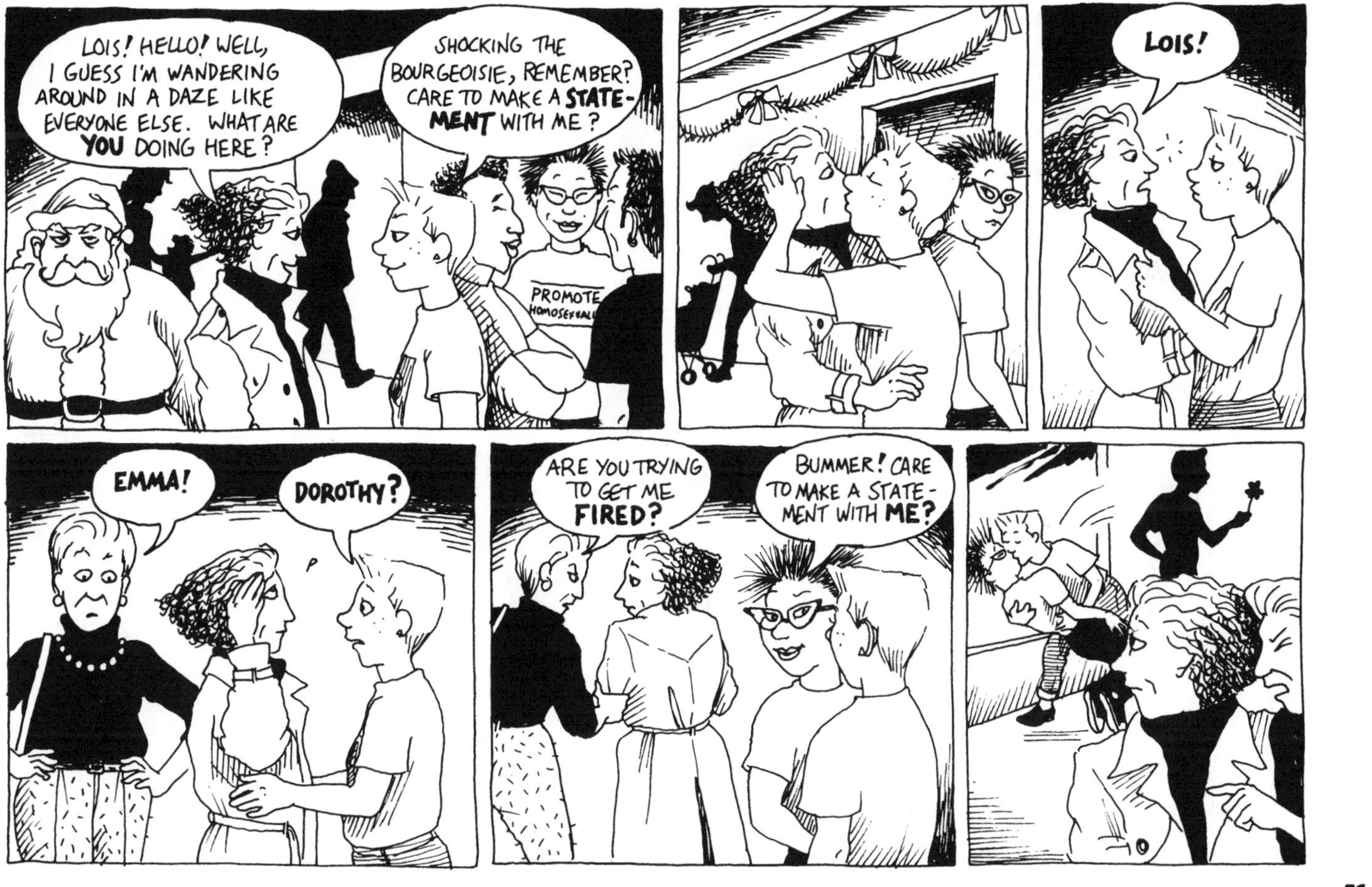
LOIS! HELLO! WELL, I GUESS I'M WANDERING AROUND IN A DAZE LIKE EVERYONE ELSE. WHAT ARE **YOU** DOING HERE?
SHOCKING THE BOURGEOISIE, REMEMBER? CARE TO MAKE A **STATE-MENT** WITH ME?
PROMOTE
LOIS!
EMMA!
DOROTHY?
ARE YOU TRYING TO GET ME **FIRED**?
BUMMER! CARE TO MAKE A STATE-MENT WITH **ME**?

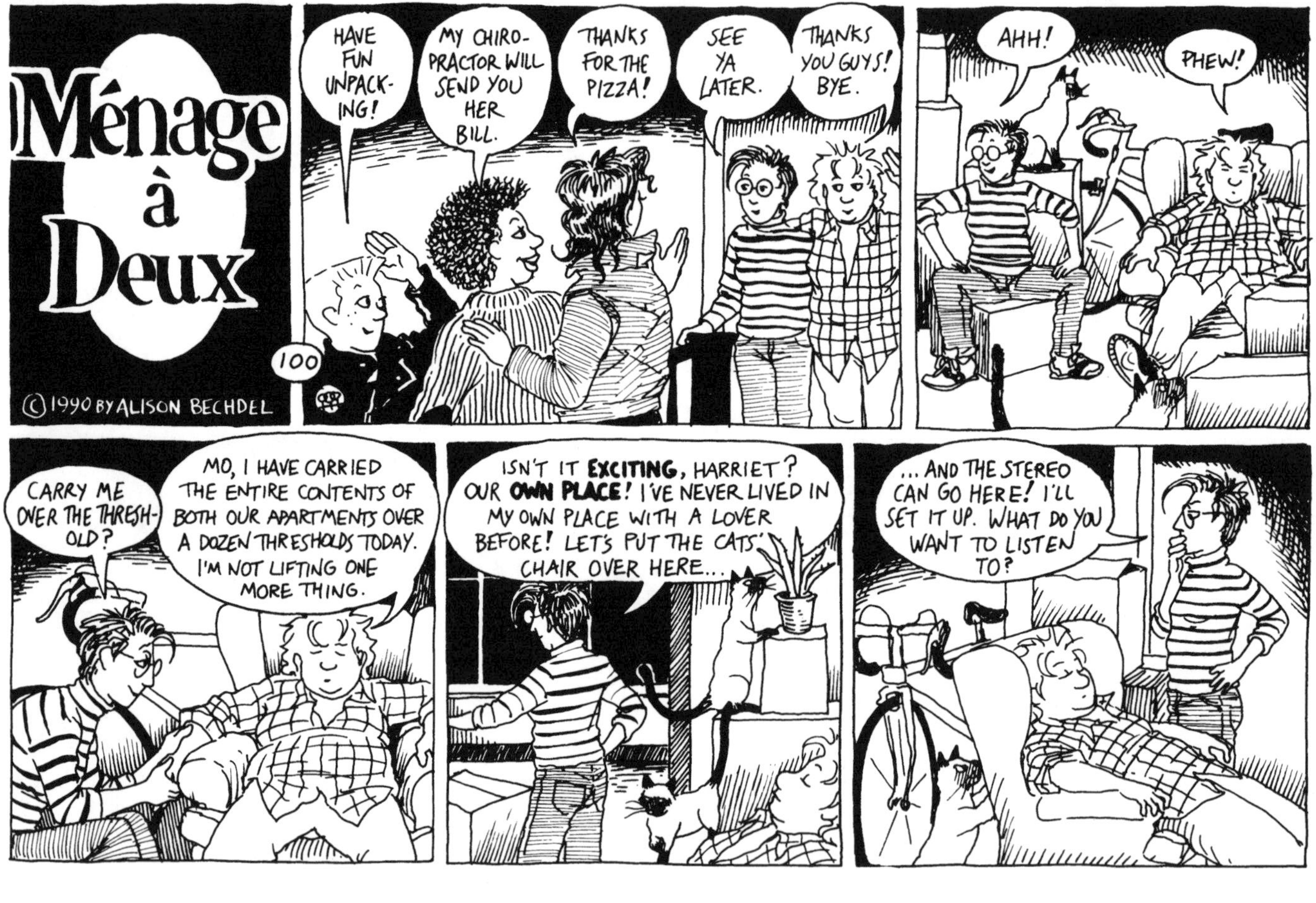
Ménage à Deux
100
©1990 BY ALISON BECHDEL
HAVE FUN UNPACKING!
MY CHIROPRACTOR WILL SEND YOU HER BILL.
THANKS FOR THE PIZZA!
SEE YA LATER.
THANKS YOU GUYS! BYE.
AHH!
PHEW!
CARRY ME OVER THE THRESHOLD?
MO, I HAVE CARRIED THE ENTIRE CONTENTS OF BOTH OUR APARTMENTS OVER A DOZEN THRESHOLDS TODAY. I'M NOT LIFTING ONE MORE THING.
ISN'T IT **EXCITING**, HARRIET? OUR **OWN PLACE**! I'VE NEVER LIVED IN MY OWN PLACE WITH A LOVER BEFORE! LET'S PUT THE CATS' CHAIR OVER HERE...
...AND THE STEREO CAN GO HERE! I'LL SET IT UP. WHAT DO YOU WANT TO LISTEN TO?

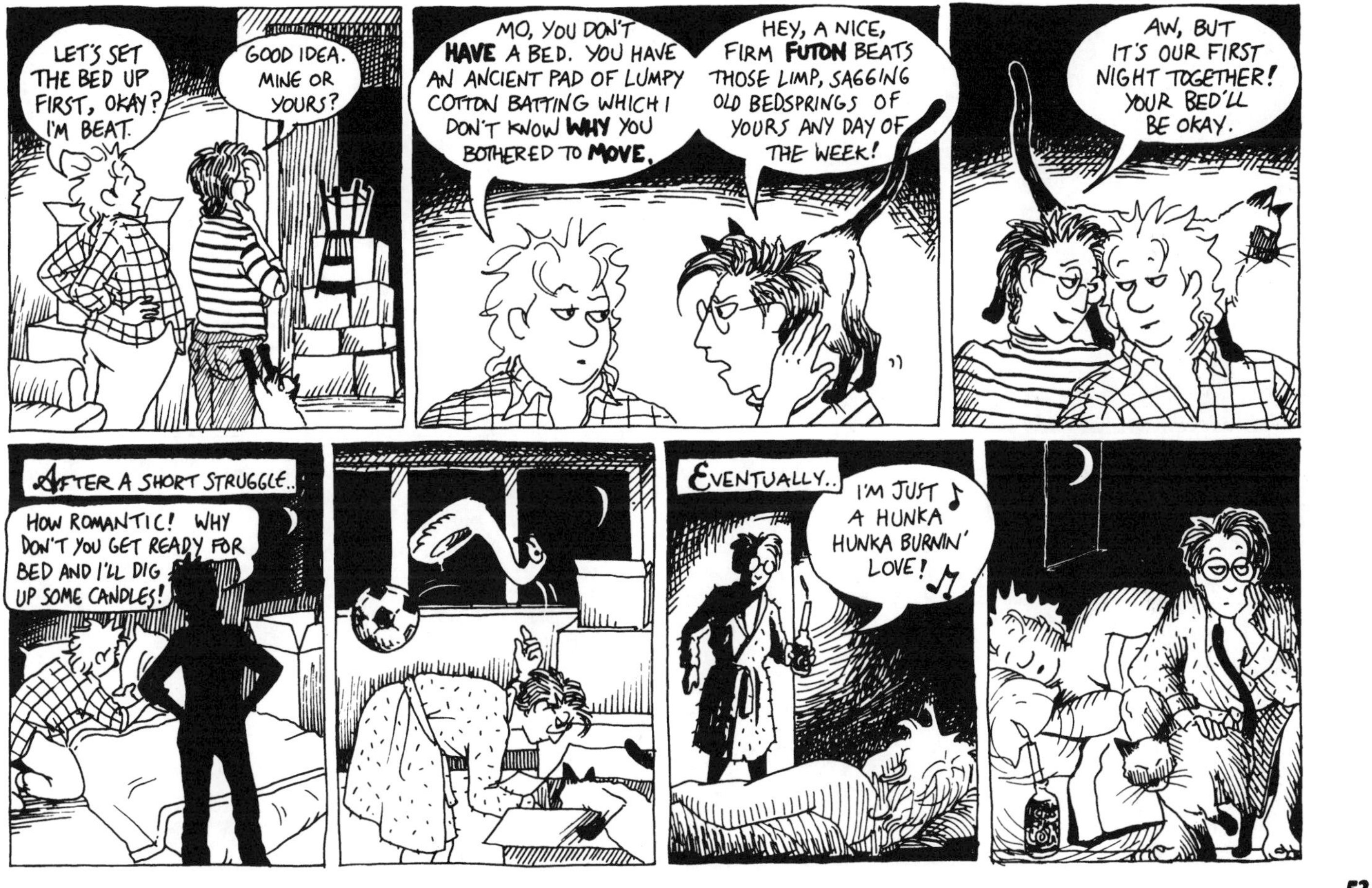
LET'S SET THE BED UP FIRST, OKAY? I'M BEAT.
GOOD IDEA. MINE OR YOURS?
MO, YOU DON'T **HAVE** A BED. YOU HAVE AN ANCIENT PAD OF LUMPY COTTON BATTING WHICH I DON'T KNOW **WHY** YOU BOTHERED TO **MOVE**.
HEY, A NICE, FIRM **FUTON** BEATS THOSE LIMP, SAGGING OLD BEDSPRINGS OF YOURS ANY DAY OF THE WEEK!
AW, BUT IT'S OUR FIRST NIGHT TOGETHER! YOUR BED'LL BE OKAY.
AFTER A SHORT STRUGGLE..
HOW ROMANTIC! WHY DON'T YOU GET READY FOR BED AND I'LL DIG UP SOME CANDLES!
EVENTUALLY..
I'M JUST A HUNKA HUNKA BURNIN' LOVE!

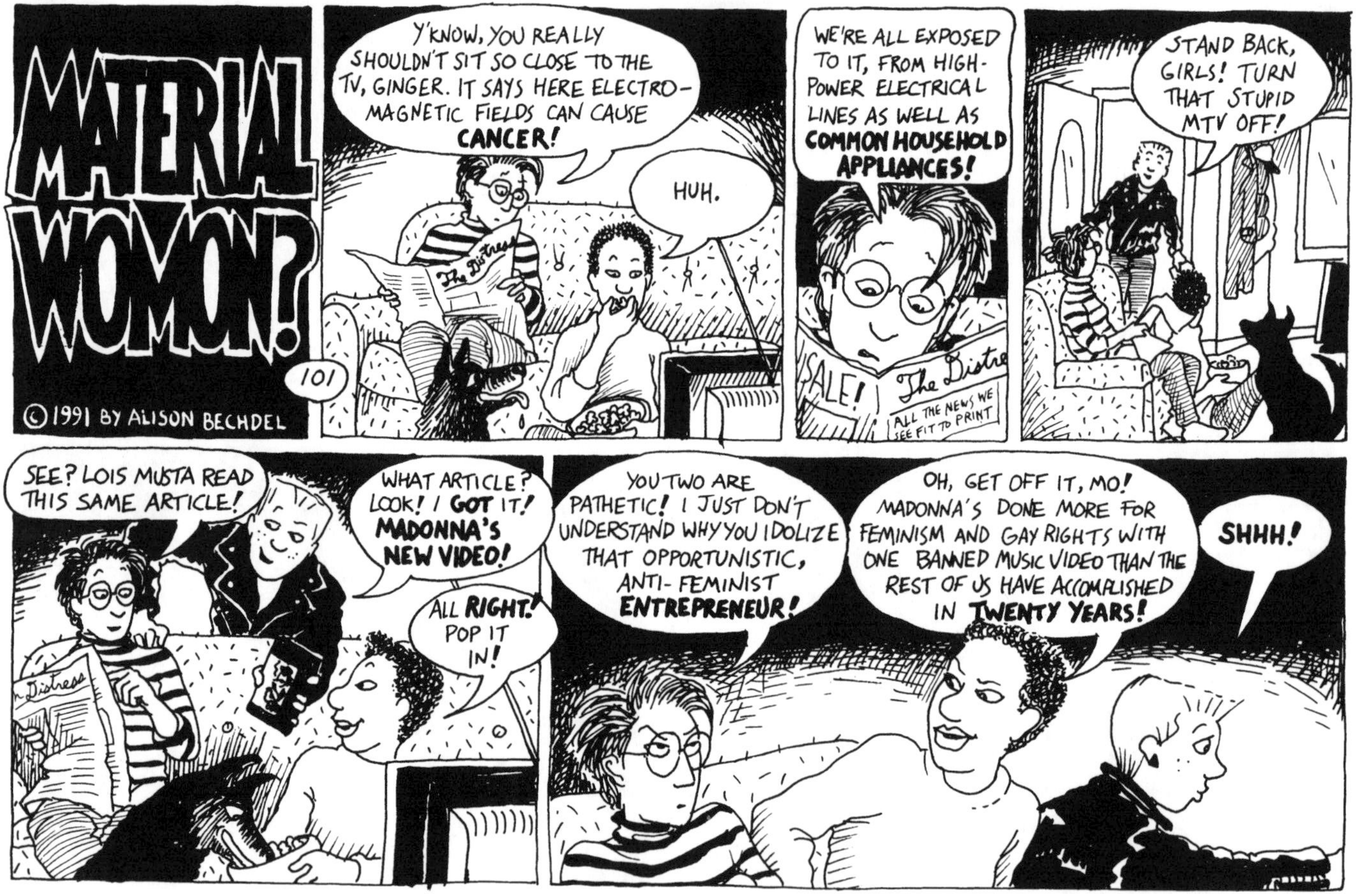
MATERIAL WOMON?
101
©1991 BY ALISON BECHDEL
Y'KNOW, YOU REALLY SHOULDN'T SIT SO CLOSE TO THE TV, GINGER. IT SAYS HERE ELECTRO-MAGNETIC FIELDS CAN CAUSE **CANCER!**
HUH.
The Distress
WE'RE ALL EXPOSED TO IT, FROM HIGH-POWER ELECTRICAL LINES AS WELL AS **COMMON HOUSEHOLD APPLIANCES!**
SALE!
The Distre
ALL THE NEWS WE SEE FIT TO PRINT
STAND BACK, GIRLS! TURN THAT STUPID MTV OFF!
SEE? LOIS MUSTA READ THIS SAME ARTICLE!
WHAT ARTICLE? LOOK! I **GOT** IT! **MADONNA'S NEW VIDEO!**
ALL **RIGHT!** POP IT IN!
Distress
YOU TWO ARE PATHETIC! I JUST DON'T UNDERSTAND WHY YOU IDOLIZE THAT OPPORTUNISTIC, ANTI-FEMINIST **ENTREPRENEUR!**
OH, GET OFF IT, MO! MADONNA'S DONE MORE FOR FEMINISM AND GAY RIGHTS WITH ONE BANNED MUSIC VIDEO THAN THE REST OF US HAVE ACCOMPLISHED IN **TWENTY YEARS!**
SHHH!

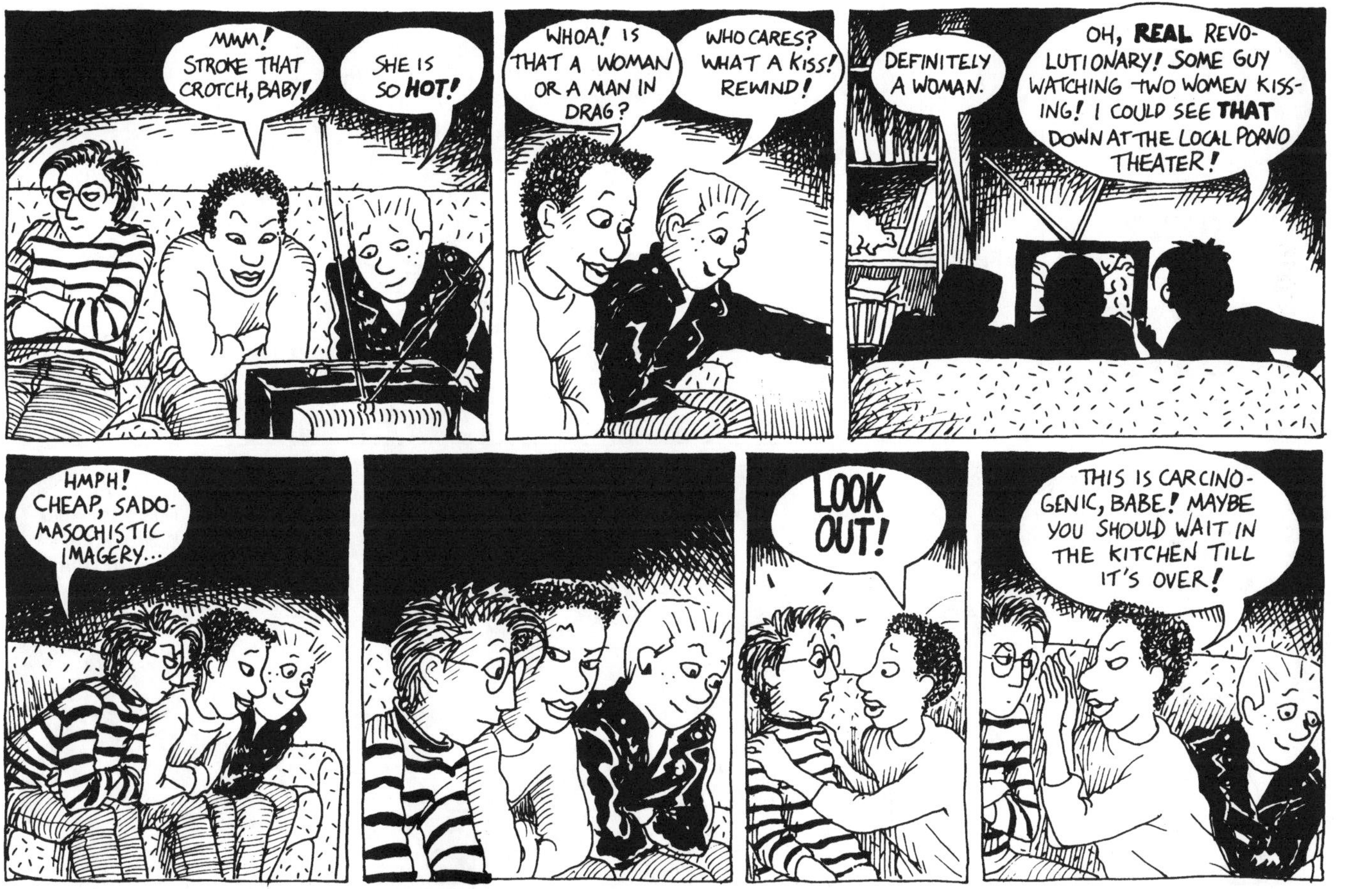
MMM! STROKE THAT CROTCH, BABY!
SHE IS SO HOT!
WHOA! IS THAT A WOMAN OR A MAN IN DRAG?
WHO CARES? WHAT A KISS! REWIND!
DEFINITELY A WOMAN.
OH, REAL REVOLUTIONARY! SOME GUY WATCHING TWO WOMEN KISSING! I COULD SEE THAT DOWN AT THE LOCAL PORNO THEATER!
HMPH! CHEAP, SADO-MASOCHISTIC IMAGERY...
LOOK OUT!
THIS IS CARCINOGENIC, BABE! MAYBE YOU SHOULD WAIT IN THE KITCHEN TILL IT'S OVER!

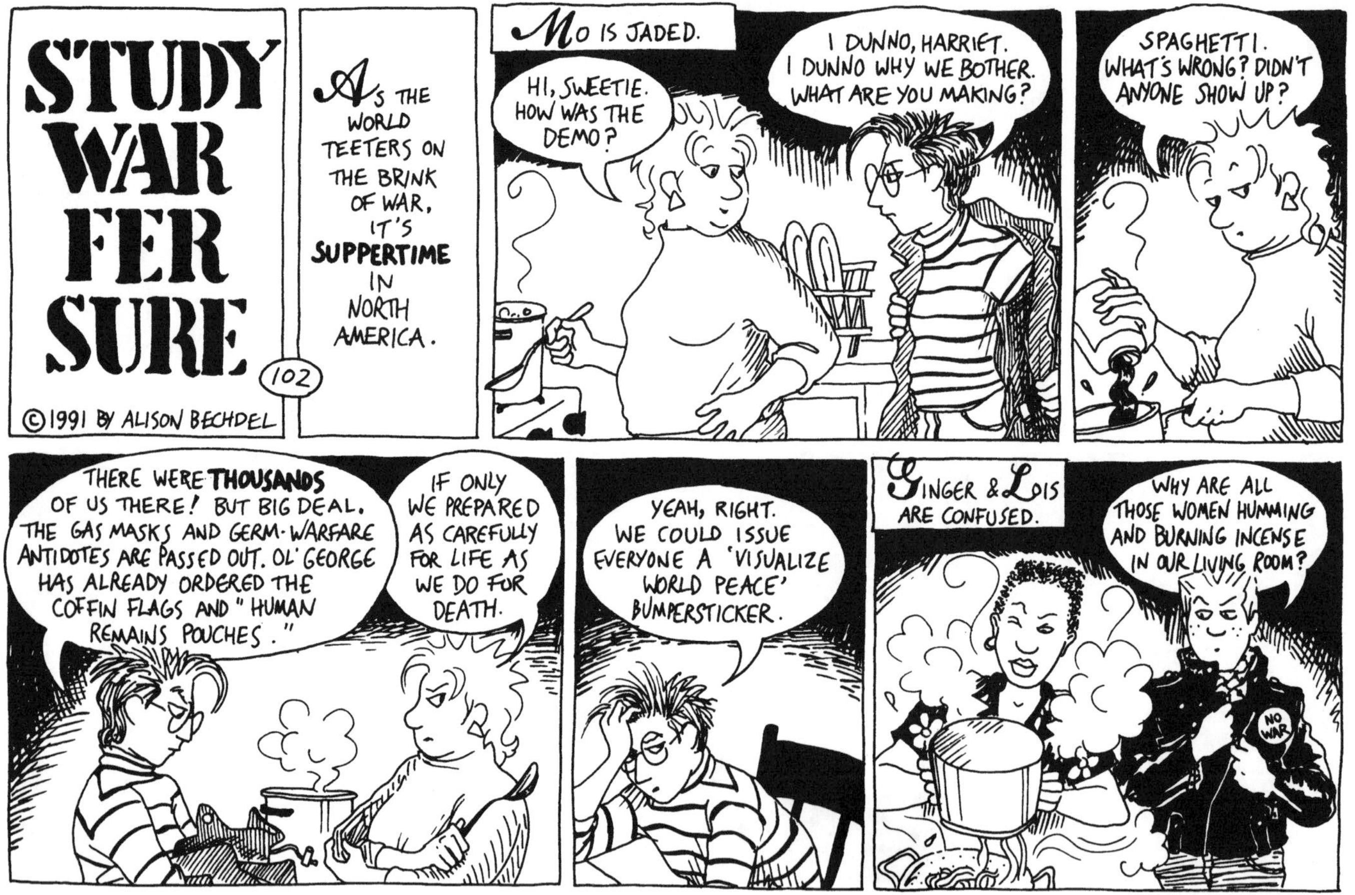
STUDY WAR FER SURE
102
©1991 BY ALISON BECHDEL
AS THE WORLD TEETERS ON THE BRINK OF WAR, IT'S SUPPERTIME IN NORTH AMERICA.
MO IS JADED.
HI, SWEETIE. HOW WAS THE DEMO?
I DUNNO, HARRIET. I DUNNO WHY WE BOTHER. WHAT ARE YOU MAKING?
SPAGHETTI. WHAT'S WRONG? DIDN'T ANYONE SHOW UP?
THERE WERE THOUSANDS OF US THERE! BUT BIG DEAL. THE GAS MASKS AND GERM-WARFARE ANTIDOTES ARE PASSED OUT. OL' GEORGE HAS ALREADY ORDERED THE COFFIN FLAGS AND "HUMAN REMAINS POUCHES."
IF ONLY WE PREPARED AS CAREFULLY FOR LIFE AS WE DO FOR DEATH.
YEAH, RIGHT. WE COULD ISSUE EVERYONE A 'VISUALIZE WORLD PEACE' BUMPERSTICKER.
GINGER & LOIS ARE CONFUSED.
WHY ARE ALL THOSE WOMEN HUMMING AND BURNING INCENSE IN OUR LIVING ROOM?
NO WAR

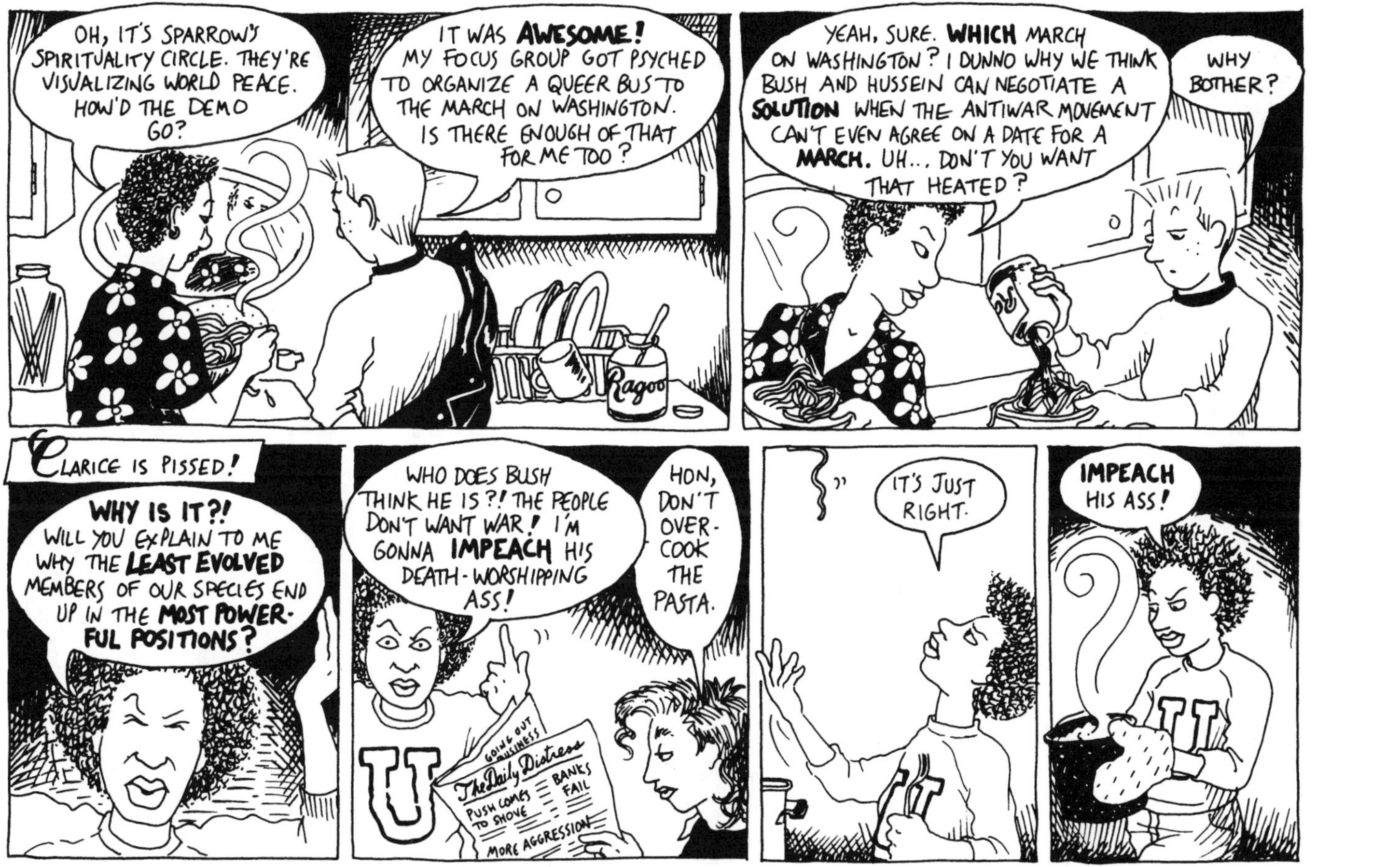
OH, IT'S SPARROW'S SPIRITUALITY CIRCLE. THEY'RE VISUALIZING WORLD PEACE. HOW'D THE DEMO GO?
IT WAS **AWESOME!** MY FOCUS GROUP GOT PSYCHED TO ORGANIZE A QUEER BUS TO THE MARCH ON WASHINGTON. IS THERE ENOUGH OF THAT FOR ME TOO?
Ragoo
YEAH, SURE. **WHICH** MARCH ON WASHINGTON? I DUNNO WHY WE THINK BUSH AND HUSSEIN CAN NEGOTIATE A **SOLUTION** WHEN THE ANTIWAR MOVEMENT CAN'T EVEN AGREE ON A DATE FOR A **MARCH.** UH... DON'T YOU WANT THAT HEATED?
WHY BOTHER?
CLARICE IS PISSED!
WHY IS IT?! WILL YOU EXPLAIN TO ME WHY THE **LEAST EVOLVED** MEMBERS OF OUR SPECIES END UP IN THE **MOST POWERFUL POSITIONS?**
WHO DOES BUSH THINK HE IS?! THE PEOPLE DON'T WANT WAR! I'M GONNA **IMPEACH** HIS DEATH-WORSHIPPING ASS!
HON, DON'T OVERCOOK THE PASTA.
GOING OUT OF BUSINESS
The Daily Distress
PUSH COMES TO SHOVE
BANKS FAIL
MORE AGGRESSION
IT'S JUST RIGHT.
IMPEACH HIS ASS!

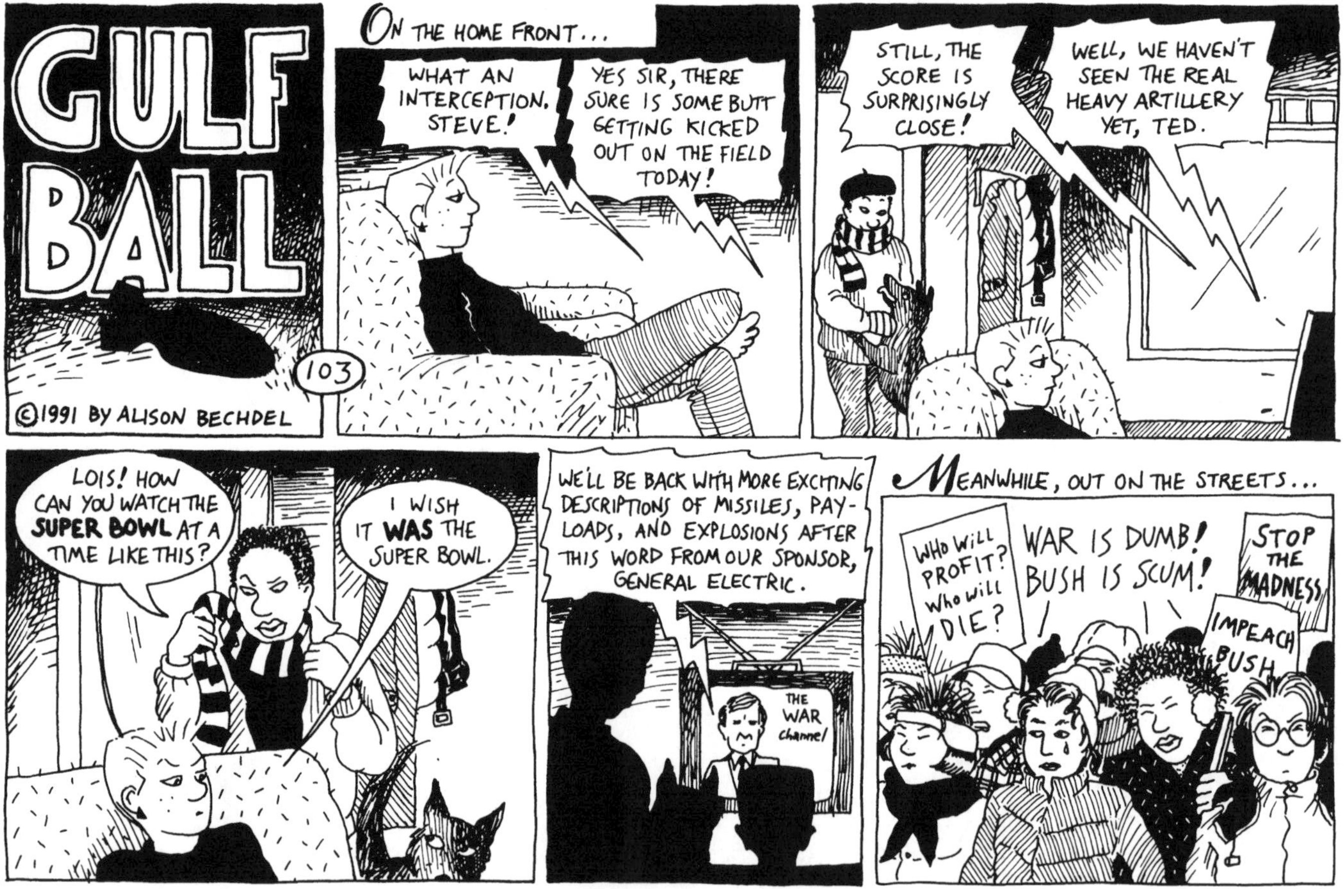
GULF BALL
D
D
103
©1991 BY ALISON BECHDEL
ON THE HOME FRONT...
WHAT AN INTERCEPTION, STEVE!
YES SIR, THERE SURE IS SOME BUTT GETTING KICKED OUT ON THE FIELD TODAY!
STILL, THE SCORE IS SURPRISINGLY CLOSE!
WELL, WE HAVEN'T SEEN THE REAL HEAVY ARTILLERY YET, TED.
LOIS! HOW CAN YOU WATCH THE **SUPER BOWL** AT A TIME LIKE THIS?
I WISH IT **WAS** THE SUPER BOWL.
WE'LL BE BACK WITH MORE EXCITING DESCRIPTIONS OF MISSILES, PAYLOADS, AND EXPLOSIONS AFTER THIS WORD FROM OUR SPONSOR, GENERAL ELECTRIC.
THE WAR Channel
MEANWHILE, OUT ON THE STREETS...
WHO WILL PROFIT? WHO WILL DIE?
WAR IS DUMB! BUSH IS SCUM!
STOP THE MADNESS
IMPEACH BUSH

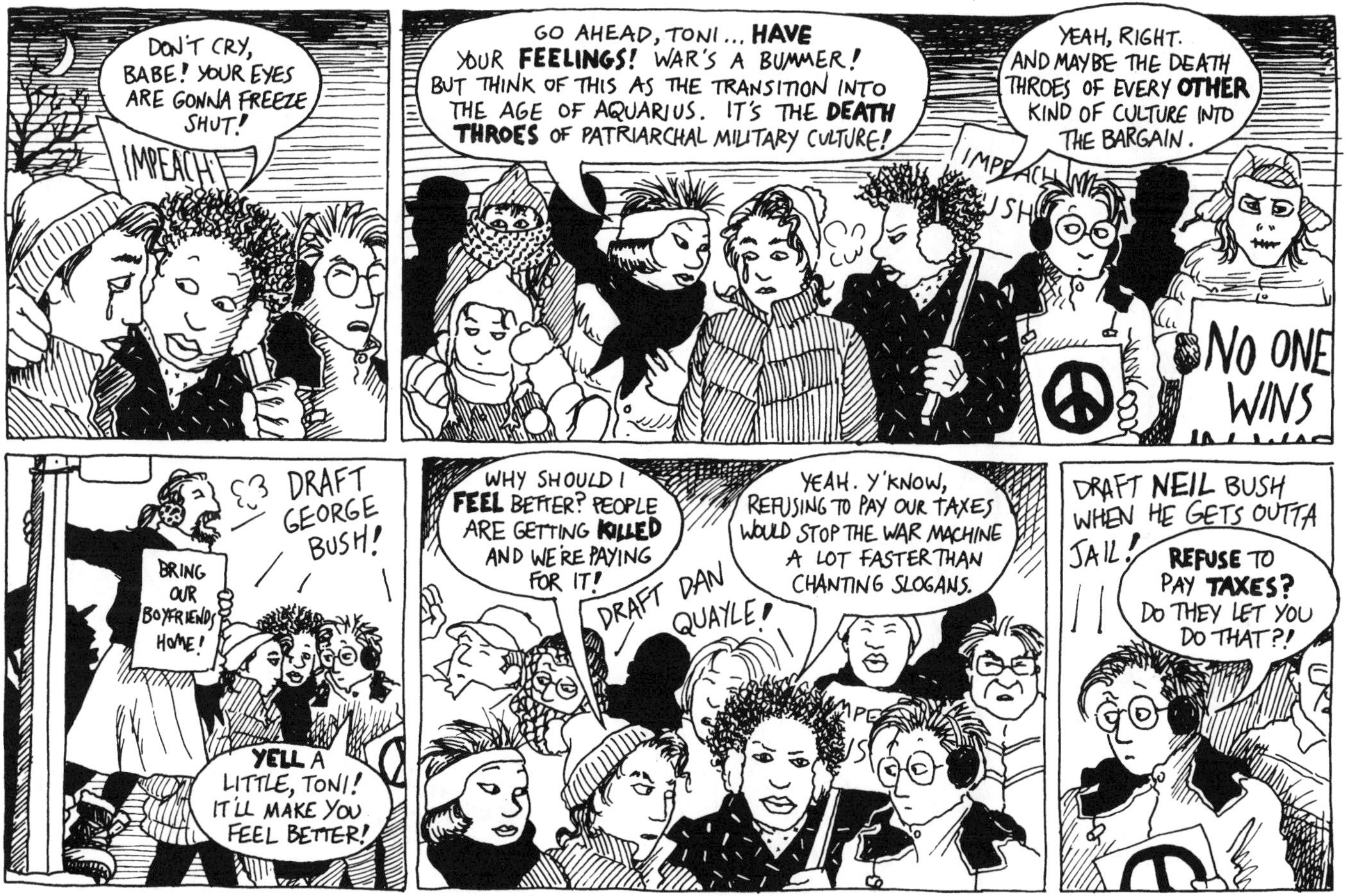
IMPEACH
DON'T CRY, BABE! YOUR EYES ARE GONNA FREEZE SHUT!
GO AHEAD, TONI... HAVE YOUR FEELINGS! WAR'S A BUMMER! BUT THINK OF THIS AS THE TRANSITION INTO THE AGE OF AQUARIUS. IT'S THE DEATH THROES OF PATRIARCHAL MILITARY CULTURE!
YEAH, RIGHT. AND MAYBE THE DEATH THROES OF EVERY OTHER KIND OF CULTURE INTO THE BARGAIN.
NO ONE WINS
DRAFT GEORGE BUSH!
BRING OUR BOYFRIENDS HOME!
YELL A LITTLE, TONI! IT'LL MAKE YOU FEEL BETTER!
WHY SHOULD I FEEL BETTER? PEOPLE ARE GETTING KILLED AND WE'RE PAYING FOR IT!
DRAFT DAN QUAYLE!
YEAH. Y'KNOW, REFUSING TO PAY OUR TAXES WOULD STOP THE WAR MACHINE A LOT FASTER THAN CHANTING SLOGANS.
DRAFT NEIL BUSH WHEN HE GETS OUTTA JAIL!
REFUSE TO PAY TAXES? DO THEY LET YOU DO THAT?!

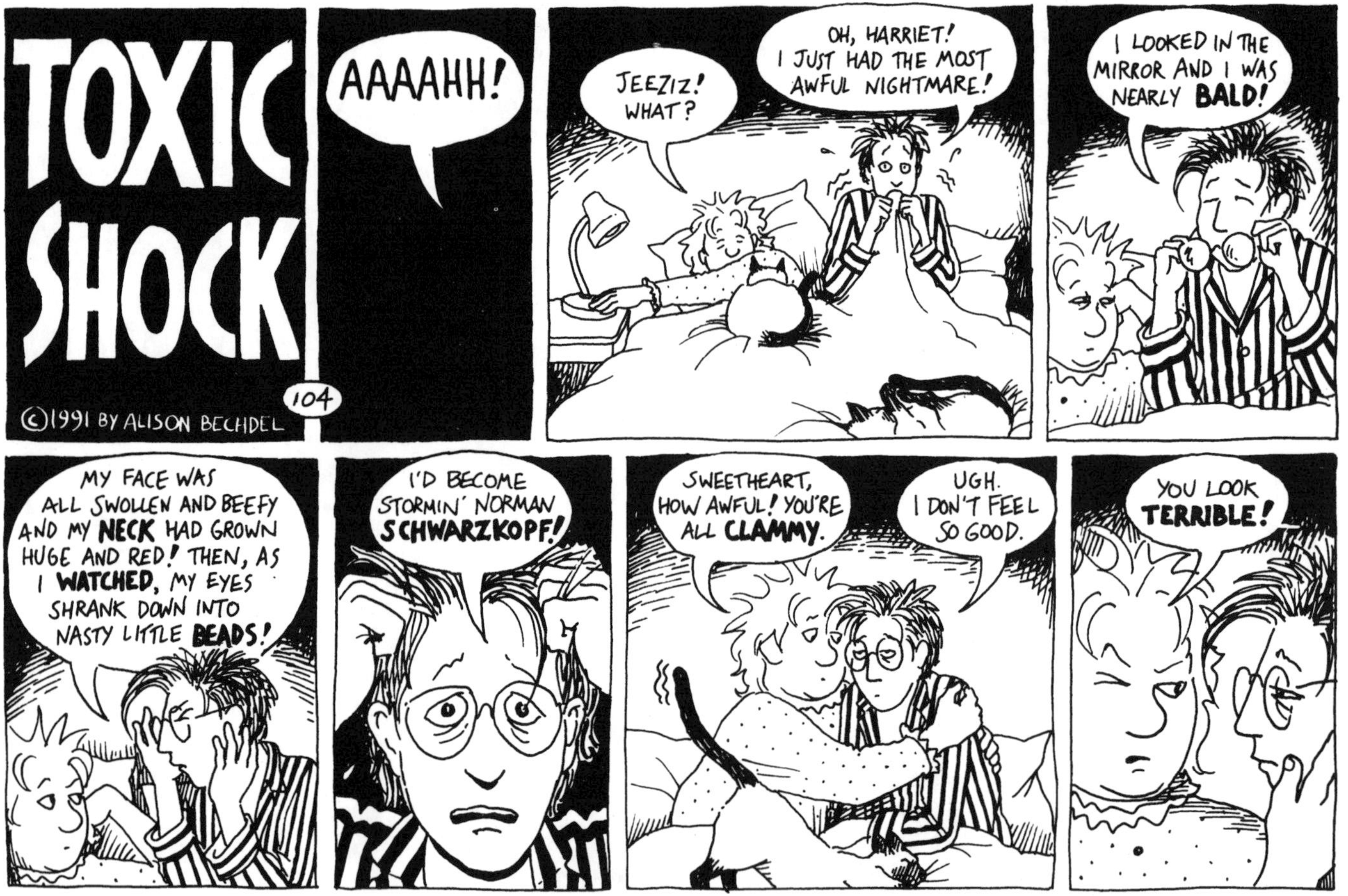
TOXIC SHOCK
©1991 BY ALISON BECHDEL
104
AAAAHH!
JEEZIZ! WHAT?
OH, HARRIET! I JUST HAD THE MOST AWFUL NIGHTMARE!
I LOOKED IN THE MIRROR AND I WAS NEARLY BALD!
MY FACE WAS ALL SWOLLEN AND BEEFY AND MY NECK HAD GROWN HUGE AND RED! THEN, AS I WATCHED, MY EYES SHRANK DOWN INTO NASTY LITTLE BEADS!
I'D BECOME STORMIN' NORMAN SCHWARZKOPF!
SWEETHEART, HOW AWFUL! YOU'RE ALL CLAMMY.
UGH. I DON'T FEEL SO GOOD.
YOU LOOK TERRIBLE!

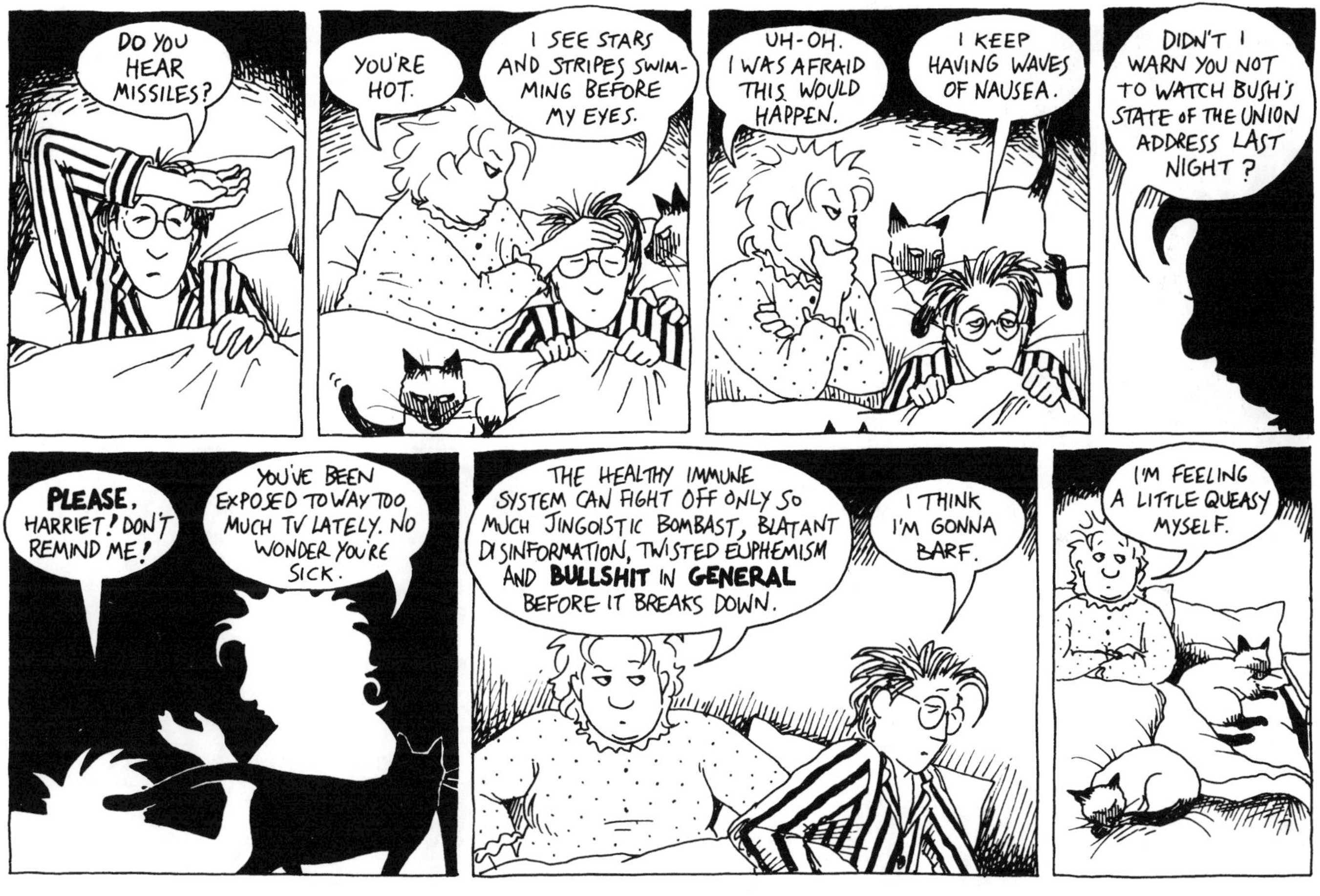
DO YOU HEAR MISSILES?
YOU'RE HOT.
I SEE STARS AND STRIPES SWIMMING BEFORE MY EYES.
UH-OH. I WAS AFRAID THIS WOULD HAPPEN.
I KEEP HAVING WAVES OF NAUSEA.
DIDN'T I WARN YOU NOT TO WATCH BUSH'S STATE OF THE UNION ADDRESS LAST NIGHT?
PLEASE, HARRIET! DON'T REMIND ME!
YOU'VE BEEN EXPOSED TO WAY TOO MUCH TV LATELY. NO WONDER YOU'RE SICK.
THE HEALTHY IMMUNE SYSTEM CAN FIGHT OFF ONLY SO MUCH JINGOISTIC BOMBAST, BLATANT DISINFORMATION, TWISTED EUPHEMISM AND **BULLSHIT** IN **GENERAL** BEFORE IT BREAKS DOWN.
I THINK I'M GONNA BARF.
I'M FEELING A LITTLE QUEASY MYSELF.

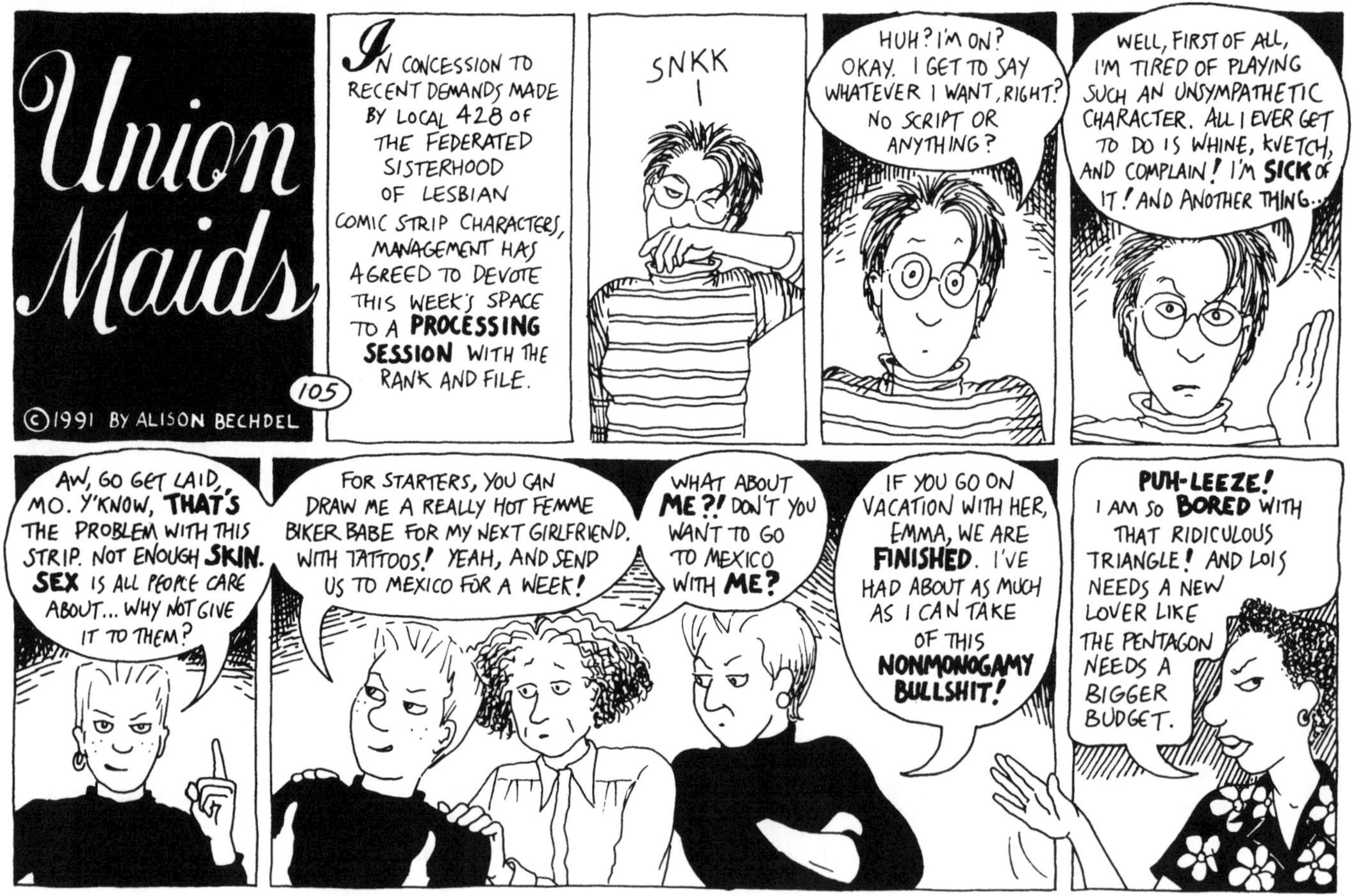
Union Maids
©1991 BY ALISON BECHDEL
105
IN CONCESSION TO RECENT DEMANDS MADE BY LOCAL 428 OF THE FEDERATED SISTERHOOD OF LESBIAN COMIC STRIP CHARACTERS, MANAGEMENT HAS AGREED TO DEVOTE THIS WEEK'S SPACE TO A **PROCESSING SESSION** WITH THE RANK AND FILE.
SNKK
HUH? I'M ON? OKAY. I GET TO SAY WHATEVER I WANT, RIGHT? NO SCRIPT OR ANYTHING?
WELL, FIRST OF ALL, I'M TIRED OF PLAYING SUCH AN UNSYMPATHETIC CHARACTER. ALL I EVER GET TO DO IS WHINE, KVETCH, AND COMPLAIN! I'M **SICK** OF IT! AND ANOTHER THING...
AW, GO GET LAID, MO. Y'KNOW, **THAT'S** THE PROBLEM WITH THIS STRIP. NOT ENOUGH **SKIN. SEX** IS ALL PEOPLE CARE ABOUT... WHY NOT GIVE IT TO THEM?
FOR STARTERS, YOU CAN DRAW ME A REALLY HOT FEMME BIKER BABE FOR MY NEXT GIRLFRIEND. WITH TATTOOS! YEAH, AND SEND US TO MEXICO FOR A WEEK!
WHAT ABOUT **ME?!** DON'T YOU WANT TO GO TO MEXICO WITH **ME?**
IF YOU GO ON VACATION WITH HER, EMMA, WE ARE **FINISHED**. I'VE HAD ABOUT AS MUCH AS I CAN TAKE OF THIS **NONMONOGAMY BULLSHIT!**
PUH-LEEZE! I AM SO **BORED** WITH THAT RIDICULOUS TRIANGLE! AND LOIS NEEDS A NEW LOVER LIKE THE PENTAGON NEEDS A BIGGER BUDGET.

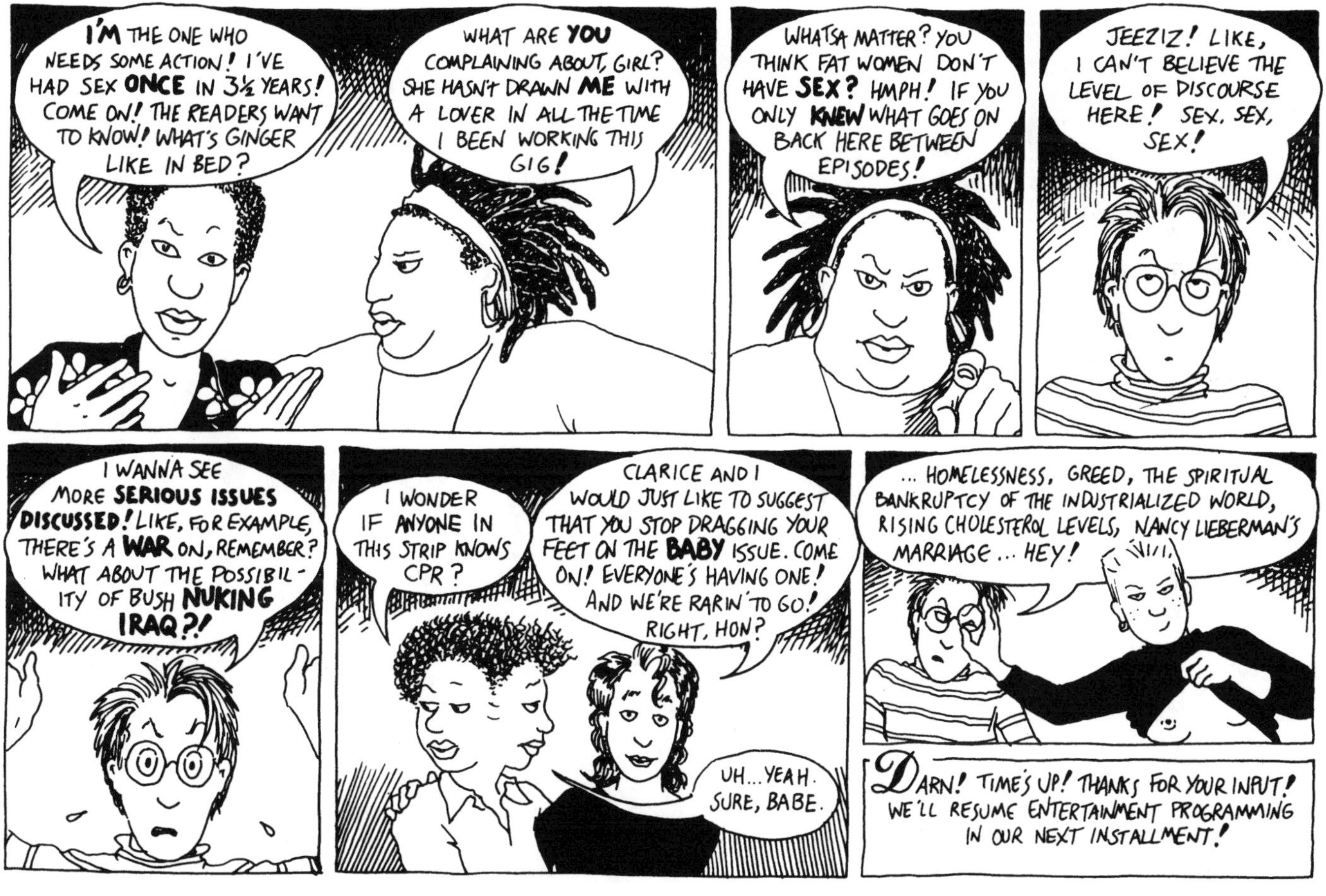
I'M THE ONE WHO NEEDS SOME ACTION! I'VE HAD SEX ONCE IN 3½ YEARS! COME ON! THE READERS WANT TO KNOW! WHAT'S GINGER LIKE IN BED?
WHAT ARE YOU COMPLAINING ABOUT, GIRL? SHE HASN'T DRAWN ME WITH A LOVER IN ALL THE TIME I BEEN WORKING THIS GIG!
WHATSA MATTER? YOU THINK FAT WOMEN DON'T HAVE SEX? HMPH! IF YOU ONLY KNEW WHAT GOES ON BACK HERE BETWEEN EPISODES!
JEEZIZ! LIKE, I CAN'T BELIEVE THE LEVEL OF DISCOURSE HERE! SEX. SEX, SEX!
I WANNA SEE MORE SERIOUS ISSUES DISCUSSED! LIKE, FOR EXAMPLE, THERE'S A WAR ON, REMEMBER? WHAT ABOUT THE POSSIBIL-ITY OF BUSH NUKING IRAQ?!
I WONDER IF ANYONE IN THIS STRIP KNOWS CPR?
CLARICE AND I WOULD JUST LIKE TO SUGGEST THAT YOU STOP DRAGGING YOUR FEET ON THE BABY ISSUE. COME ON! EVERYONE'S HAVING ONE! AND WE'RE RARIN' TO GO! RIGHT, HON?
UH... YEAH. SURE, BABE.
... HOMELESSNESS, GREED, THE SPIRITUAL BANKRUPTCY OF THE INDUSTRIALIZED WORLD, RISING CHOLESTEROL LEVELS, NANCY LIEBERMAN'S MARRIAGE ... HEY!
DARN! TIME'S UP! THANKS FOR YOUR INPUT! WE'LL RESUME ENTERTAINMENT PROGRAMMING IN OUR NEXT INSTALLMENT!

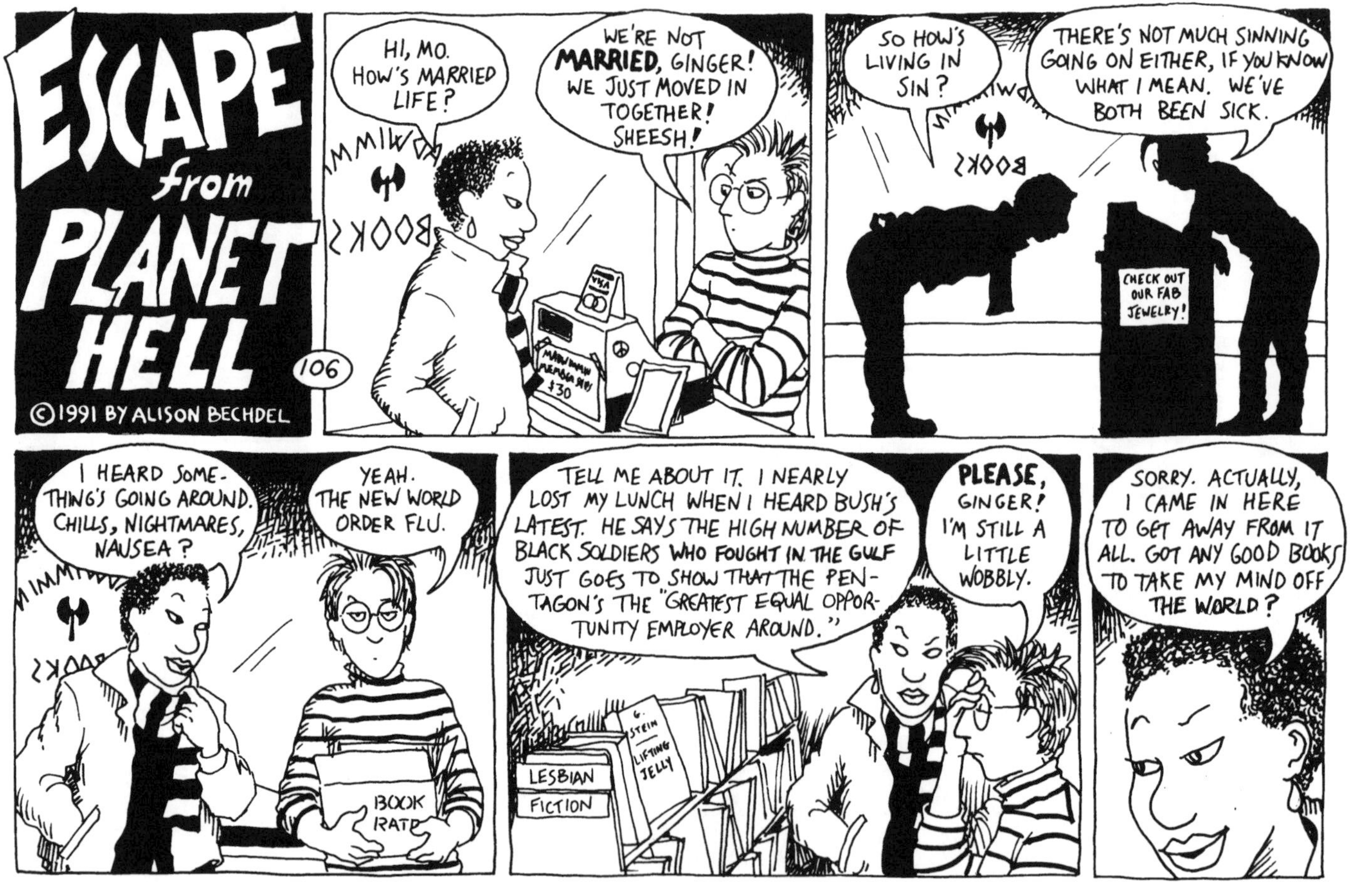
ESCAPE from PLANET HELL
106
©1991 BY ALISON BECHDEL
HI, MO. HOW'S MARRIED LIFE?
WE'RE NOT **MARRIED**, GINGER! WE JUST MOVED IN TOGETHER! SHEESH!
VISA
SO HOW'S LIVING IN SIN?
THERE'S NOT MUCH SINNING GOING ON EITHER, IF YOU KNOW WHAT I MEAN. WE'VE BOTH BEEN SICK.
CHECK OUT OUR FAB JEWELRY!
I HEARD SOMETHING'S GOING AROUND. CHILLS, NIGHTMARES, NAUSEA?
YEAH. THE NEW WORLD ORDER FLU.
BOOK RATE
TELL ME ABOUT IT. I NEARLY LOST MY LUNCH WHEN I HEARD BUSH'S LATEST. HE SAYS THE HIGH NUMBER OF BLACK SOLDIERS **WHO FOUGHT IN THE GULF** JUST GOES TO SHOW THAT THE PENTAGON'S THE "GREATEST EQUAL OPPORTUNITY EMPLOYER AROUND."
PLEASE, GINGER! I'M STILL A LITTLE WOBBLY.
G. STEIN
LIFTING JELLY
LESBIAN
FICTION
SORRY. ACTUALLY, I CAME IN HERE TO GET AWAY FROM IT ALL. GOT ANY GOOD BOOKS TO TAKE MY MIND OFF **THE WORLD**?

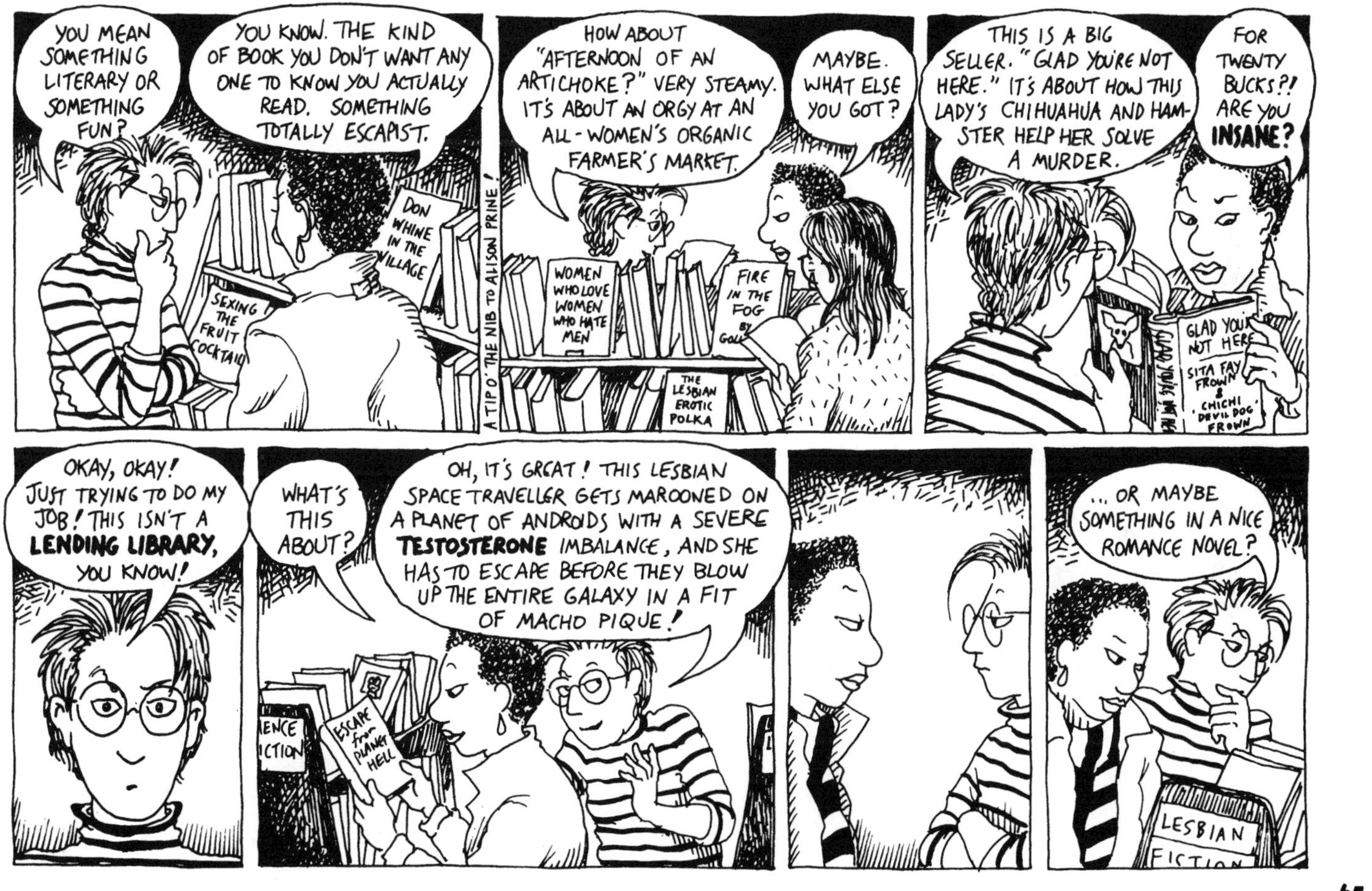
YOU MEAN SOMETHING LITERARY OR SOMETHING FUN?
YOU KNOW. THE KIND OF BOOK YOU DON'T WANT ANY ONE TO KNOW YOU ACTUALLY READ. SOMETHING TOTALLY ESCAPIST.
DON WHINE IN THE VILLAGE
SEXING THE FRUIT COCKTAIL
A TIP O' THE NIB TO ALISON PRINE!
HOW ABOUT "AFTERNOON OF AN ARTICHOKE?" VERY STEAMY. IT'S ABOUT AN ORGY AT AN ALL-WOMEN'S ORGANIC FARMER'S MARKET.
MAYBE. WHAT ELSE YOU GOT?
WOMEN WHO LOVE WOMEN WHO HATE MEN
FIRE IN THE FOG
THE LESBIAN EROTIC POLKA
THIS IS A BIG SELLER. "GLAD YOU'RE NOT HERE." IT'S ABOUT HOW THIS LADY'S CHIHUAHUA AND HAMSTER HELP HER SOLVE A MURDER.
FOR TWENTY BUCKS?! ARE YOU **INSANE?**
SITA FAY FROWN & CHICHI 'DEVIL DOG' FROWN
OKAY, OKAY! JUST TRYING TO DO MY JOB! THIS ISN'T A **LENDING LIBRARY,** YOU KNOW!
WHAT'S THIS ABOUT?
OH, IT'S GREAT! THIS LESBIAN SPACE TRAVELLER GETS MAROONED ON A PLANET OF ANDROIDS WITH A SEVERE **TESTOSTERONE** IMBALANCE, AND SHE HAS TO ESCAPE BEFORE THEY BLOW UP THE ENTIRE GALAXY IN A FIT OF MACHO PIQUE!
ESCAPE from PLANET HELL
... OR MAYBE SOMETHING IN A NICE ROMANCE NOVEL?
LESBIAN

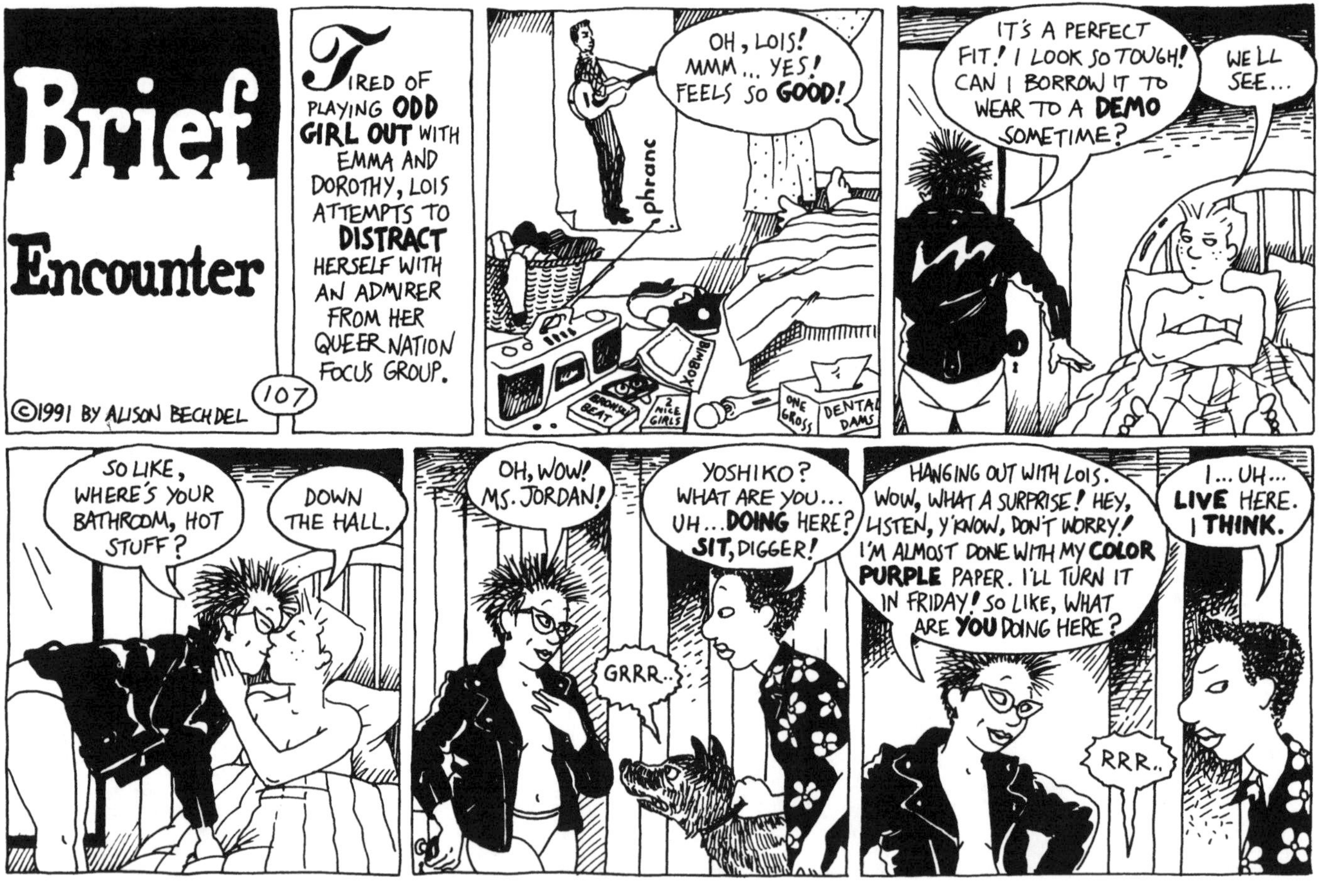

Brief
Encounter
©1991 BY ALISON BECHDEL
107
TIRED OF PLAYING ODD GIRL OUT WITH EMMA AND DOROTHY, LOIS ATTEMPTS TO DISTRACT HERSELF WITH AN ADMIRER FROM HER QUEER NATION FOCUS GROUP.
OH, LOIS! MMM... YES! FEELS SO GOOD!
phranc
BIMBOX
BRONSKI BEAT
2 NICE GIRLS
ONE GROSS DENTAL DAMS
IT'S A PERFECT FIT! I LOOK SO TOUGH! CAN I BORROW IT TO WEAR TO A DEMO SOMETIME?
WE'LL SEE...
SO LIKE, WHERE'S YOUR BATHROOM, HOT STUFF?
DOWN THE HALL.
OH, WOW! MS. JORDAN!
YOSHIKO? WHAT ARE YOU... UH... DOING HERE? SIT, DIGGER!
GRRR..
HANGING OUT WITH LOIS. WOW, WHAT A SURPRISE! HEY, LISTEN, Y'KNOW, DON'T WORRY! I'M ALMOST DONE WITH MY COLOR PURPLE PAPER. I'LL TURN IT IN FRIDAY! SO LIKE, WHAT ARE YOU DOING HERE?
I... UH... LIVE HERE. I THINK.
RRR..

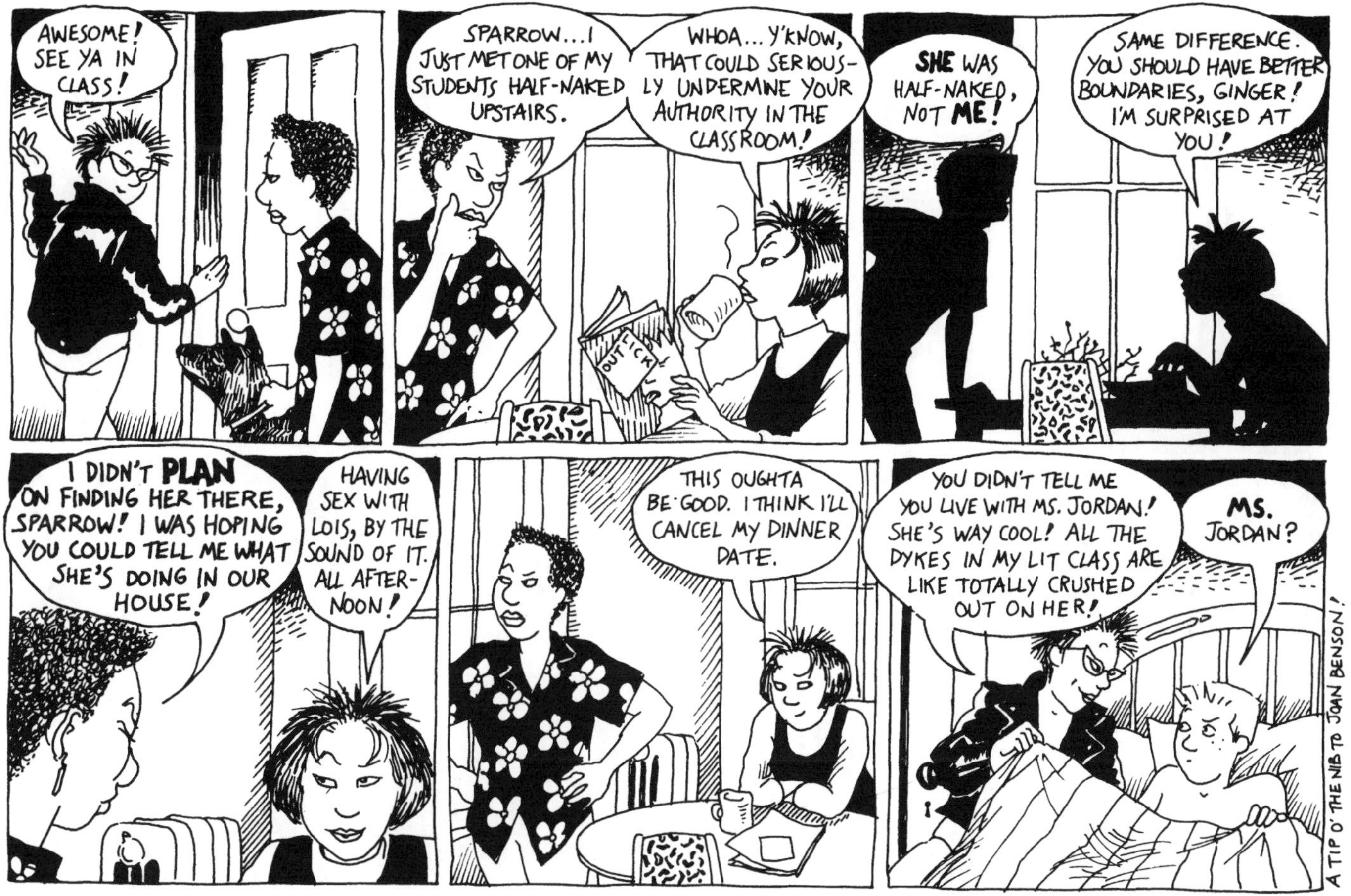
AWESOME! SEE YA IN CLASS!
SPARROW... I JUST MET ONE OF MY STUDENTS HALF-NAKED UPSTAIRS.
WHOA... Y'KNOW, THAT COULD SERIOUSLY UNDERMINE YOUR AUTHORITY IN THE CLASSROOM!
OUT LICK
SHE WAS HALF-NAKED, NOT ME!
SAME DIFFERENCE. YOU SHOULD HAVE BETTER BOUNDARIES, GINGER! I'M SURPRISED AT YOU!
I DIDN'T PLAN ON FINDING HER THERE, SPARROW! I WAS HOPING YOU COULD TELL ME WHAT SHE'S DOING IN OUR HOUSE!
HAVING SEX WITH LOIS, BY THE SOUND OF IT. ALL AFTERNOON!
THIS OUGHTA BE GOOD. I THINK I'LL CANCEL MY DINNER DATE.
YOU DIDN'T TELL ME YOU LIVE WITH MS. JORDAN! SHE'S WAY COOL! ALL THE DYKES IN MY LIT CLASS ARE LIKE TOTALLY CRUSHED OUT ON HER!
MS. JORDAN?
A TIP O' THE NIB TO JOAN BENSON!

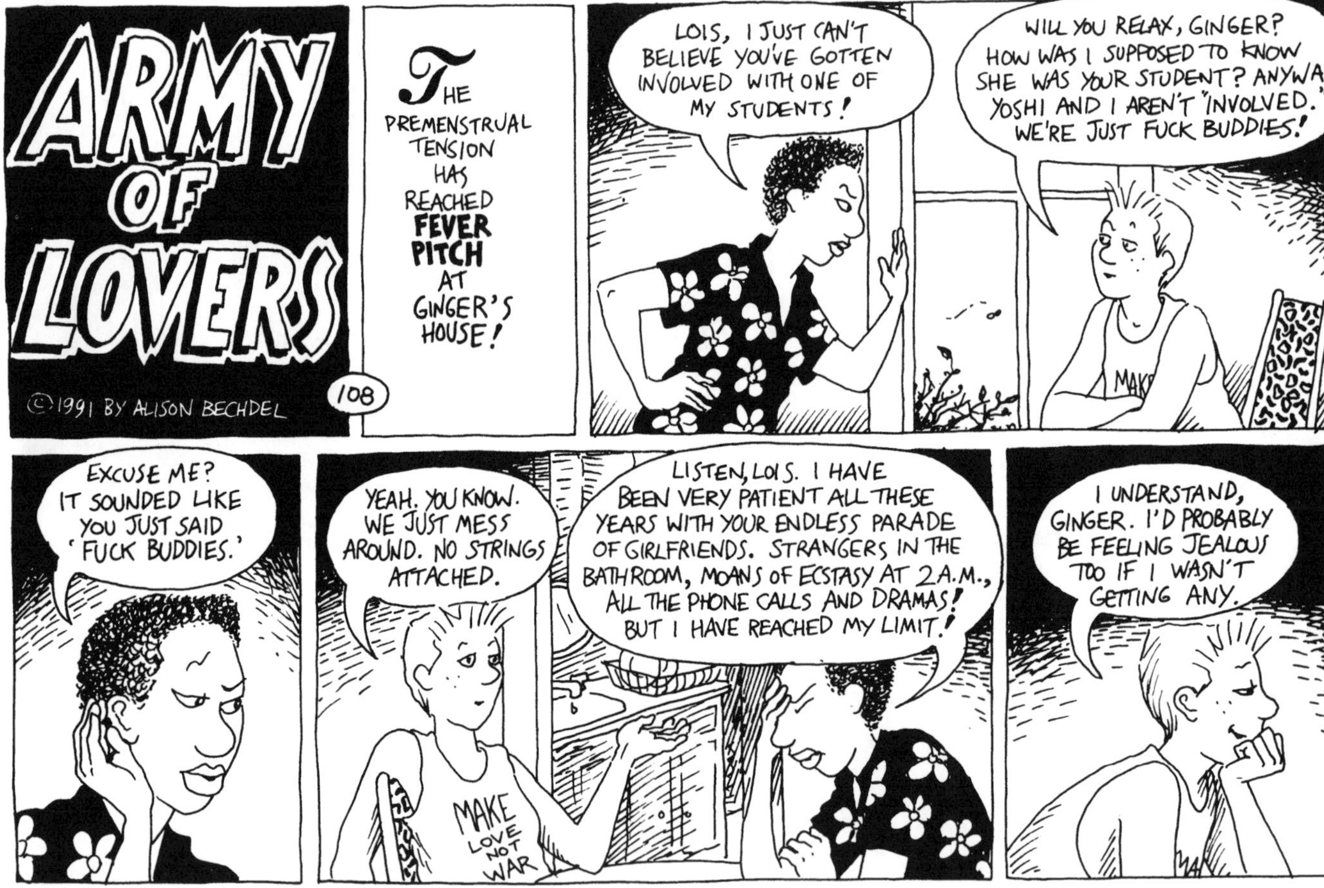
ARMY OF LOVERS
©1991 BY ALISON BECHDEL
108
THE PREMENSTRUAL TENSION HAS REACHED **FEVER PITCH** AT GINGER'S HOUSE!
LOIS, I JUST CAN'T BELIEVE YOU'VE GOTTEN INVOLVED WITH ONE OF MY STUDENTS!
WILL YOU RELAX, GINGER? HOW WAS I SUPPOSED TO KNOW SHE WAS YOUR STUDENT? ANYWAY, YOSHI AND I AREN'T "INVOLVED." WE'RE JUST FUCK BUDDIES!
EXCUSE ME? IT SOUNDED LIKE YOU JUST SAID 'FUCK BUDDIES.'
YEAH. YOU KNOW. WE JUST MESS AROUND. NO STRINGS ATTACHED.
MAKE LOVE NOT WAR
LISTEN, LOIS. I HAVE BEEN VERY PATIENT ALL THESE YEARS WITH YOUR ENDLESS PARADE OF GIRLFRIENDS. STRANGERS IN THE BATHROOM, MOANS OF ECSTASY AT 2 A.M., ALL THE PHONE CALLS AND DRAMAS! BUT I HAVE REACHED MY LIMIT!
I UNDERSTAND, GINGER. I'D PROBABLY BE FEELING JEALOUS TOO IF I WASN'T GETTING ANY.

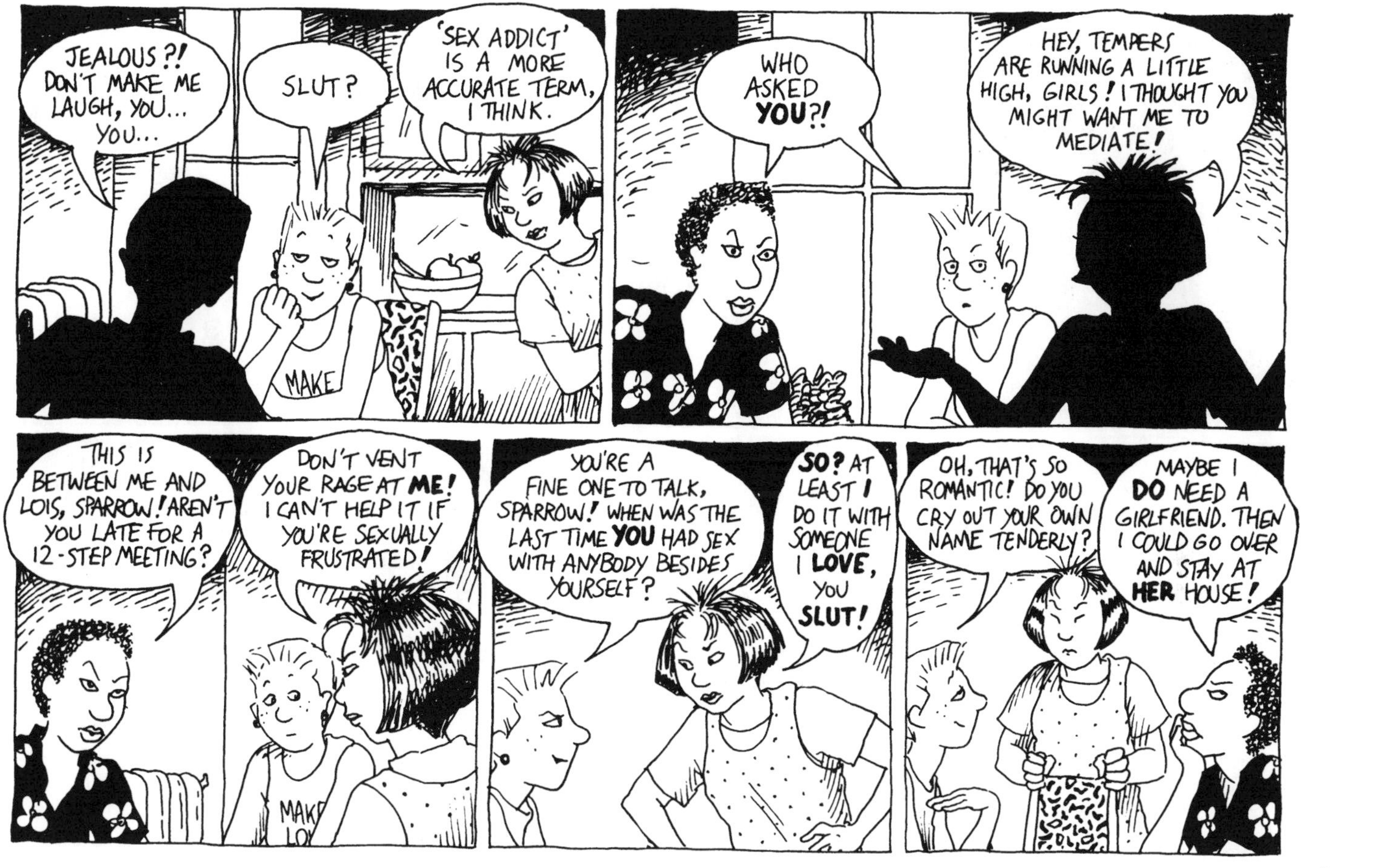
JEALOUS?! DON'T MAKE ME LAUGH, YOU... YOU...
SLUT?
'SEX ADDICT' IS A MORE ACCURATE TERM, I THINK.
MAKE
WHO ASKED **YOU**?!
HEY, TEMPERS ARE RUNNING A LITTLE HIGH, GIRLS! I THOUGHT YOU MIGHT WANT ME TO MEDIATE!
THIS IS BETWEEN ME AND LOIS, SPARROW! AREN'T YOU LATE FOR A 12-STEP MEETING?
DON'T VENT YOUR RAGE AT **ME**! I CAN'T HELP IT IF YOU'RE SEXUALLY FRUSTRATED!
YOU'RE A FINE ONE TO TALK, SPARROW! WHEN WAS THE LAST TIME **YOU** HAD SEX WITH ANYBODY BESIDES YOURSELF?
SO? AT LEAST **I** DO IT WITH SOMEONE I **LOVE**, YOU **SLUT!**
OH, THAT'S SO ROMANTIC! DO YOU CRY OUT YOUR OWN NAME TENDERLY?
MAYBE I **DO** NEED A GIRLFRIEND. THEN I COULD GO OVER AND STAY AT **HER** HOUSE!

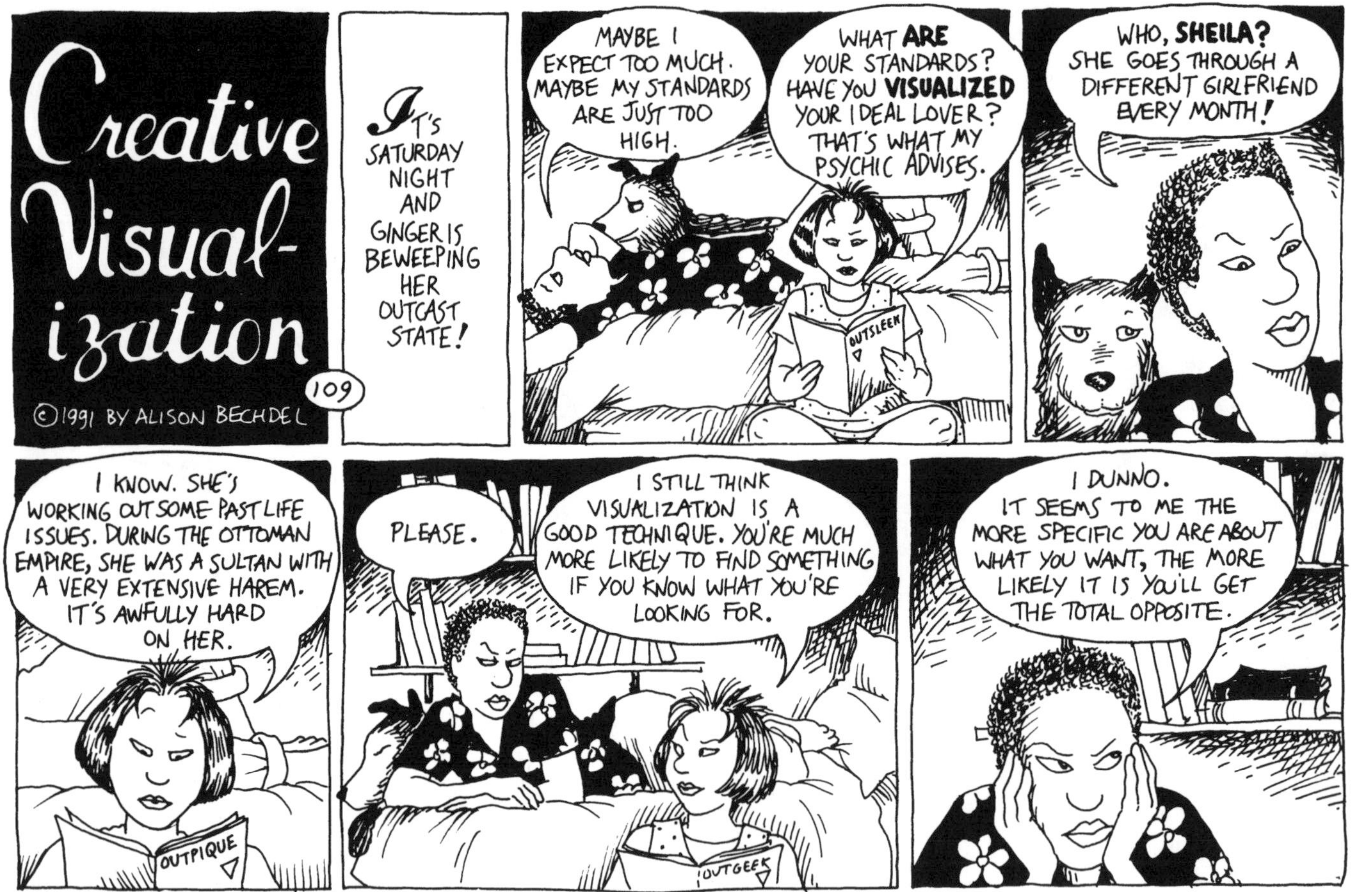

Creative Visual-ization
109
©1991 BY ALISON BECHDEL
IT'S SATURDAY NIGHT AND GINGER IS BEWEEPING HER OUTCAST STATE!
MAYBE I EXPECT TOO MUCH. MAYBE MY STANDARDS ARE JUST TOO HIGH.
WHAT **ARE** YOUR STANDARDS? HAVE YOU **VISUALIZED** YOUR IDEAL LOVER? THAT'S WHAT MY PSYCHIC ADVISES.
OUTSLEEK
WHO, **SHEILA?** SHE GOES THROUGH A DIFFERENT GIRLFRIEND EVERY MONTH!
I KNOW. SHE'S WORKING OUT SOME PAST LIFE ISSUES. DURING THE OTTOMAN EMPIRE, SHE WAS A SULTAN WITH A VERY EXTENSIVE HAREM. IT'S AWFULLY HARD ON HER.
OUTPIQUE
PLEASE.
I STILL THINK VISUALIZATION IS A GOOD TECHNIQUE. YOU'RE MUCH MORE LIKELY TO FIND SOMETHING IF YOU KNOW WHAT YOU'RE LOOKING FOR.
OUTGEEK
I DUNNO. IT SEEMS TO ME THE MORE SPECIFIC YOU ARE ABOUT WHAT YOU WANT, THE MORE LIKELY IT IS YOU'LL GET THE TOTAL OPPOSITE.

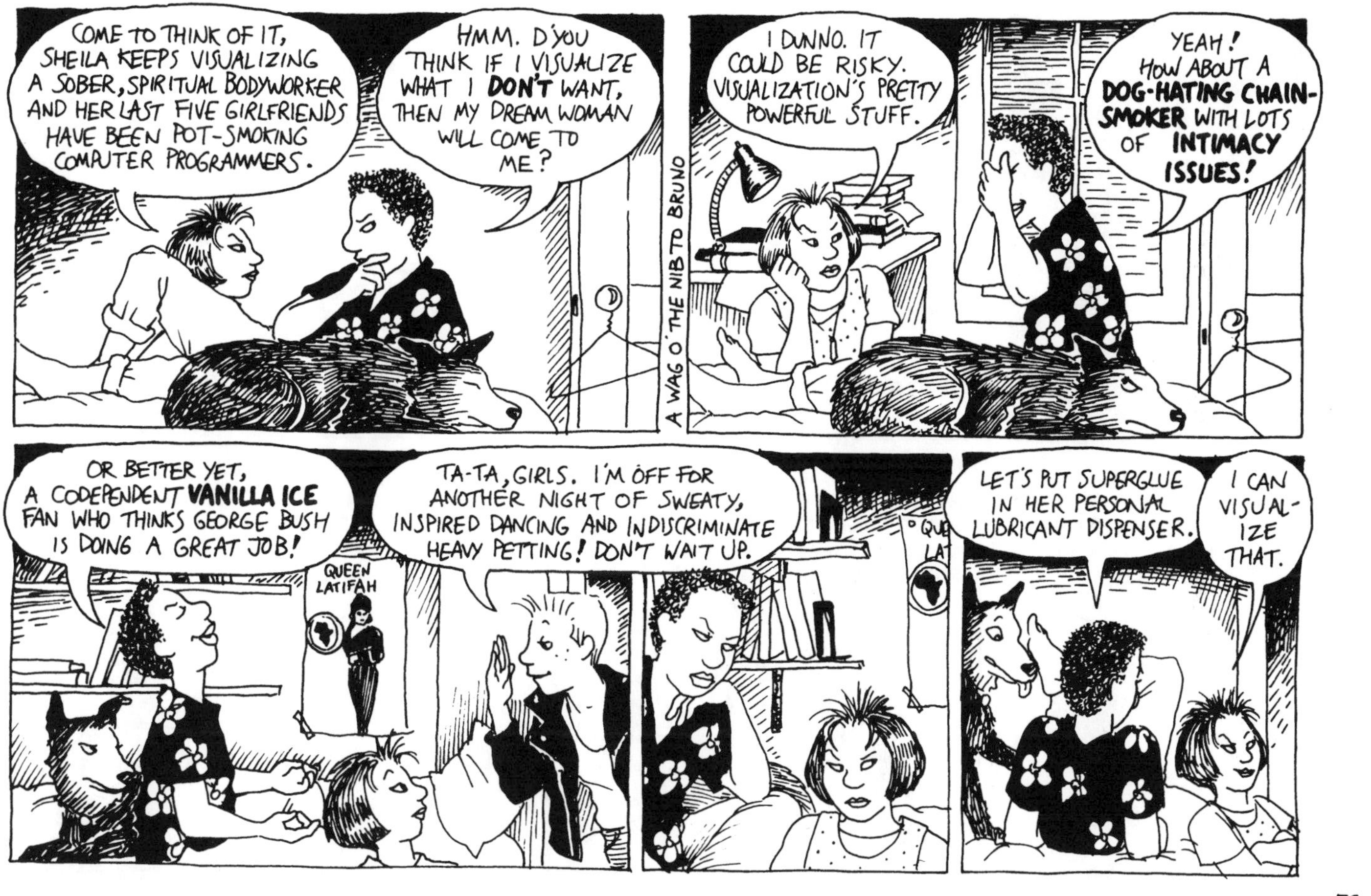
COME TO THINK OF IT, SHEILA KEEPS VISUALIZING A SOBER, SPIRITUAL BODYWORKER AND HER LAST FIVE GIRLFRIENDS HAVE BEEN POT-SMOKING COMPUTER PROGRAMMERS.
HMM. D'YOU THINK IF I VISUALIZE WHAT I **DON'T** WANT, THEN MY DREAM WOMAN WILL COME TO ME?
A WAG O' THE NIB TO BRUNO
I DUNNO. IT COULD BE RISKY. VISUALIZATION'S PRETTY POWERFUL STUFF.
YEAH! HOW ABOUT A **DOG-HATING CHAIN-SMOKER** WITH LOTS OF **INTIMACY ISSUES**!
OR BETTER YET, A CODEPENDENT **VANILLA ICE** FAN WHO THINKS GEORGE BUSH IS DOING A GREAT JOB!
QUEEN LATIFAH
TA-TA, GIRLS. I'M OFF FOR ANOTHER NIGHT OF SWEATY, INSPIRED DANCING AND INDISCRIMINATE HEAVY PETTING! DON'T WAIT UP.
LET'S PUT SUPERGLUE IN HER PERSONAL LUBRICANT DISPENSER.
I CAN VISUALIZE THAT.

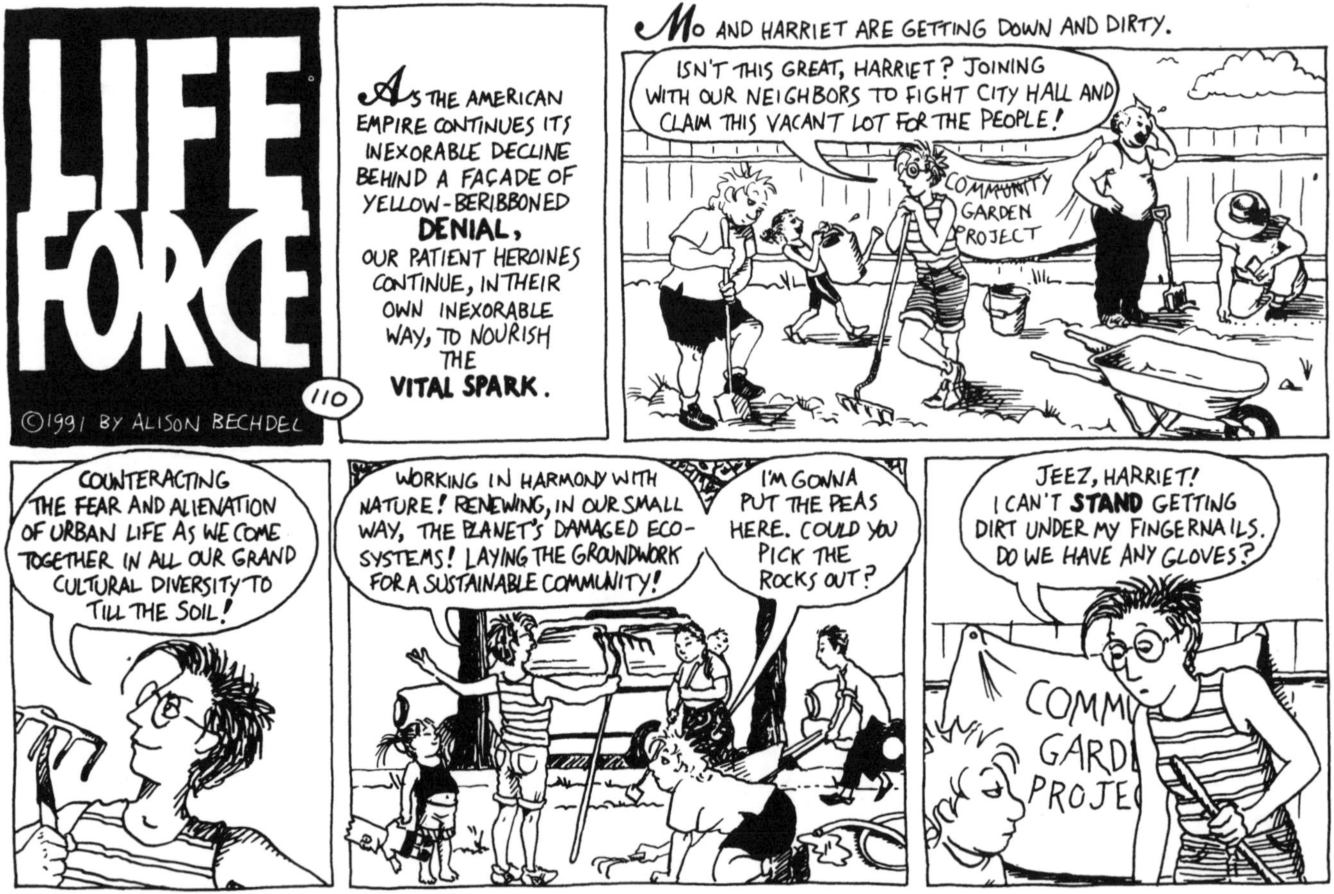
LIFE FORCE
©1991 BY ALISON BECHDEL
110
AS THE AMERICAN EMPIRE CONTINUES ITS INEXORABLE DECLINE BEHIND A FAÇADE OF YELLOW-BERIBBONED DENIAL, OUR PATIENT HEROINES CONTINUE, IN THEIR OWN INEXORABLE WAY, TO NOURISH THE VITAL SPARK.
MO AND HARRIET ARE GETTING DOWN AND DIRTY.
ISN'T THIS GREAT, HARRIET? JOINING WITH OUR NEIGHBORS TO FIGHT CITY HALL AND CLAIM THIS VACANT LOT FOR THE PEOPLE!
COMMUNITY GARDEN PROJECT
COUNTERACTING THE FEAR AND ALIENATION OF URBAN LIFE AS WE COME TOGETHER IN ALL OUR GRAND CULTURAL DIVERSITY TO TILL THE SOIL!
WORKING IN HARMONY WITH NATURE! RENEWING, IN OUR SMALL WAY, THE PLANET'S DAMAGED ECO-SYSTEMS! LAYING THE GROUNDWORK FOR A SUSTAINABLE COMMUNITY!
I'M GONNA PUT THE PEAS HERE. COULD YOU PICK THE ROCKS OUT?
JEEZ, HARRIET! I CAN'T STAND GETTING DIRT UNDER MY FINGERNAILS. DO WE HAVE ANY GLOVES?
COMMU GARD PROJE

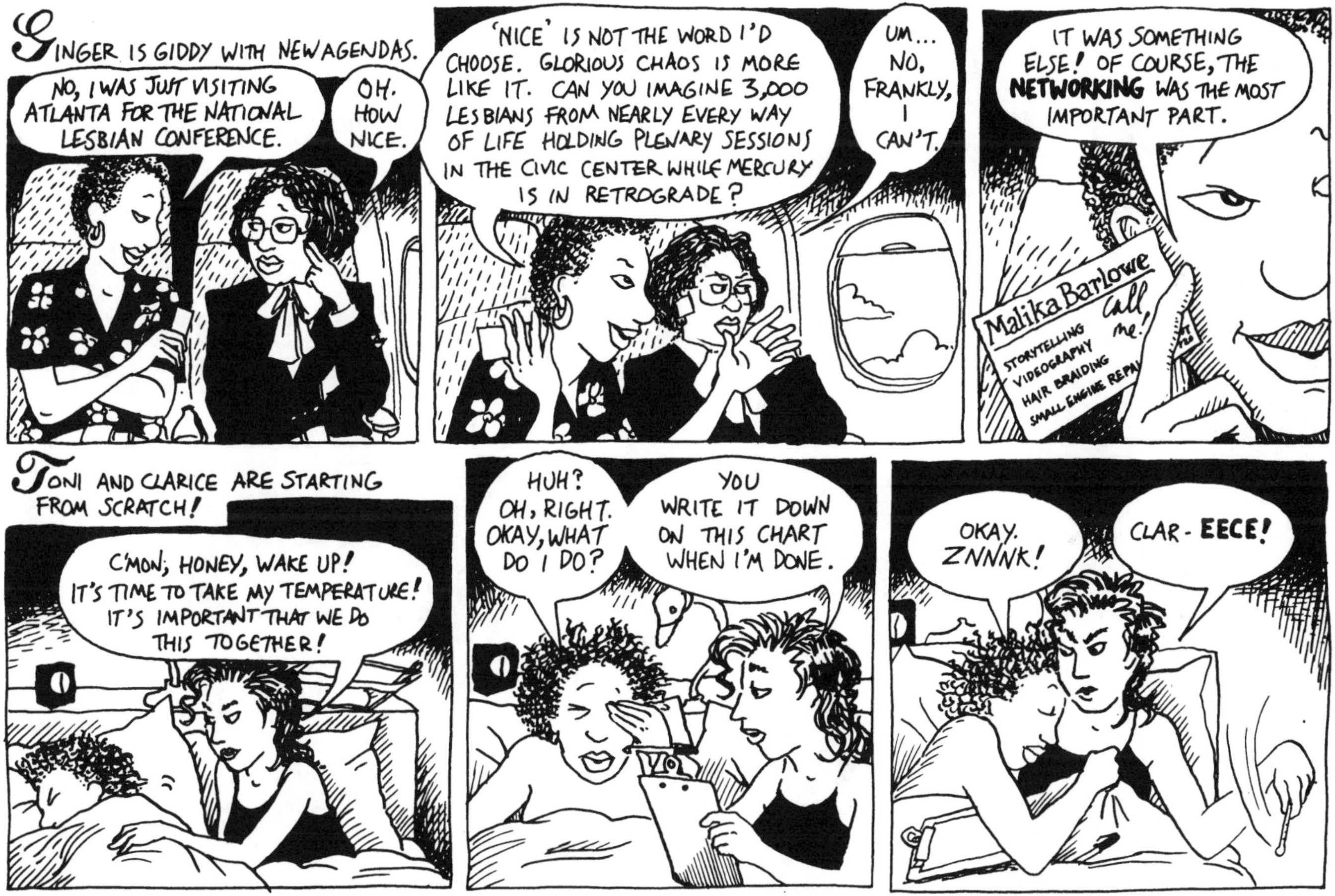
GINGER IS GIDDY WITH NEW AGENDAS.
NO, I WAS JUST VISITING ATLANTA FOR THE NATIONAL LESBIAN CONFERENCE.
OH. HOW NICE.
'NICE' IS NOT THE WORD I'D CHOOSE. GLORIOUS CHAOS IS MORE LIKE IT. CAN YOU IMAGINE 3,000 LESBIANS FROM NEARLY EVERY WAY OF LIFE HOLDING PLENARY SESSIONS IN THE CIVIC CENTER WHILE MERCURY IS IN RETROGRADE?
UM... NO, FRANKLY, I CAN'T.
IT WAS SOMETHING ELSE! OF COURSE, THE **NETWORKING** WAS THE MOST IMPORTANT PART.
Malika Barlowe
Call me!
STORYTELLING
VIDEOGRAPHY
HAIR BRAIDING
SMALL ENGINE REPAI
TONI AND CLARICE ARE STARTING FROM SCRATCH!
C'MON, HONEY, WAKE UP! IT'S TIME TO TAKE MY TEMPERATURE! IT'S IMPORTANT THAT WE DO THIS TOGETHER!
HUH? OH, RIGHT. OKAY, WHAT DO I DO?
YOU WRITE IT DOWN ON THIS CHART WHEN I'M DONE.
OKAY. ZNNNK!
CLAR-**EECE**!

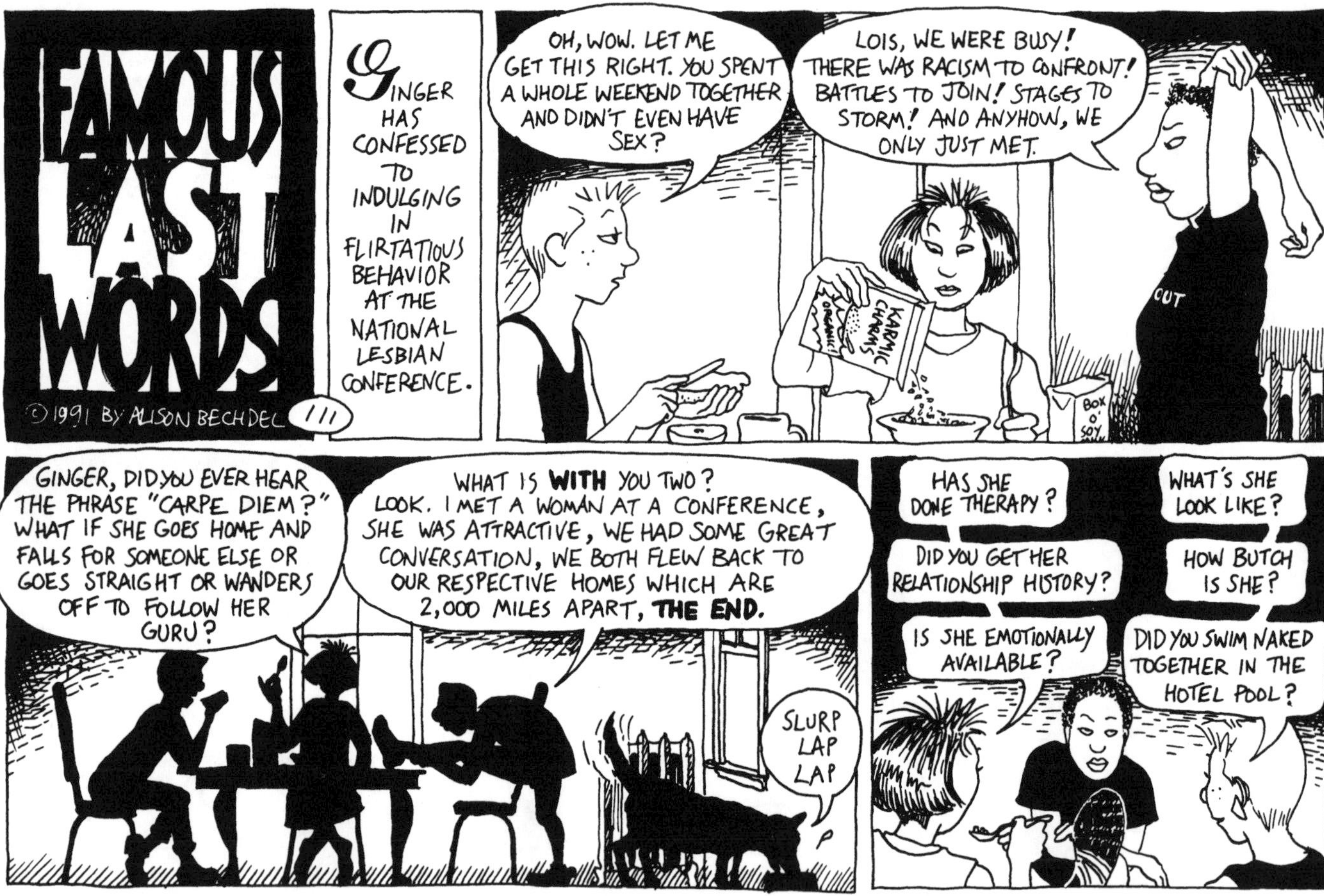
FAMOUS LAST WORDS
© 1991 BY ALISON BECHDEL
111
GINGER HAS CONFESSED TO INDULGING IN FLIRTATIOUS BEHAVIOR AT THE NATIONAL LESBIAN CONFERENCE.
OH, WOW. LET ME GET THIS RIGHT. YOU SPENT A WHOLE WEEKEND TOGETHER AND DIDN'T EVEN HAVE SEX?
LOIS, WE WERE BUSY! THERE WAS RACISM TO CONFRONT! BATTLES TO JOIN! STAGES TO STORM! AND ANYHOW, WE ONLY JUST MET.
KARMIC CHARMS
ORGANIC!
OUT
BOX O' SOY
GINGER, DID YOU EVER HEAR THE PHRASE "CARPE DIEM?" WHAT IF SHE GOES HOME AND FALLS FOR SOMEONE ELSE OR GOES STRAIGHT OR WANDERS OFF TO FOLLOW HER GURU?
WHAT IS **WITH** YOU TWO? LOOK. I MET A WOMAN AT A CONFERENCE, SHE WAS ATTRACTIVE, WE HAD SOME GREAT CONVERSATION, WE BOTH FLEW BACK TO OUR RESPECTIVE HOMES WHICH ARE 2,000 MILES APART, **THE END.**
SLURP LAP LAP
HAS SHE DONE THERAPY?
WHAT'S SHE LOOK LIKE?
DID YOU GET HER RELATIONSHIP HISTORY?
HOW BUTCH IS SHE?
IS SHE EMOTIONALLY AVAILABLE?
DID YOU SWIM NAKED TOGETHER IN THE HOTEL POOL?

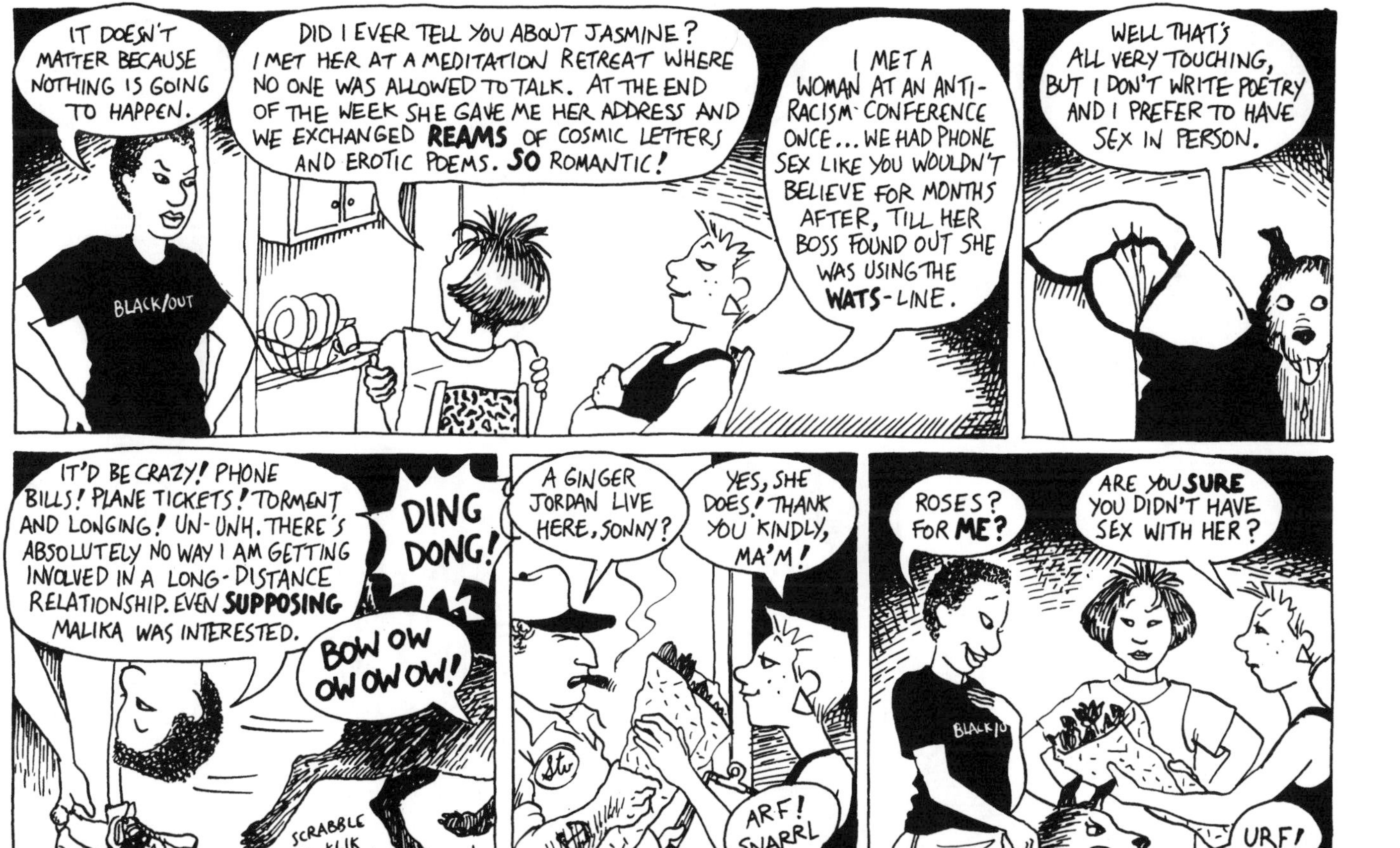
IT DOESN'T MATTER BECAUSE NOTHING IS GOING TO HAPPEN.
DID I EVER TELL YOU ABOUT JASMINE? I MET HER AT A MEDITATION RETREAT WHERE NO ONE WAS ALLOWED TO TALK. AT THE END OF THE WEEK SHE GAVE ME HER ADDRESS AND WE EXCHANGED **REAMS** OF COSMIC LETTERS AND EROTIC POEMS. **SO** ROMANTIC!
I MET A WOMAN AT AN ANTI-RACISM CONFERENCE ONCE... WE HAD PHONE SEX LIKE YOU WOULDN'T BELIEVE FOR MONTHS AFTER, TILL HER BOSS FOUND OUT SHE WAS USING THE **WATS**-LINE.
BLACK/OUT
WELL THAT'S ALL VERY TOUCHING, BUT I DON'T WRITE POETRY AND I PREFER TO HAVE SEX IN PERSON.
IT'D BE CRAZY! PHONE BILLS! PLANE TICKETS! TORMENT AND LONGING! UN-UNH. THERE'S ABSOLUTELY NO WAY I AM GETTING INVOLVED IN A LONG-DISTANCE RELATIONSHIP. EVEN **SUPPOSING** MALIKA WAS INTERESTED.
DING DONG!
BOW OW OW OW OW!
SCRABBLE KLIK KLIK
A GINGER JORDAN LIVE HERE, SONNY?
YES, SHE DOES! THANK YOU KINDLY, MA'M!
ARF! SNARRL
ROSES? FOR **ME**?
ARE YOU **SURE** YOU DIDN'T HAVE SEX WITH HER?
BLACK/OUT
URF!

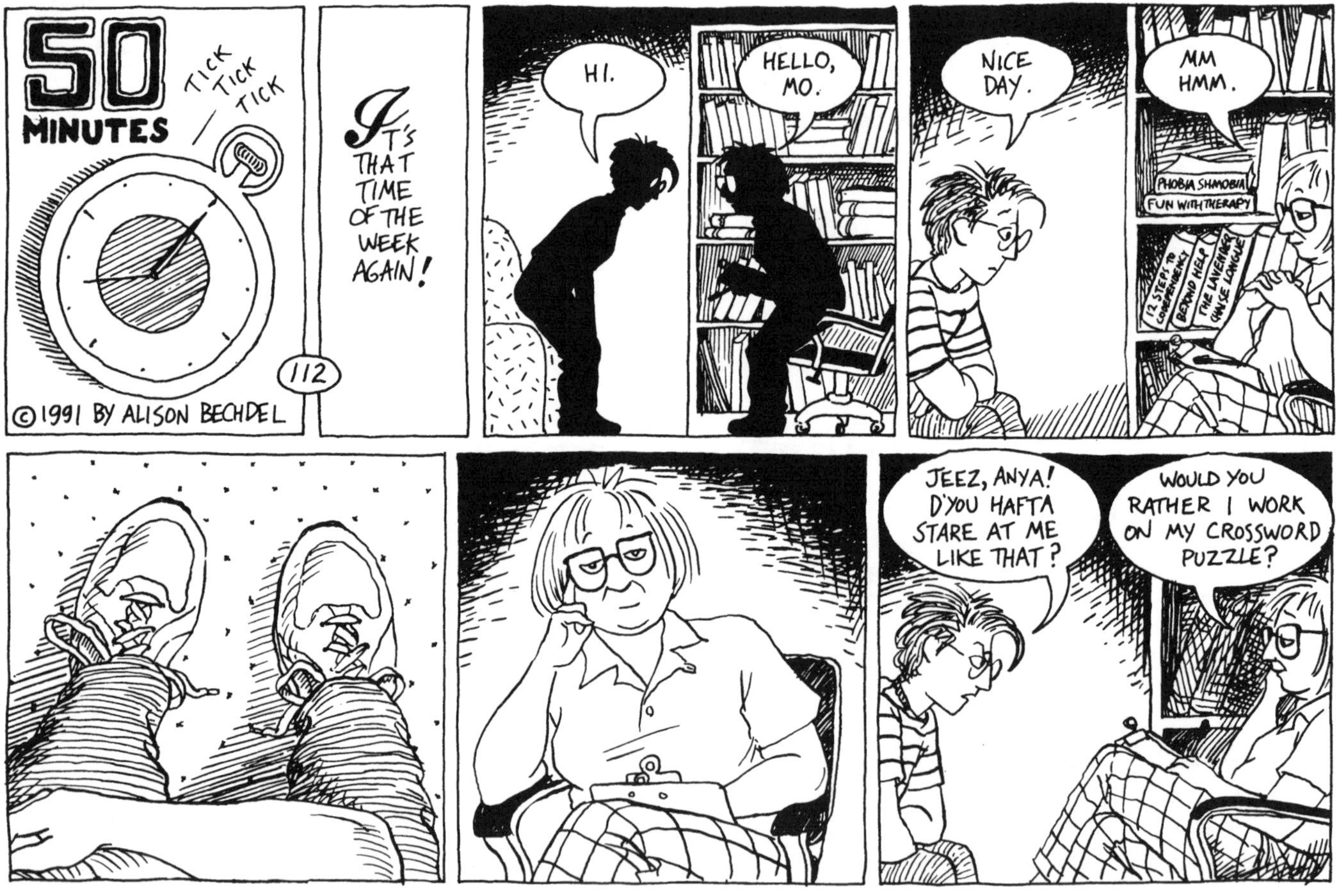
50 MINUTES
TICK TICK TICK
112
©1991 BY ALISON BECHDEL
IT'S THAT TIME OF THE WEEK AGAIN!
HI.
HELLO, MO.
NICE DAY.
MM HMM.
PHOBIA SHMOBIA
FUN WITH THERAPY
12 STEPS TO CODEPENDENCY
BEYOND HELP
THE LAVENDER CHAISE LONGUE
JEEZ, ANYA! D'YOU HAFTA STARE AT ME LIKE THAT?
WOULD YOU RATHER I WORK ON MY CROSSWORD PUZZLE?

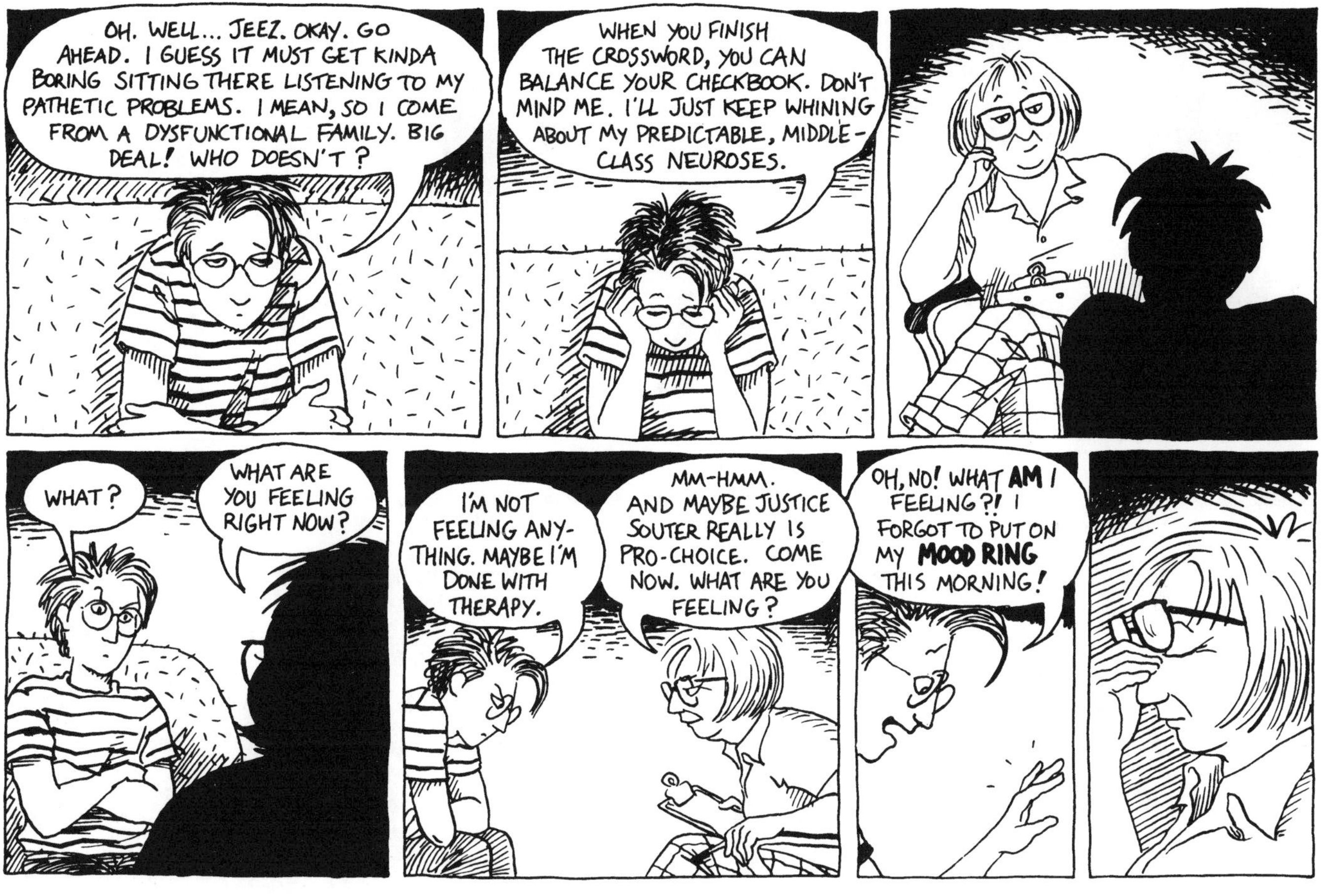
OH. WELL... JEEZ. OKAY. GO AHEAD. I GUESS IT MUST GET KINDA BORING SITTING THERE LISTENING TO MY PATHETIC PROBLEMS. I MEAN, SO I COME FROM A DYSFUNCTIONAL FAMILY. BIG DEAL! WHO DOESN'T?
WHEN YOU FINISH THE CROSSWORD, YOU CAN BALANCE YOUR CHECKBOOK. DON'T MIND ME. I'LL JUST KEEP WHINING ABOUT MY PREDICTABLE, MIDDLE-CLASS NEUROSES.
WHAT?
WHAT ARE YOU FEELING RIGHT NOW?
I'M NOT FEELING ANYTHING. MAYBE I'M DONE WITH THERAPY.
MM-HMM. AND MAYBE JUSTICE SOUTER REALLY IS PRO-CHOICE. COME NOW. WHAT ARE YOU FEELING?
OH, NO! WHAT **AM** I FEELING?! I FORGOT TO PUT ON MY **MOOD RING** THIS MORNING!

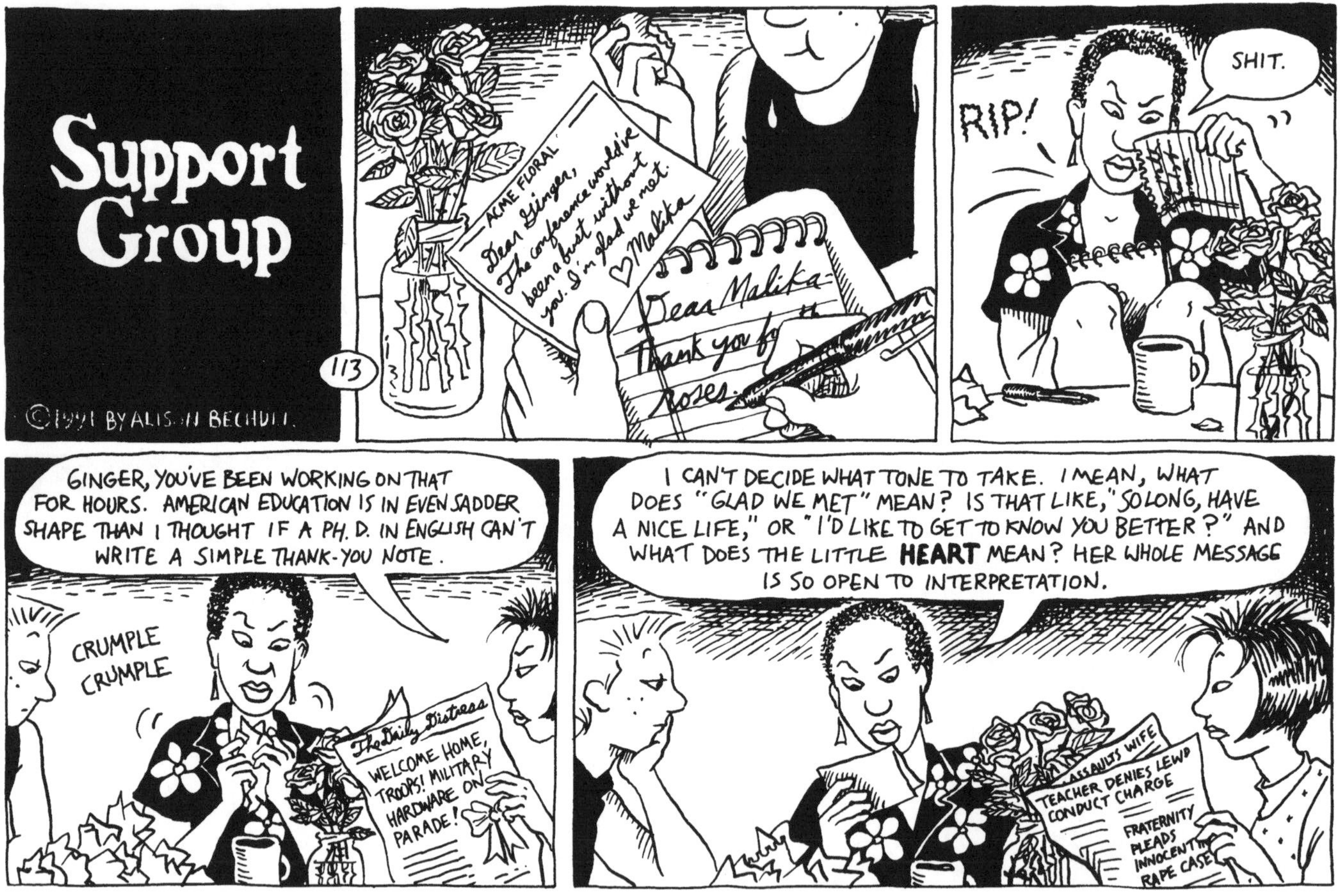
Support Group
113
©1991 BY ALISON BECHDEL.
ACME FLORAL
Dear Ginger, The conference would've been a bust without you. I'm glad we met. ♡ Malika
Dear Malika
Roses.
RIP!
SHIT.
GINGER, YOU'VE BEEN WORKING ON THAT FOR HOURS. AMERICAN EDUCATION IS IN EVEN SADDER SHAPE THAN I THOUGHT IF A PH. D. IN ENGLISH CAN'T WRITE A SIMPLE THANK-YOU NOTE.
CRUMPLE CRUMPLE
The Daily Distress
WELCOME HOME, TROOPS! MILITARY HARDWARE ON PARADE!
I CAN'T DECIDE WHAT TONE TO TAKE. I MEAN, WHAT DOES "GLAD WE MET" MEAN? IS THAT LIKE, "SO LONG, HAVE A NICE LIFE," OR "I'D LIKE TO GET TO KNOW YOU BETTER?" AND WHAT DOES THE LITTLE **HEART** MEAN? HER WHOLE MESSAGE IS SO OPEN TO INTERPRETATION.
ASSAULTS WIFE
TEACHER DENIES LEWD CONDUCT CHARGE
FRATERNITY PLEADS INNOCENT
RAPE CASE

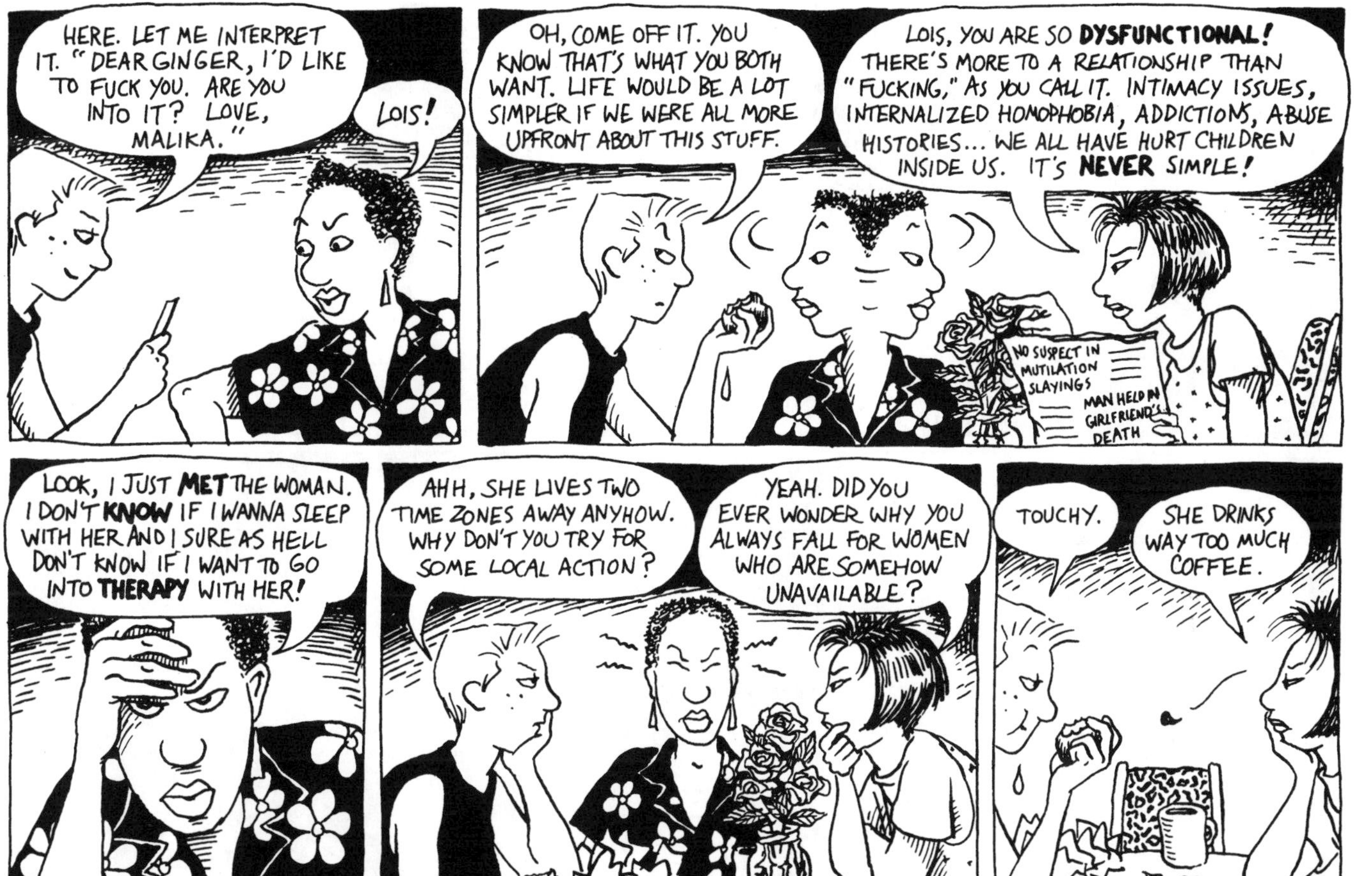
HERE. LET ME INTERPRET IT. "DEAR GINGER, I'D LIKE TO FUCK YOU. ARE YOU INTO IT? LOVE, MALIKA."
LOIS!
OH, COME OFF IT. YOU KNOW THAT'S WHAT YOU BOTH WANT. LIFE WOULD BE A LOT SIMPLER IF WE WERE ALL MORE UPFRONT ABOUT THIS STUFF.
LOIS, YOU ARE SO DYSFUNCTIONAL! THERE'S MORE TO A RELATIONSHIP THAN "FUCKING," AS YOU CALL IT. INTIMACY ISSUES, INTERNALIZED HOMOPHOBIA, ADDICTIONS, ABUSE HISTORIES... WE ALL HAVE HURT CHILDREN INSIDE US. IT'S NEVER SIMPLE!
NO SUSPECT IN MUTILATION SLAYINGS
MAN HELD IN GIRLFRIEND'S DEATH
LOOK, I JUST MET THE WOMAN. I DON'T KNOW IF I WANNA SLEEP WITH HER AND I SURE AS HELL DON'T KNOW IF I WANT TO GO INTO THERAPY WITH HER!
AHH, SHE LIVES TWO TIME ZONES AWAY ANYHOW. WHY DON'T YOU TRY FOR SOME LOCAL ACTION?
YEAH. DID YOU EVER WONDER WHY YOU ALWAYS FALL FOR WOMEN WHO ARE SOMEHOW UNAVAILABLE?
TOUCHY.
SHE DRINKS WAY TOO MUCH COFFEE.

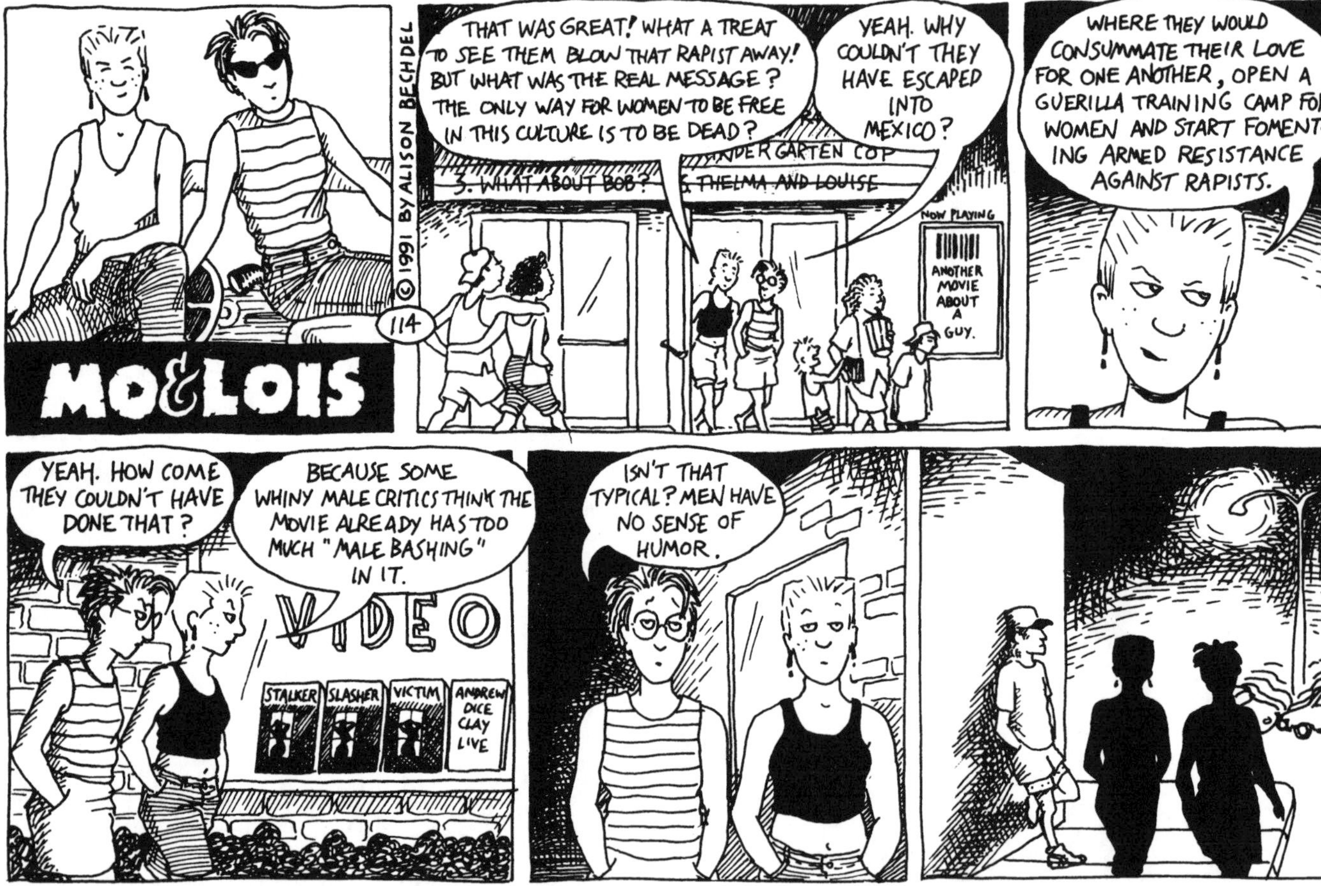
MO&LOIS
114
© 1991 BY ALISON BECHDEL
THAT WAS GREAT! WHAT A TREAT TO SEE THEM BLOW THAT RAPIST AWAY! BUT WHAT WAS THE REAL MESSAGE? THE ONLY WAY FOR WOMEN TO BE FREE IN THIS CULTURE IS TO BE DEAD?
YEAH. WHY COULDN'T THEY HAVE ESCAPED INTO MEXICO?
3. WHAT ABOUT BOB?
THELMA AND LOUISE
NOW PLAYING
ANOTHER MOVIE ABOUT A GUY.
WHERE THEY WOULD CONSUMMATE THEIR LOVE FOR ONE ANOTHER, OPEN A GUERILLA TRAINING CAMP FOR WOMEN AND START FOMENTING ARMED RESISTANCE AGAINST RAPISTS.
YEAH. HOW COME THEY COULDN'T HAVE DONE THAT?
BECAUSE SOME WHINY MALE CRITICS THINK THE MOVIE ALREADY HAS TOO MUCH "MALE BASHING" IN IT.
VIDEO
STALKER
SLASHER
VICTIM
ANDREW DICE CLAY LIVE
ISN'T THAT TYPICAL? MEN HAVE NO SENSE OF HUMOR.

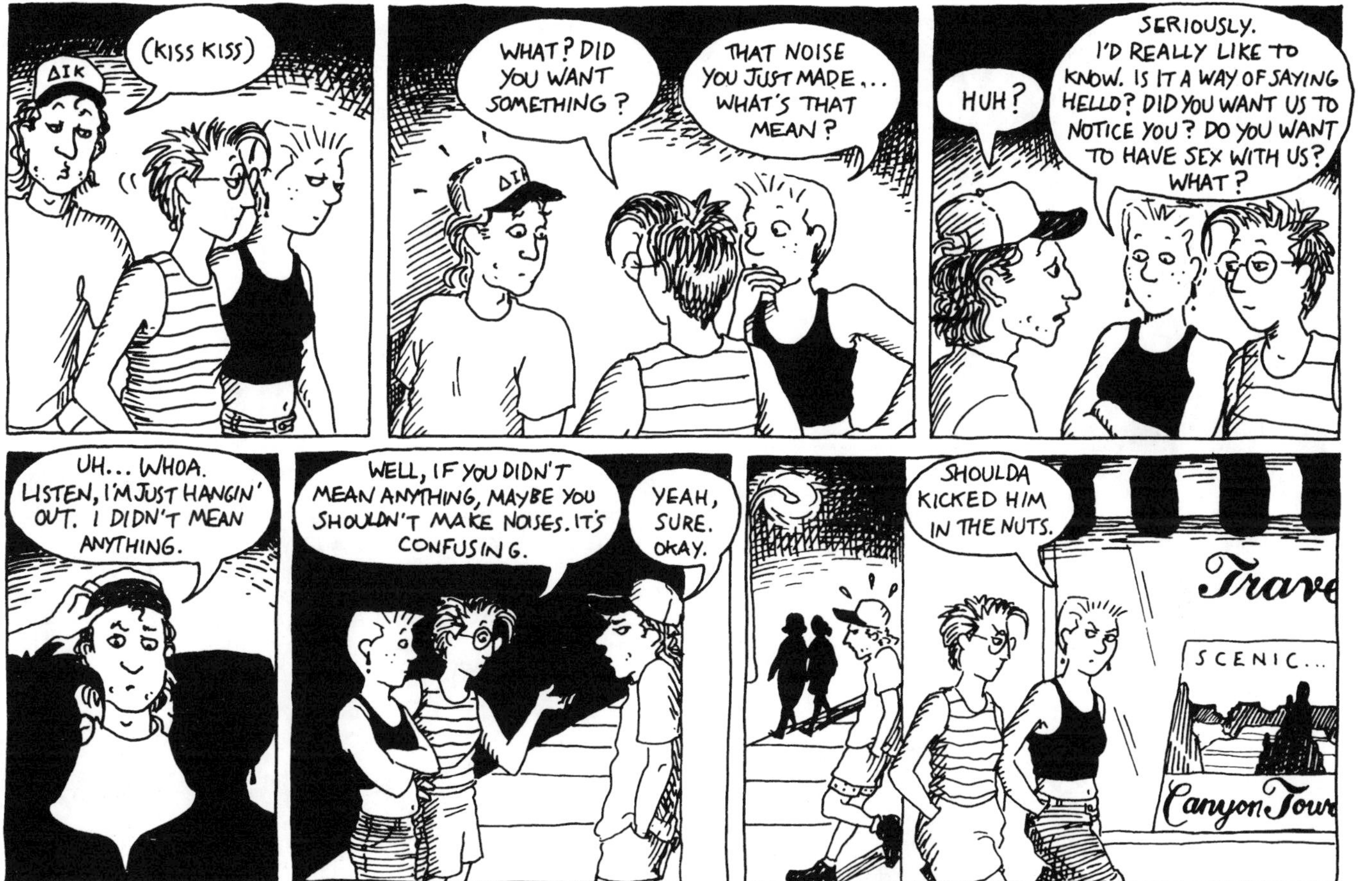
ΔIK
(KISS KISS)
WHAT? DID YOU WANT SOMETHING?
ΔIK
THAT NOISE YOU JUST MADE... WHAT'S THAT MEAN?
HUH?
SERIOUSLY. I'D REALLY LIKE TO KNOW. IS IT A WAY OF SAYING HELLO? DID YOU WANT US TO NOTICE YOU? DO YOU WANT TO HAVE SEX WITH US? WHAT?
UH... WHOA. LISTEN, I'M JUST HANGIN' OUT. I DIDN'T MEAN ANYTHING.
WELL, IF YOU DIDN'T MEAN ANYTHING, MAYBE YOU SHOULDN'T MAKE NOISES. IT'S CONFUSING.
YEAH, SURE. OKAY.
SHOULDA KICKED HIM IN THE NUTS.
Trave
SCENIC...
Canyon Tour

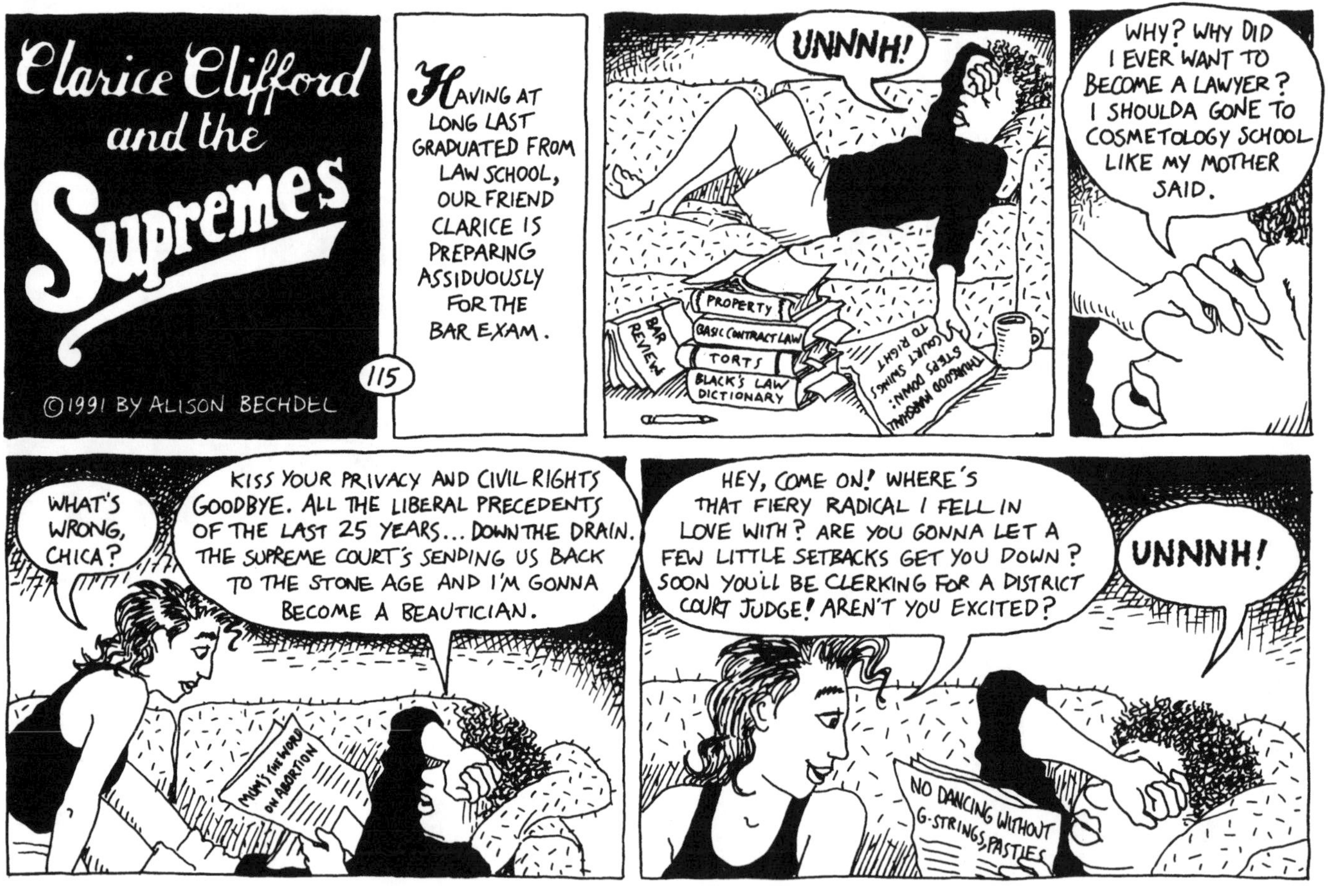
Clarice Clifford and the Supremes
©1991 BY ALISON BECHDEL
115
HAVING AT LONG LAST GRADUATED FROM LAW SCHOOL, OUR FRIEND CLARICE IS PREPARING ASSIDUOUSLY FOR THE BAR EXAM.
UNNNH!
BAR REVIEW
PROPERTY
BASIC CONTRACT LAW
TORTS
BLACK'S LAW DICTIONARY
THURGOOD MARSHALL STEPS DOWN: COURT SWINGS TO RIGHT
WHY? WHY DID I EVER WANT TO BECOME A LAWYER? I SHOULDA GONE TO COSMETOLOGY SCHOOL LIKE MY MOTHER SAID.
WHAT'S WRONG, CHICA?
KISS YOUR PRIVACY AND CIVIL RIGHTS GOODBYE. ALL THE LIBERAL PRECEDENTS OF THE LAST 25 YEARS... DOWN THE DRAIN. THE SUPREME COURT'S SENDING US BACK TO THE STONE AGE AND I'M GONNA BECOME A BEAUTICIAN.
MUM'S THE WORD ON ABORTION
HEY, COME ON! WHERE'S THAT FIERY RADICAL I FELL IN LOVE WITH? ARE YOU GONNA LET A FEW LITTLE SETBACKS GET YOU DOWN? SOON YOU'LL BE CLERKING FOR A DISTRICT COURT JUDGE! AREN'T YOU EXCITED?
UNNNH!
NO DANCING WITHOUT G-STRINGS, PASTIES

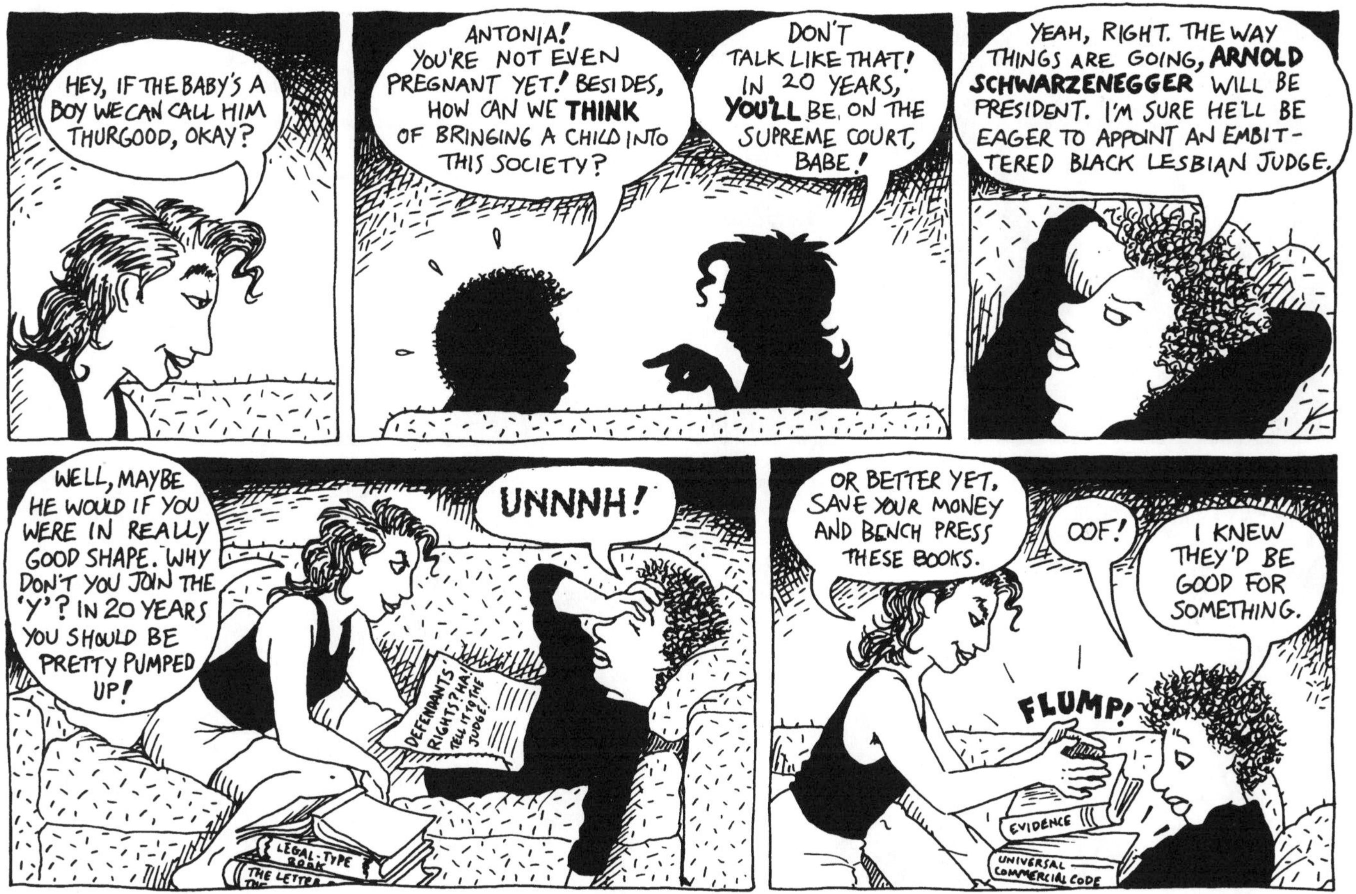

HEY, IF THE BABY'S A BOY WE CAN CALL HIM THURGOOD, OKAY?
ANTONIA! YOU'RE NOT EVEN PREGNANT YET! BESIDES, HOW CAN WE **THINK** OF BRINGING A CHILD INTO THIS SOCIETY?
DON'T TALK LIKE THAT! IN 20 YEARS, **YOU'LL** BE ON THE SUPREME COURT, BABE!
YEAH, RIGHT. THE WAY THINGS ARE GOING, **ARNOLD SCHWARZENEGGER** WILL BE PRESIDENT. I'M SURE HE'LL BE EAGER TO APPOINT AN EMBITTERED BLACK LESBIAN JUDGE.
WELL, MAYBE HE WOULD IF YOU WERE IN REALLY GOOD SHAPE. WHY DON'T YOU JOIN THE 'Y'? IN 20 YEARS YOU SHOULD BE PRETTY PUMPED UP!
UNNNH!
DEFENDANTS' RIGHTS? HA! TELL IT TO THE JUDGE!
LEGAL-TYPE BOOK
THE LETTER
OR BETTER YET, SAVE YOUR MONEY AND BENCH PRESS THESE BOOKS.
OOF!
I KNEW THEY'D BE GOOD FOR SOMETHING.
FLUMP!
EVIDENCE
UNIVERSAL COMMERCIAL CODE

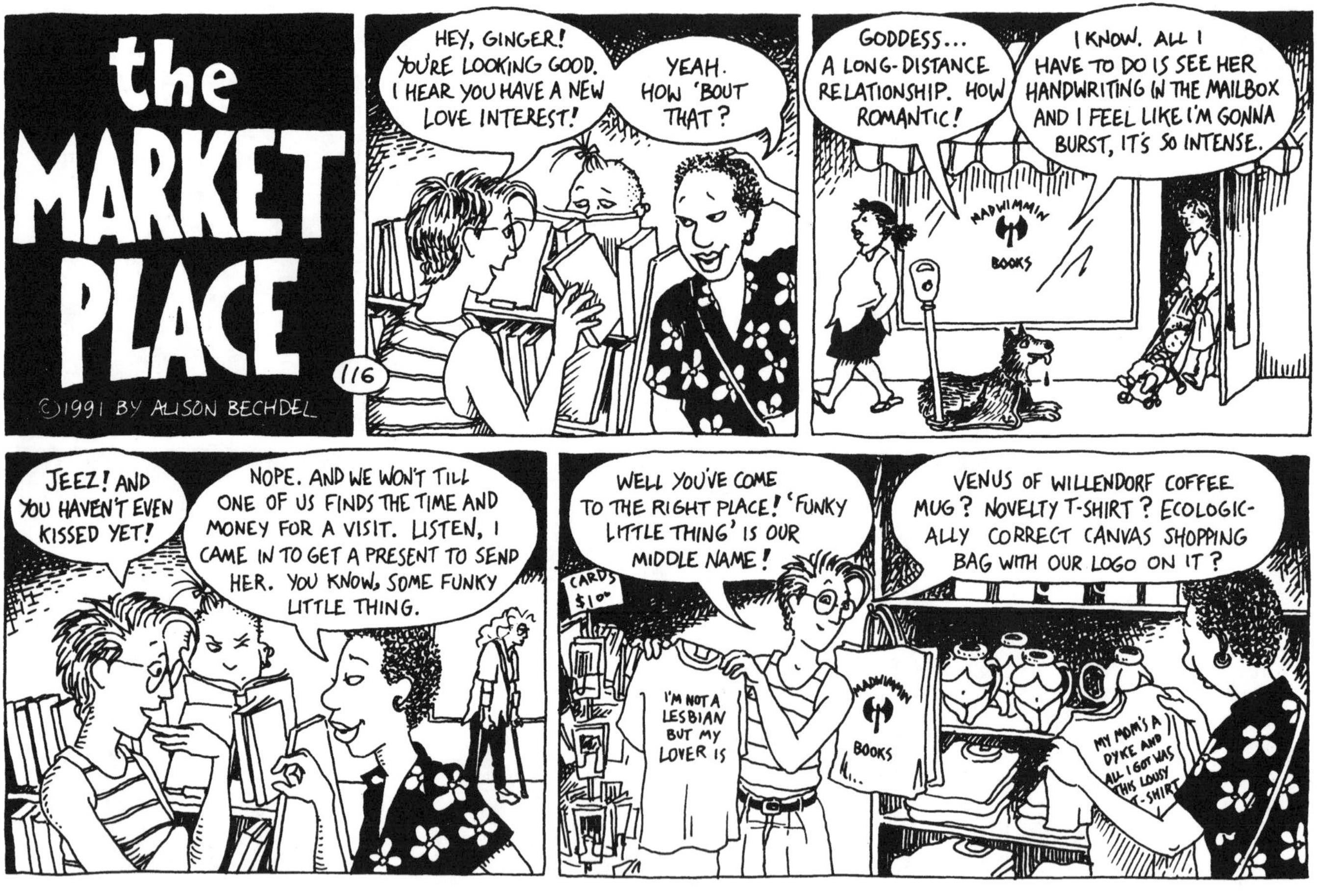
the MARKET PLACE
116
©1991 BY ALISON BECHDEL
HEY, GINGER! YOU'RE LOOKING GOOD. I HEAR YOU HAVE A NEW LOVE INTEREST!
YEAH. HOW 'BOUT THAT?
GODDESS... A LONG-DISTANCE RELATIONSHIP. HOW ROMANTIC!
I KNOW. ALL I HAVE TO DO IS SEE HER HANDWRITING IN THE MAILBOX AND I FEEL LIKE I'M GONNA BURST, IT'S SO INTENSE.
MADWIMMIN BOOKS
JEEZ! AND YOU HAVEN'T EVEN KISSED YET!
NOPE. AND WE WON'T TILL ONE OF US FINDS THE TIME AND MONEY FOR A VISIT. LISTEN, I CAME IN TO GET A PRESENT TO SEND HER. YOU KNOW, SOME FUNKY LITTLE THING.
WELL YOU'VE COME TO THE RIGHT PLACE! 'FUNKY LITTLE THING' IS OUR MIDDLE NAME!
VENUS OF WILLENDORF COFFEE MUG? NOVELTY T-SHIRT? ECOLOGIC-ALLY CORRECT CANVAS SHOPPING BAG WITH OUR LOGO ON IT?
CARDS $1.00
I'M NOT A LESBIAN BUT MY LOVER IS
MADWIMMIN BOOKS
MY MOM'S A DYKE AND ALL I GOT WAS THIS LOUSY T-SHIRT

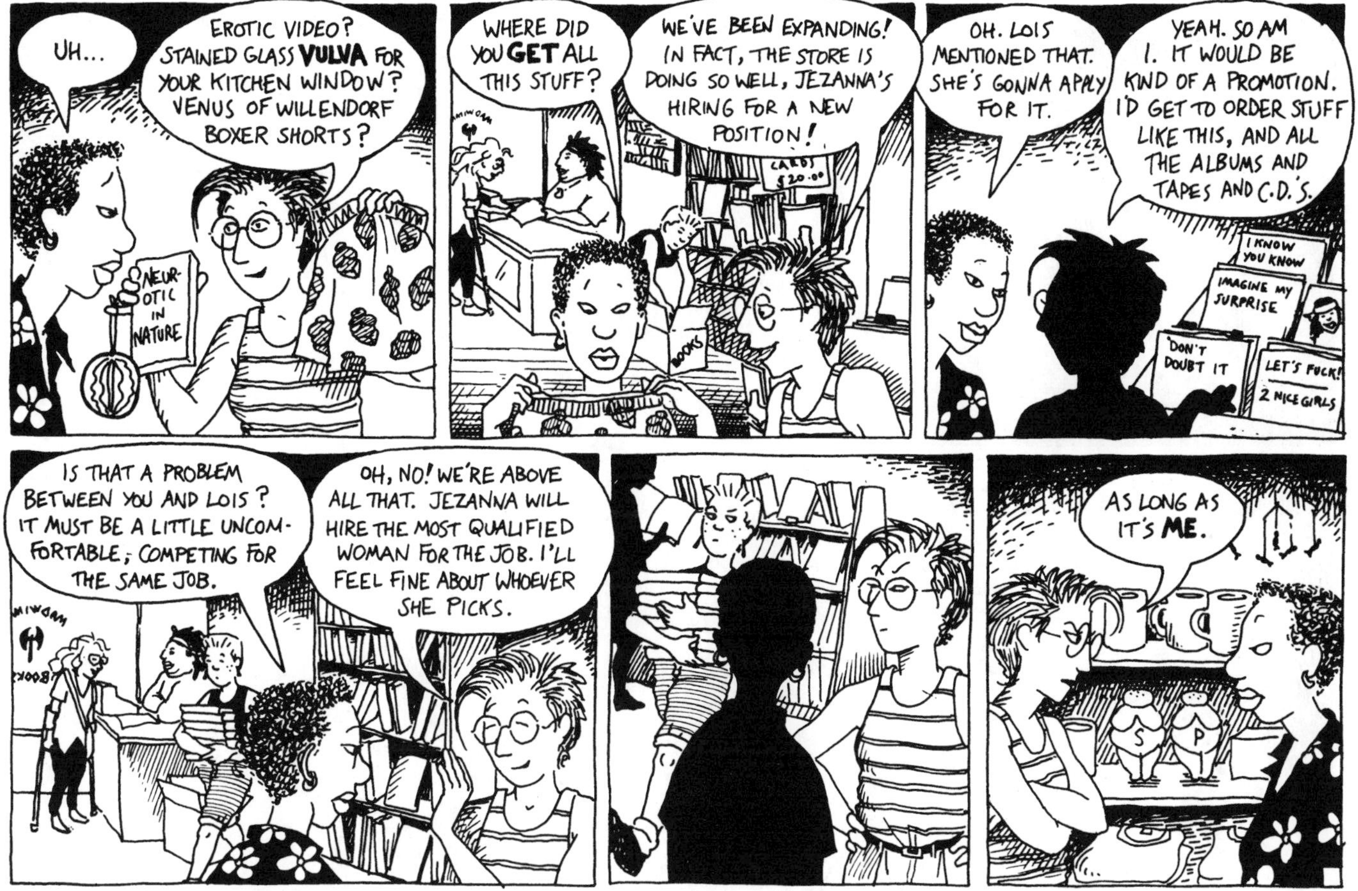
UH...
EROTIC VIDEO? STAINED GLASS **VULVA** FOR YOUR KITCHEN WINDOW? VENUS OF WILLENDORF BOXER SHORTS?
NEUROTIC IN NATURE
WHERE DID YOU **GET** ALL THIS STUFF?
WE'VE BEEN EXPANDING! IN FACT, THE STORE IS DOING SO WELL, JEZANNA'S HIRING FOR A NEW POSITION!
CARDS $20.00
BOOKS
OH. LOIS MENTIONED THAT. SHE'S GONNA APPLY FOR IT.
YEAH. SO AM I. IT WOULD BE KIND OF A PROMOTION. I'D GET TO ORDER STUFF LIKE THIS, AND ALL THE ALBUMS AND TAPES AND C.D.'S.
I KNOW YOU KNOW
IMAGINE MY SURPRISE
DON'T DOUBT IT
LET'S FUCK!
2 NICE GIRLS
IS THAT A PROBLEM BETWEEN YOU AND LOIS? IT MUST BE A LITTLE UNCOMFORTABLE; COMPETING FOR THE SAME JOB.
OH, NO! WE'RE ABOVE ALL THAT. JEZANNA WILL HIRE THE MOST QUALIFIED WOMAN FOR THE JOB. I'LL FEEL FINE ABOUT WHOEVER SHE PICKS.
AS LONG AS IT'S **ME**.
S
P

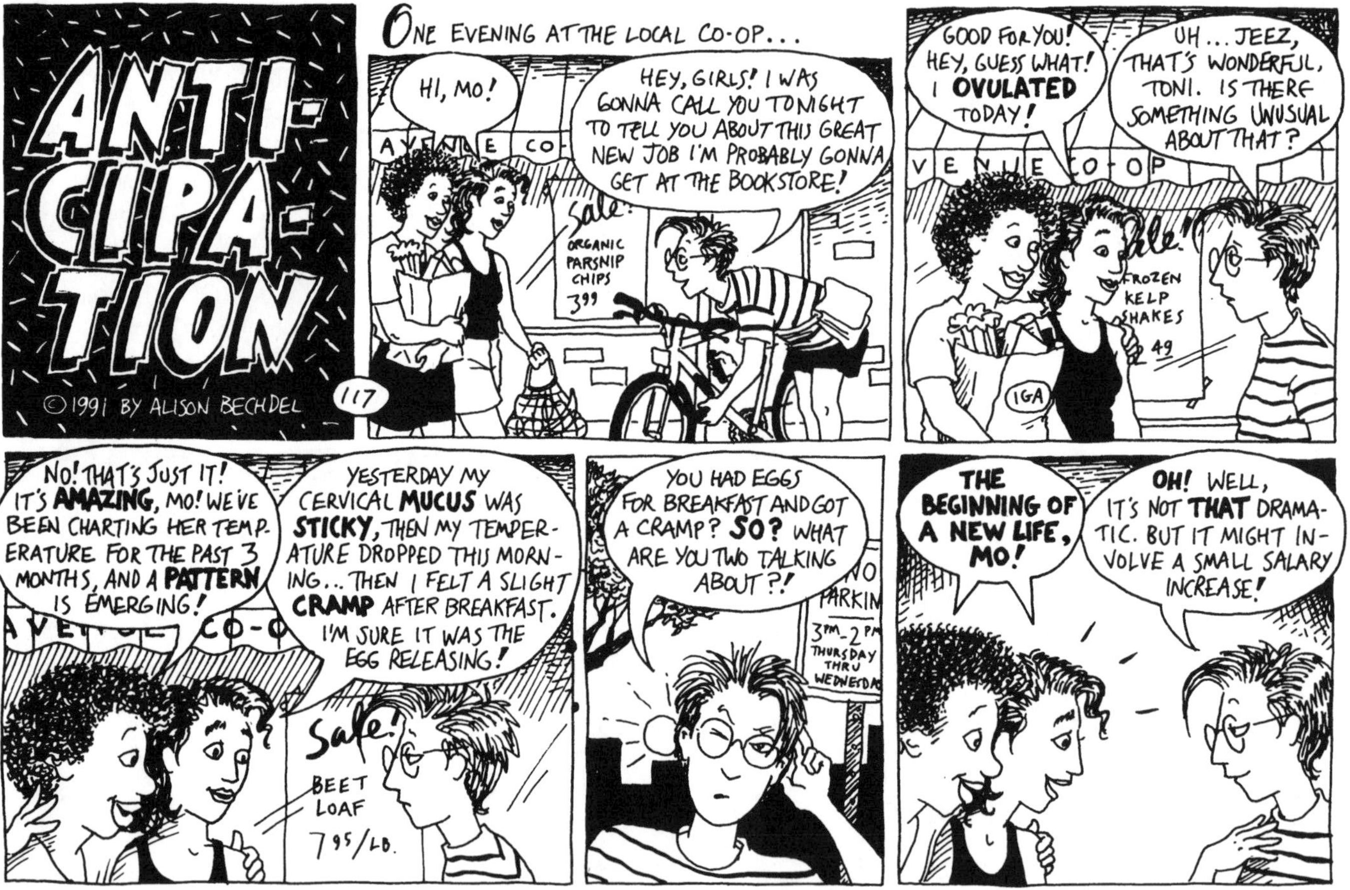
ANTI-CIPA-TION
©1991 BY ALISON BECHDEL
117
ONE EVENING AT THE LOCAL CO-OP...
HI, MO!
HEY, GIRLS! I WAS GONNA CALL YOU TONIGHT TO TELL YOU ABOUT THIS GREAT NEW JOB I'M PROBABLY GONNA GET AT THE BOOKSTORE!
SALE! ORGANIC PARSNIP CHIPS 3.99
GOOD FOR YOU! HEY, GUESS WHAT! I **OVULATED** TODAY!
UH... JEEZ, THAT'S WONDERFUL, TONI. IS THERE SOMETHING UNUSUAL ABOUT THAT?
SALE! FROZEN KELP SHAKES .49
IGA
NO! THAT'S JUST IT! IT'S **AMAZING**, MO! WE'VE BEEN CHARTING HER TEMPERATURE FOR THE PAST 3 MONTHS, AND A **PATTERN** IS EMERGING!
YESTERDAY MY CERVICAL **MUCUS** WAS **STICKY**, THEN MY TEMPERATURE DROPPED THIS MORNING... THEN I FELT A SLIGHT **CRAMP** AFTER BREAKFAST. I'M SURE IT WAS THE EGG RELEASING!
SALE! BEET LOAF 7.95/LB.
YOU HAD EGGS FOR BREAKFAST AND GOT A CRAMP? **SO?** WHAT ARE YOU TWO TALKING ABOUT?!
3PM-2PM THURSDAY THRU WEDNESDAY
THE BEGINNING OF A NEW LIFE, MO!
OH! WELL, IT'S NOT **THAT** DRAMATIC. BUT IT MIGHT INVOLVE A SMALL SALARY INCREASE!

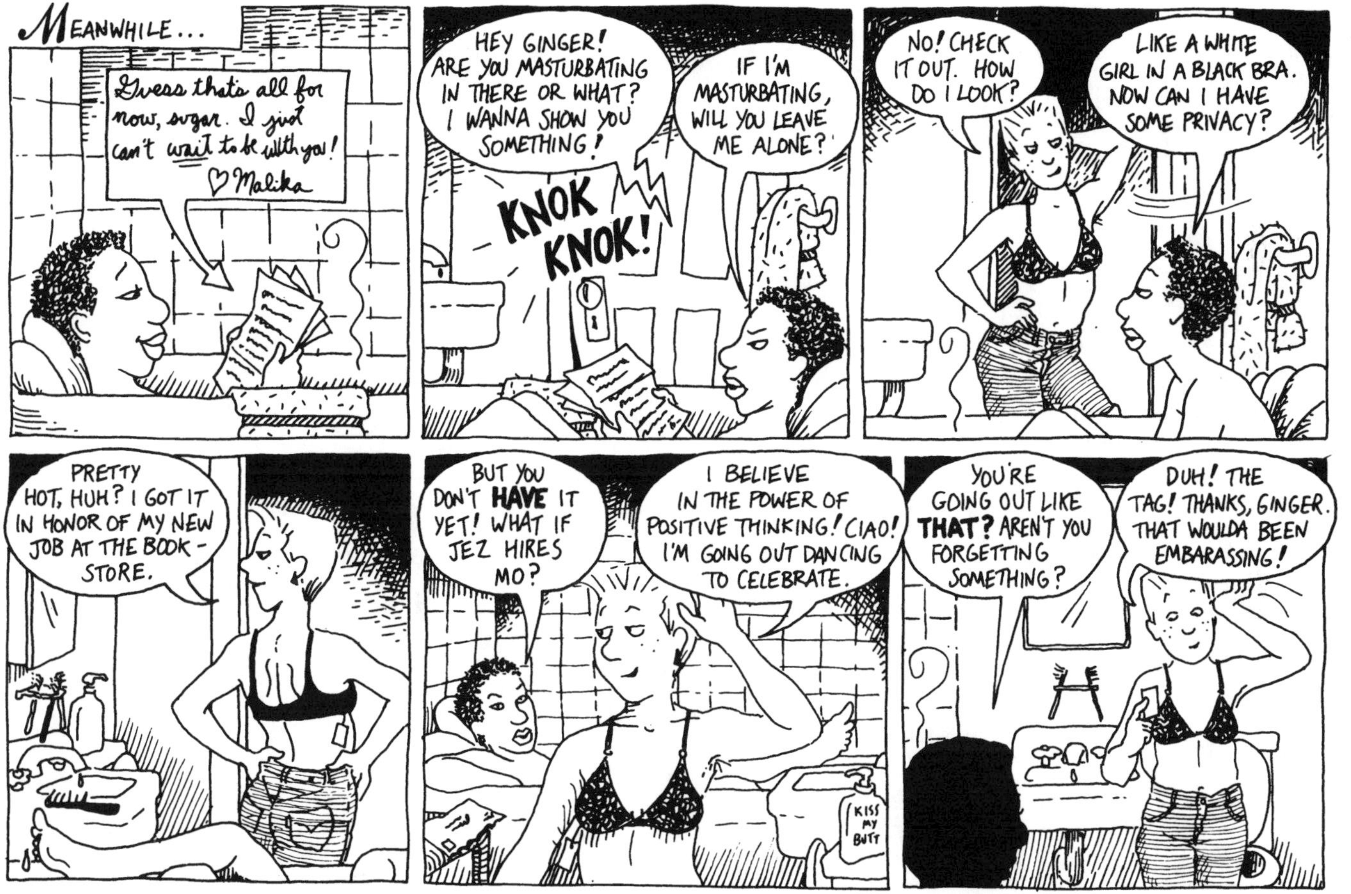
MEANWHILE...
Guess that's all for now, sugar. I just can't wait to be with you! ♡ Malika
HEY GINGER! ARE YOU MASTURBATING IN THERE OR WHAT? I WANNA SHOW YOU SOMETHING!
KNOK KNOK!
IF I'M MASTURBATING, WILL YOU LEAVE ME ALONE?
NO! CHECK IT OUT. HOW DO I LOOK?
LIKE A WHITE GIRL IN A BLACK BRA. NOW CAN I HAVE SOME PRIVACY?
PRETTY HOT, HUH? I GOT IT IN HONOR OF MY NEW JOB AT THE BOOK-STORE.
BUT YOU DON'T HAVE IT YET! WHAT IF JEZ HIRES MO?
I BELIEVE IN THE POWER OF POSITIVE THINKING! CIAO! I'M GOING OUT DANCING TO CELEBRATE.
KISS MY BUTT
YOU'RE GOING OUT LIKE THAT? AREN'T YOU FORGETTING SOMETHING?
DUH! THE TAG! THANKS, GINGER. THAT WOULDA BEEN EMBARASSING!

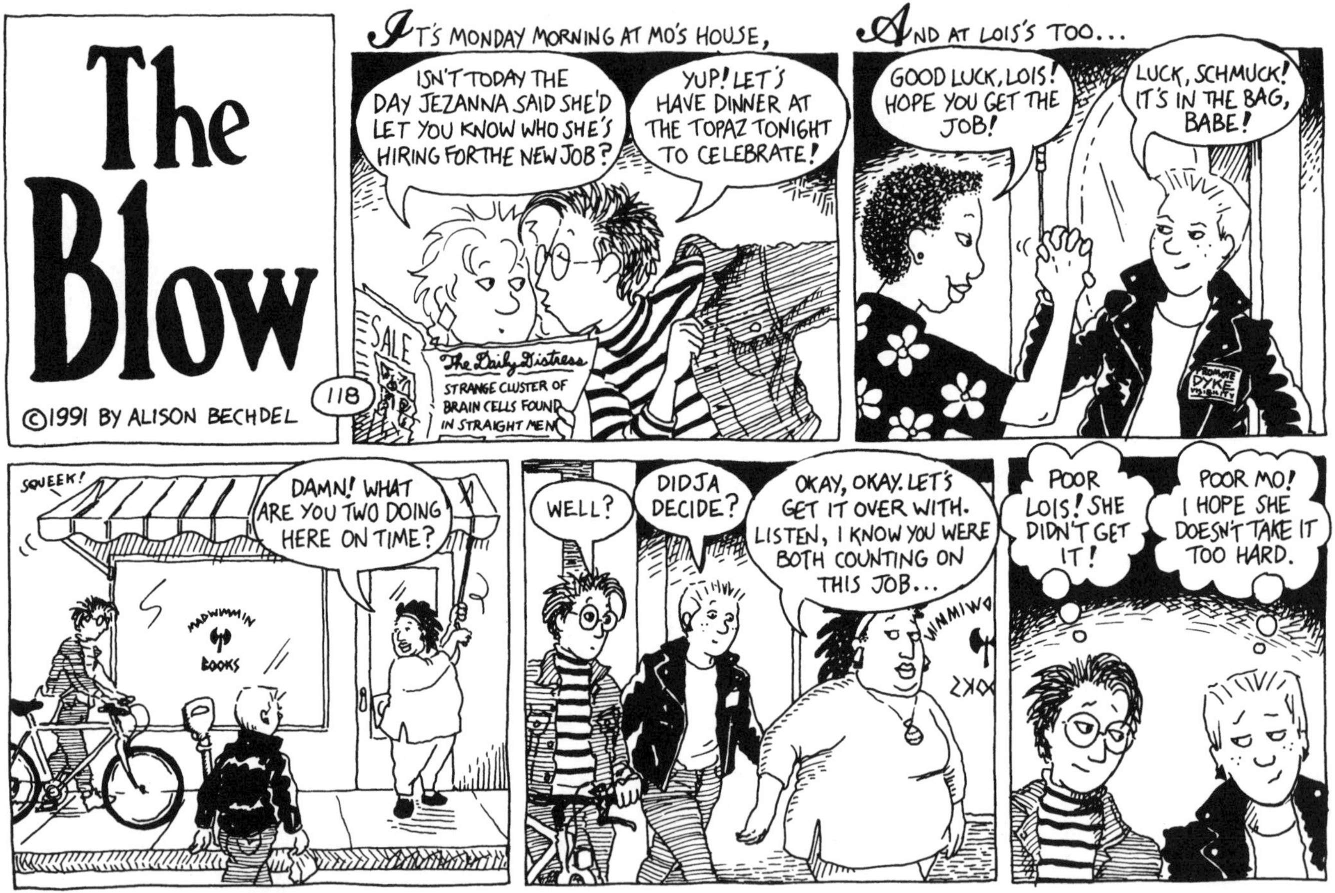
The Blow
©1991 BY ALISON BECHDEL
118
IT'S MONDAY MORNING AT MO'S HOUSE,
ISN'T TODAY THE DAY JEZANNA SAID SHE'D LET YOU KNOW WHO SHE'S HIRING FOR THE NEW JOB?
YUP! LET'S HAVE DINNER AT THE TOPAZ TONIGHT TO CELEBRATE!
SALE
The Daily Distress
STRANGE CLUSTER OF BRAIN CELLS FOUND IN STRAIGHT MEN
AND AT LOIS'S TOO...
GOOD LUCK, LOIS! HOPE YOU GET THE JOB!
LUCK, SCHMUCK! IT'S IN THE BAG, BABE!
PROMOTE DYKE VISIBILITY
SQUEEK!
DAMN! WHAT ARE YOU TWO DOING HERE ON TIME?
MADWIMMIN BOOKS
WELL?
DIDJA DECIDE?
OKAY, OKAY. LET'S GET IT OVER WITH. LISTEN, I KNOW YOU WERE BOTH COUNTING ON THIS JOB...
POOR LOIS! SHE DIDN'T GET IT!
POOR MO! I HOPE SHE DOESN'T TAKE IT TOO HARD.

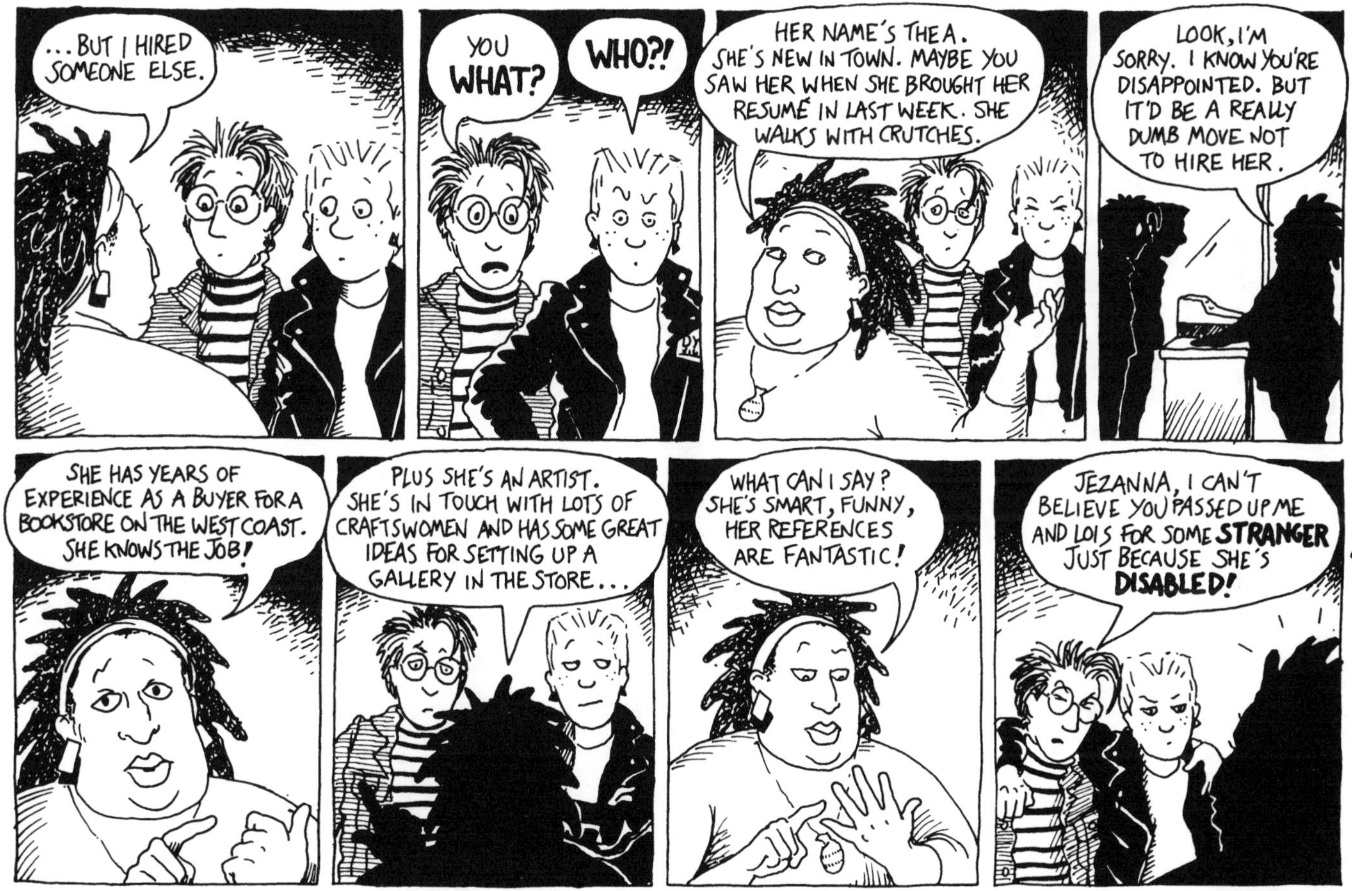

...BUT I HIRED SOMEONE ELSE.
YOU WHAT?
WHO?!
HER NAME'S THEA. SHE'S NEW IN TOWN. MAYBE YOU SAW HER WHEN SHE BROUGHT HER RESUMÉ IN LAST WEEK. SHE WALKS WITH CRUTCHES.
LOOK, I'M SORRY. I KNOW YOU'RE DISAPPOINTED. BUT IT'D BE A REALLY DUMB MOVE NOT TO HIRE HER.
SHE HAS YEARS OF EXPERIENCE AS A BUYER FOR A BOOKSTORE ON THE WEST COAST. SHE KNOWS THE JOB!
PLUS SHE'S AN ARTIST. SHE'S IN TOUCH WITH LOTS OF CRAFTSWOMEN AND HAS SOME GREAT IDEAS FOR SETTING UP A GALLERY IN THE STORE...
WHAT CAN I SAY? SHE'S SMART, FUNNY, HER REFERENCES ARE FANTASTIC!
JEZANNA, I CAN'T BELIEVE YOU PASSED UP ME AND LOIS FOR SOME STRANGER JUST BECAUSE SHE'S DISABLED!

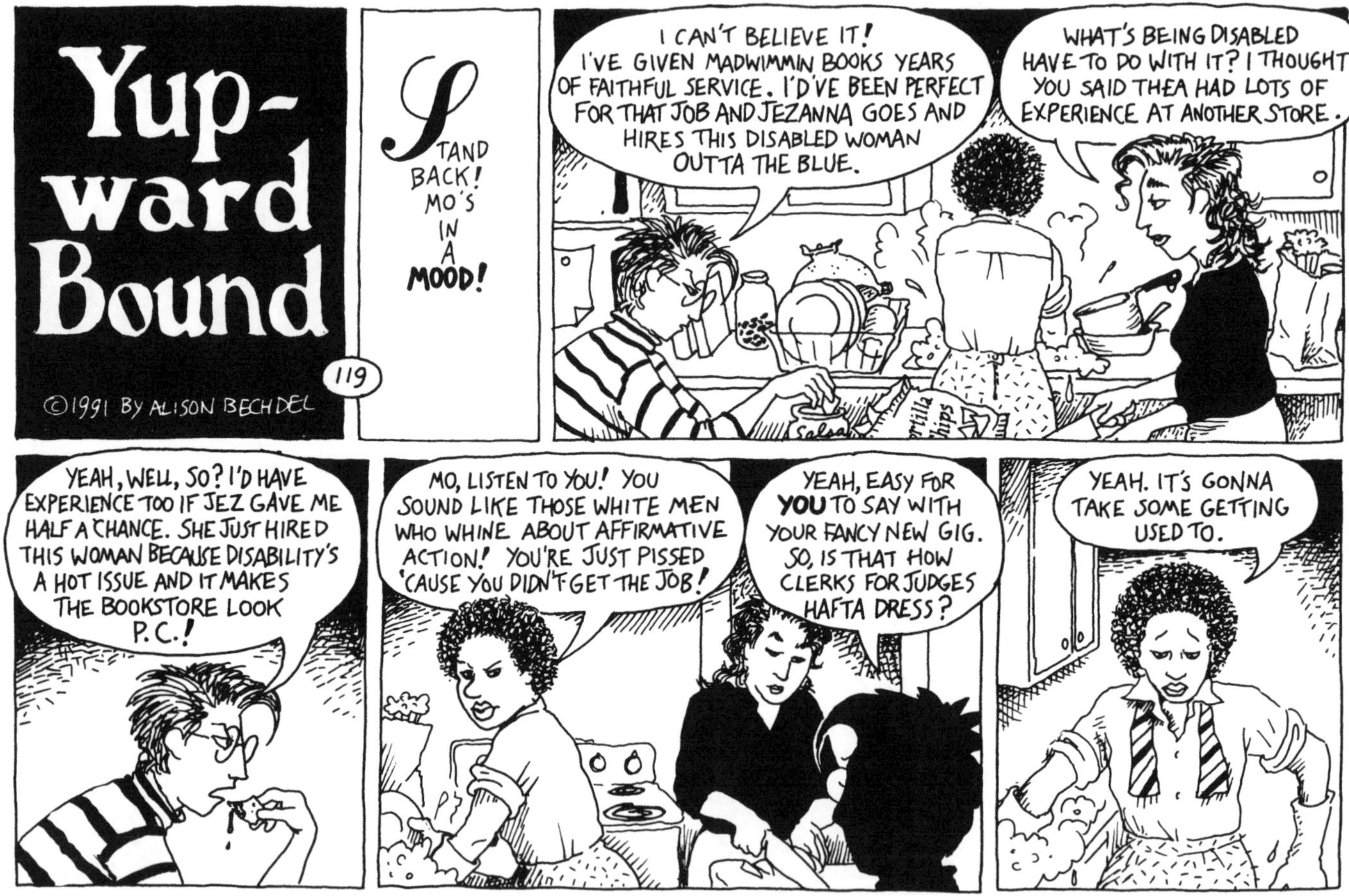
Yup-ward Bound
©1991 BY ALISON BECHDEL
119
STAND BACK! MO'S IN A MOOD!
I CAN'T BELIEVE IT! I'VE GIVEN MADWIMMIN BOOKS YEARS OF FAITHFUL SERVICE. I'D'VE BEEN PERFECT FOR THAT JOB AND JEZANNA GOES AND HIRES THIS DISABLED WOMAN OUTTA THE BLUE.
WHAT'S BEING DISABLED HAVE TO DO WITH IT? I THOUGHT YOU SAID THEA HAD LOTS OF EXPERIENCE AT ANOTHER STORE.
Salsa
Tortilla Chips
YEAH, WELL, SO? I'D HAVE EXPERIENCE TOO IF JEZ GAVE ME HALF A CHANCE. SHE JUST HIRED THIS WOMAN BECAUSE DISABILITY'S A HOT ISSUE AND IT MAKES THE BOOKSTORE LOOK P.C.!
MO, LISTEN TO YOU! YOU SOUND LIKE THOSE WHITE MEN WHO WHINE ABOUT AFFIRMATIVE ACTION! YOU'RE JUST PISSED 'CAUSE YOU DIDN'T GET THE JOB!
YEAH, EASY FOR YOU TO SAY WITH YOUR FANCY NEW GIG. SO, IS THAT HOW CLERKS FOR JUDGES HAFTA DRESS?
YEAH. IT'S GONNA TAKE SOME GETTING USED TO.

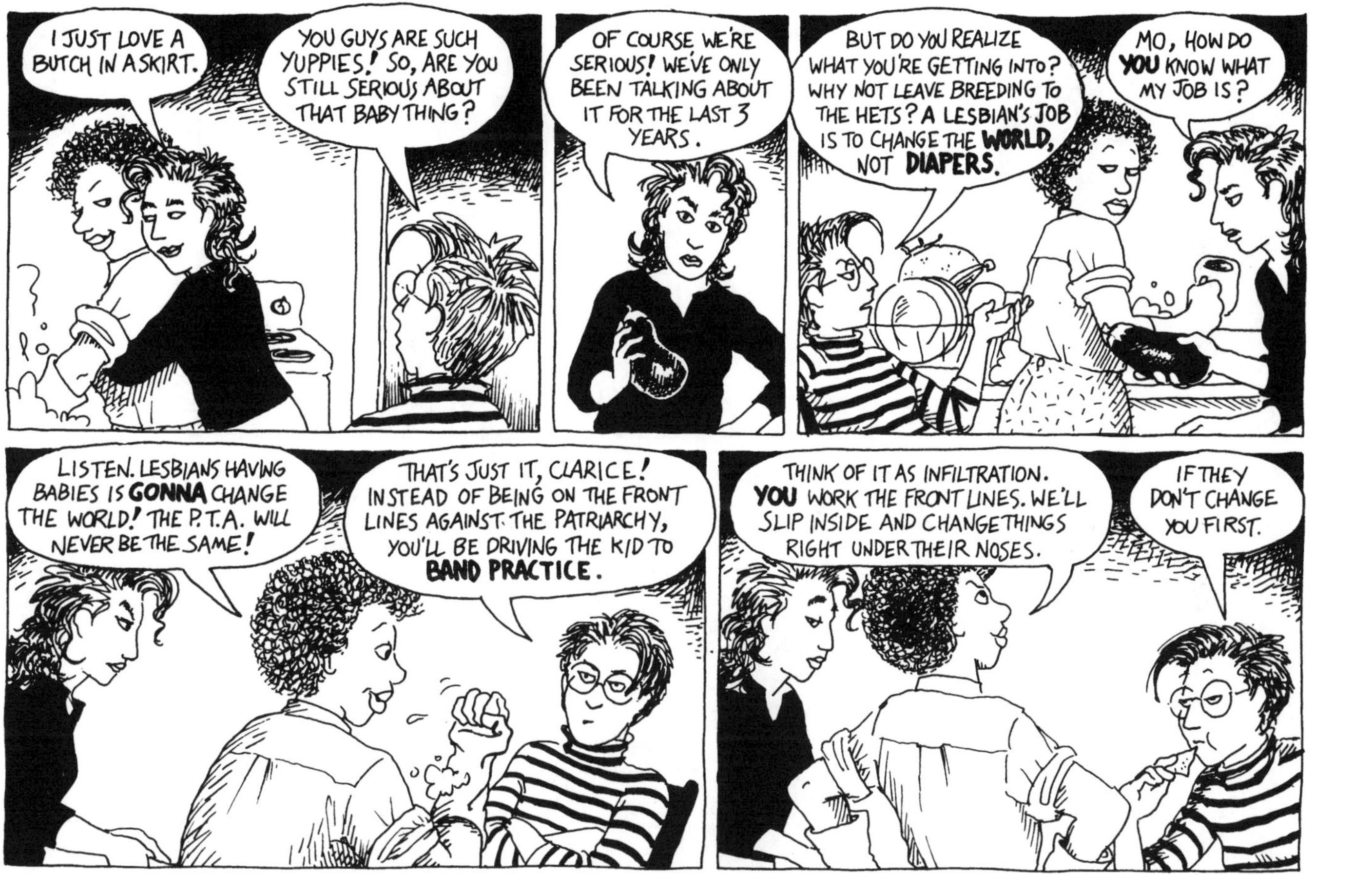
I JUST LOVE A BUTCH IN A SKIRT.
YOU GUYS ARE SUCH YUPPIES! SO, ARE YOU STILL SERIOUS ABOUT THAT BABY THING?
OF COURSE WE'RE SERIOUS! WE'VE ONLY BEEN TALKING ABOUT IT FOR THE LAST 3 YEARS.
BUT DO YOU REALIZE WHAT YOU'RE GETTING INTO? WHY NOT LEAVE BREEDING TO THE HETS? A LESBIAN'S JOB IS TO CHANGE THE **WORLD**, NOT **DIAPERS**.
MO, HOW DO **YOU** KNOW WHAT MY JOB IS?
LISTEN. LESBIANS HAVING BABIES IS **GONNA** CHANGE THE WORLD! THE P.T.A. WILL NEVER BE THE SAME!
THAT'S JUST IT, CLARICE! INSTEAD OF BEING ON THE FRONT LINES AGAINST THE PATRIARCHY, YOU'LL BE DRIVING THE KID TO **BAND PRACTICE**.
THINK OF IT AS INFILTRATION. **YOU** WORK THE FRONT LINES. WE'LL SLIP INSIDE AND CHANGE THINGS RIGHT UNDER THEIR NOSES.
IF THEY DON'T CHANGE YOU FIRST.

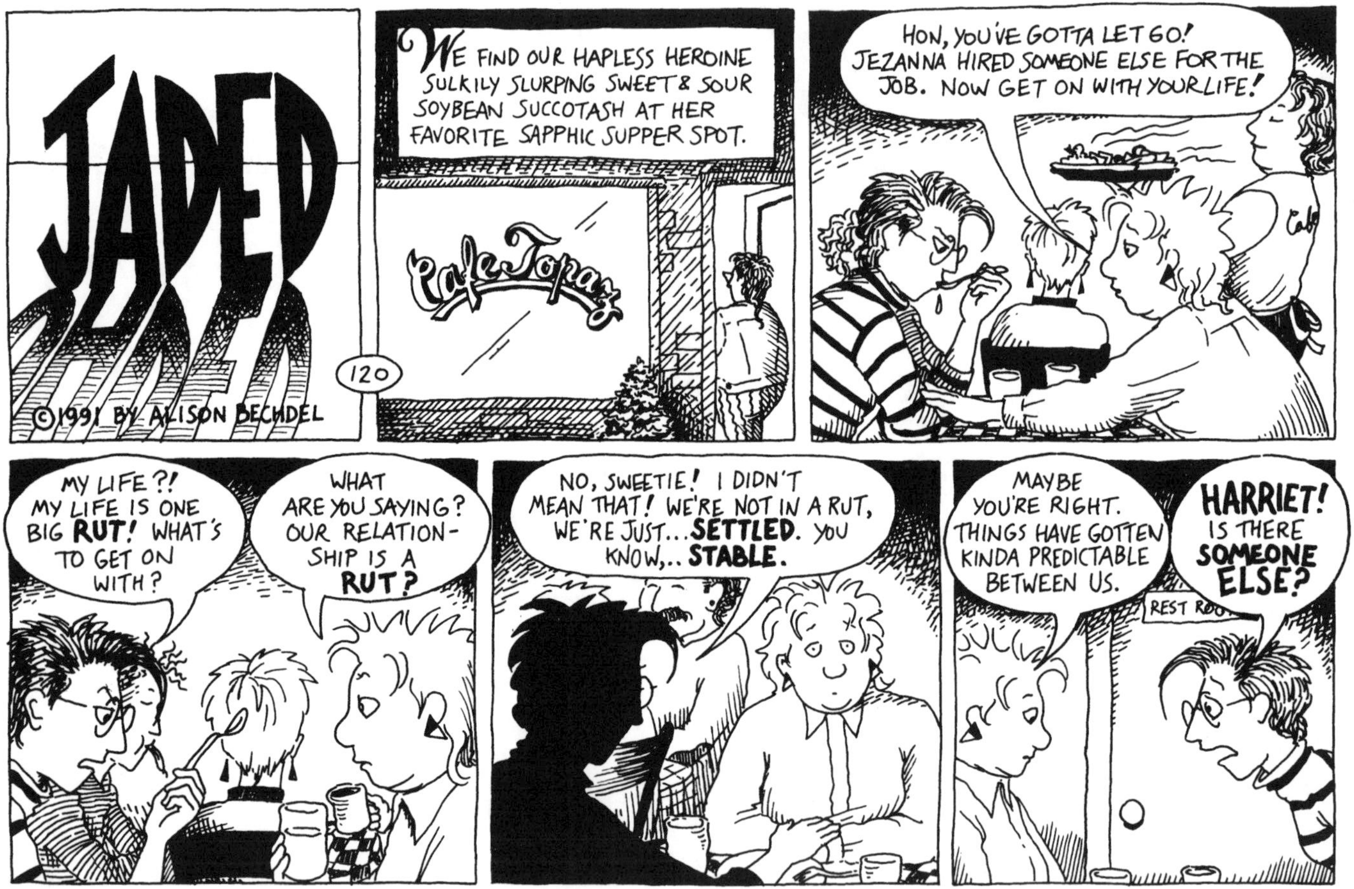

JADED
©1991 BY ALISON BECHDEL
120
WE FIND OUR HAPLESS HEROINE SULKILY SLURPING SWEET & SOUR SOYBEAN SUCCOTASH AT HER FAVORITE SAPPHIC SUPPER SPOT.
Cafe Topaz
HON, YOU'VE GOTTA LET GO! JEZANNA HIRED SOMEONE ELSE FOR THE JOB. NOW GET ON WITH YOUR LIFE!
MY LIFE?! MY LIFE IS ONE BIG **RUT**! WHAT'S TO GET ON WITH?
WHAT ARE YOU SAYING? OUR RELATIONSHIP IS A **RUT?**
NO, SWEETIE! I DIDN'T MEAN THAT! WE'RE NOT IN A RUT, WE'RE JUST... **SETTLED**. YOU KNOW,.. **STABLE**.
MAYBE YOU'RE RIGHT. THINGS HAVE GOTTEN KINDA PREDICTABLE BETWEEN US.
HARRIET! IS THERE **SOMEONE ELSE?**

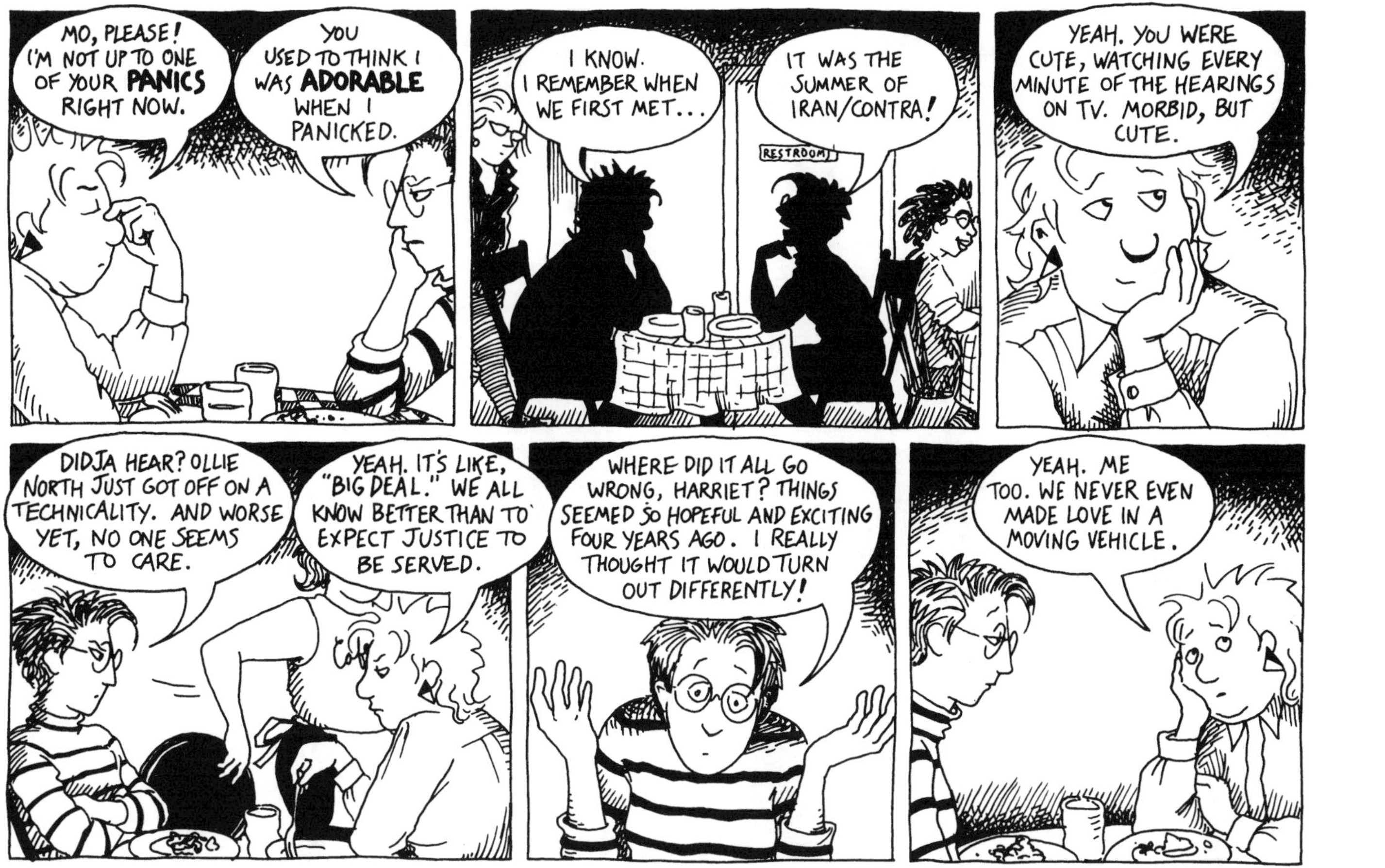
MO, PLEASE! I'M NOT UP TO ONE OF YOUR **PANICS** RIGHT NOW.
YOU USED TO THINK I WAS **ADORABLE** WHEN I PANICKED.
I KNOW. I REMEMBER WHEN WE FIRST MET...
IT WAS THE SUMMER OF IRAN/CONTRA!
RESTROOM
YEAH. YOU WERE CUTE, WATCHING EVERY MINUTE OF THE HEARINGS ON TV. MORBID, BUT CUTE.
DIDJA HEAR? OLLIE NORTH JUST GOT OFF ON A TECHNICALITY. AND WORSE YET, NO ONE SEEMS TO CARE.
YEAH. IT'S LIKE, "BIG DEAL." WE ALL KNOW BETTER THAN TO EXPECT JUSTICE TO BE SERVED.
WHERE DID IT ALL GO WRONG, HARRIET? THINGS SEEMED SO HOPEFUL AND EXCITING FOUR YEARS AGO. I REALLY THOUGHT IT WOULD TURN OUT DIFFERENTLY!
YEAH. ME TOO. WE NEVER EVEN MADE LOVE IN A MOVING VEHICLE.

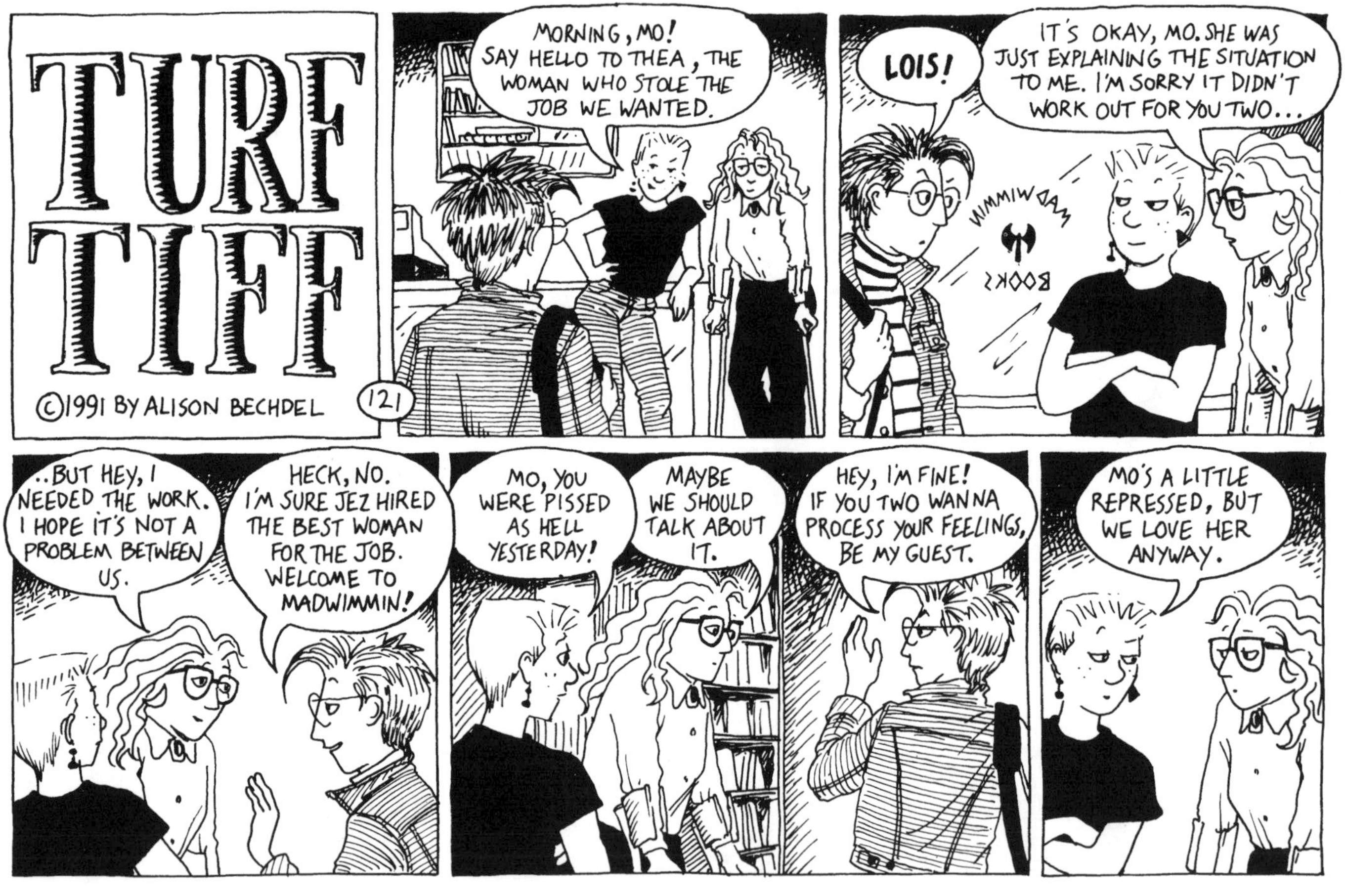
TURF TIFF
©1991 BY ALISON BECHDEL
121
MORNING, MO! SAY HELLO TO THEA, THE WOMAN WHO STOLE THE JOB WE WANTED.
LOIS!
IT'S OKAY, MO. SHE WAS JUST EXPLAINING THE SITUATION TO ME. I'M SORRY IT DIDN'T WORK OUT FOR YOU TWO...
..BUT HEY, I NEEDED THE WORK. I HOPE IT'S NOT A PROBLEM BETWEEN US.
HECK, NO. I'M SURE JEZ HIRED THE BEST WOMAN FOR THE JOB. WELCOME TO MADWIMMIN!
MO, YOU WERE PISSED AS HELL YESTERDAY!
MAYBE WE SHOULD TALK ABOUT IT.
HEY, I'M FINE! IF YOU TWO WANNA PROCESS YOUR FEELINGS, BE MY GUEST.
MO'S A LITTLE REPRESSED, BUT WE LOVE HER ANYWAY.

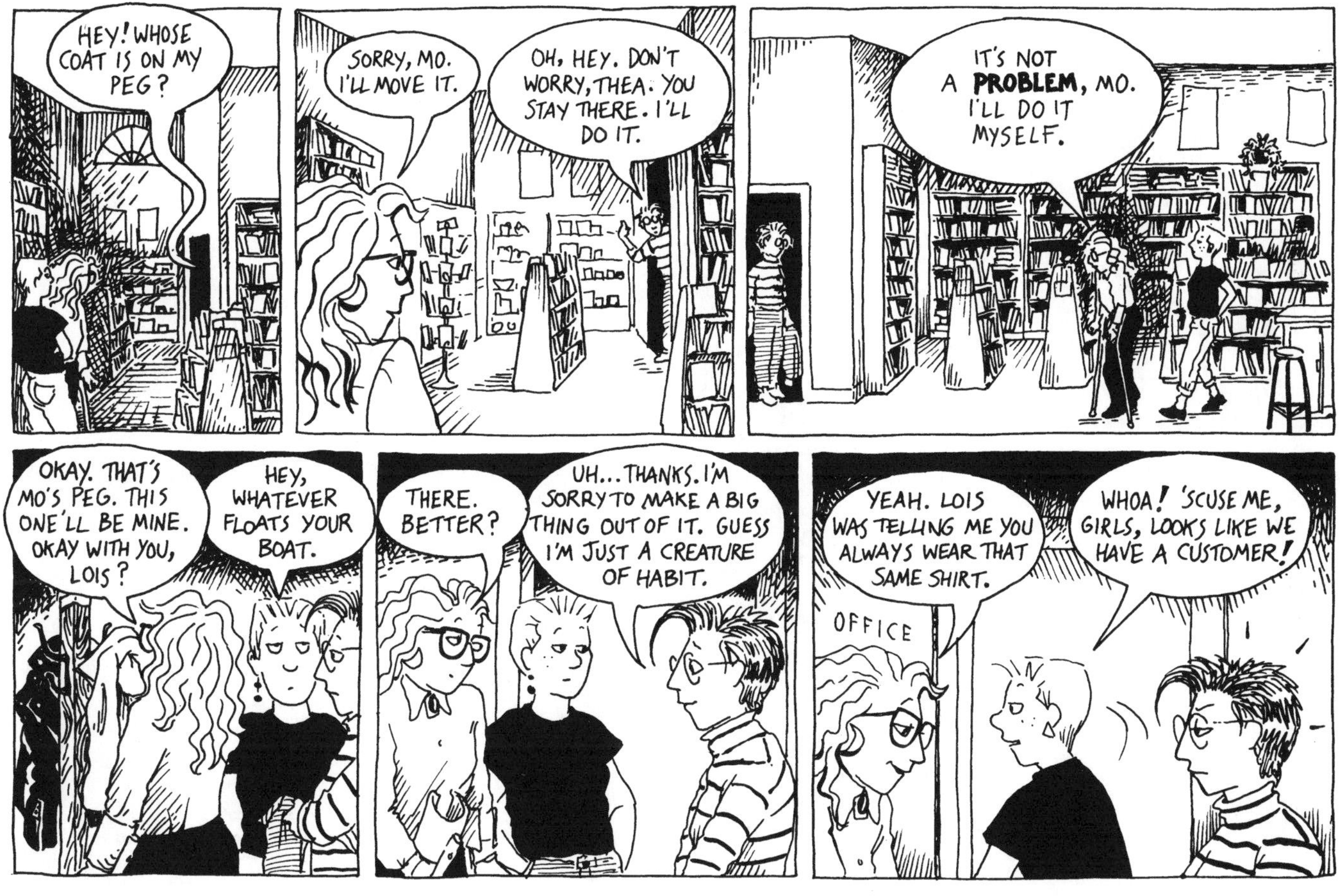
HEY! WHOSE COAT IS ON MY PEG?
SORRY, MO. I'LL MOVE IT.
OH, HEY. DON'T WORRY, THEA. YOU STAY THERE. I'LL DO IT.
IT'S NOT A **PROBLEM**, MO. I'LL DO IT MYSELF.
OKAY. THAT'S MO'S PEG. THIS ONE'LL BE MINE. OKAY WITH YOU, LOIS?
HEY, WHATEVER FLOATS YOUR BOAT.
THERE. BETTER?
UH... THANKS. I'M SORRY TO MAKE A BIG THING OUT OF IT. GUESS I'M JUST A CREATURE OF HABIT.
YEAH. LOIS WAS TELLING ME YOU ALWAYS WEAR THAT SAME SHIRT.
WHOA! 'SCUSE ME, GIRLS, LOOKS LIKE WE HAVE A CUSTOMER!
OFFICE

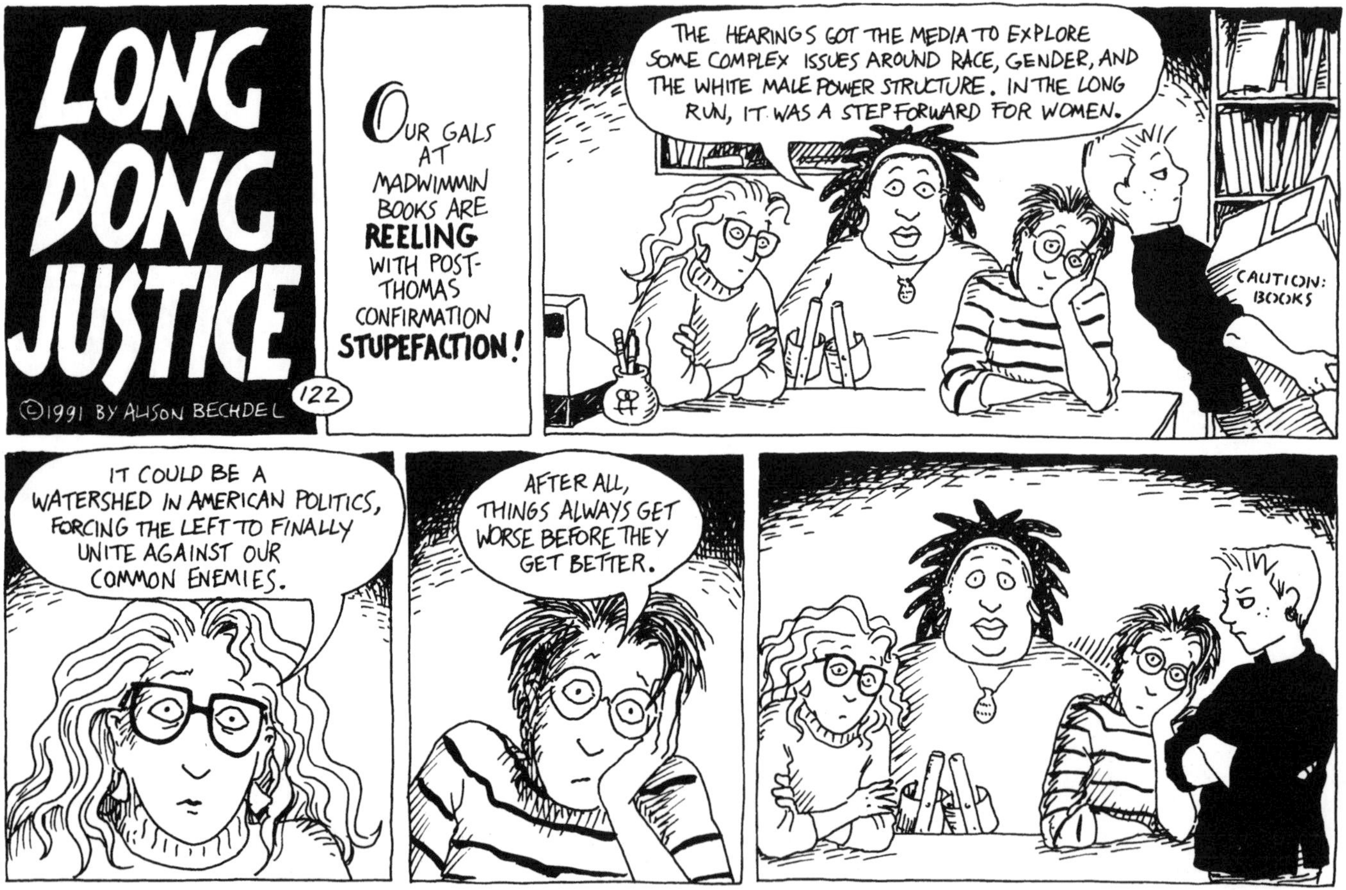
LONG DONG JUSTICE
©1991 BY ALISON BECHDEL
122
OUR GALS AT MADWIMMIN BOOKS ARE REELING WITH POST-THOMAS CONFIRMATION STUPEFACTION!
THE HEARINGS GOT THE MEDIA TO EXPLORE SOME COMPLEX ISSUES AROUND RACE, GENDER, AND THE WHITE MALE POWER STRUCTURE. IN THE LONG RUN, IT WAS A STEP FORWARD FOR WOMEN.
CAUTION: BOOKS
IT COULD BE A WATERSHED IN AMERICAN POLITICS, FORCING THE LEFT TO FINALLY UNITE AGAINST OUR COMMON ENEMIES.
AFTER ALL, THINGS ALWAYS GET WORSE BEFORE THEY GET BETTER.

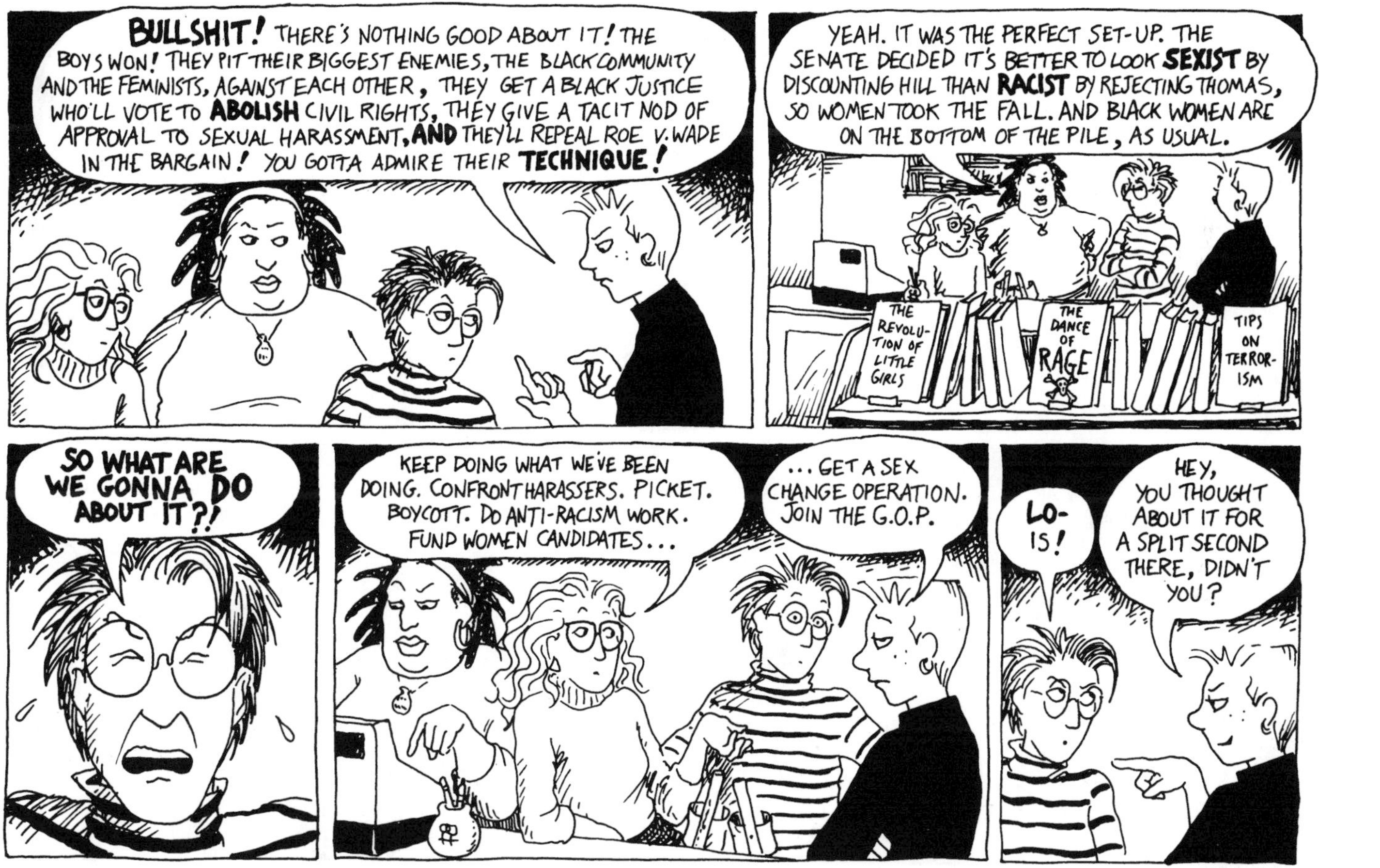

BULLSHIT! THERE'S NOTHING GOOD ABOUT IT! THE BOYS WON! THEY PIT THEIR BIGGEST ENEMIES, THE BLACK COMMUNITY AND THE FEMINISTS, AGAINST EACH OTHER, THEY GET A BLACK JUSTICE WHO'LL VOTE TO ABOLISH CIVIL RIGHTS, THEY GIVE A TACIT NOD OF APPROVAL TO SEXUAL HARASSMENT, AND THEY'LL REPEAL ROE V. WADE IN THE BARGAIN! YOU GOTTA ADMIRE THEIR TECHNIQUE!
YEAH. IT WAS THE PERFECT SET-UP. THE SENATE DECIDED IT'S BETTER TO LOOK SEXIST BY DISCOUNTING HILL THAN RACIST BY REJECTING THOMAS, SO WOMEN TOOK THE FALL. AND BLACK WOMEN ARE ON THE BOTTOM OF THE PILE, AS USUAL.
THE REVOLUTION OF LITTLE GIRLS
THE DANCE OF RAGE
TIPS ON TERRORISM
SO WHAT ARE WE GONNA DO ABOUT IT?!
KEEP DOING WHAT WE'VE BEEN DOING. CONFRONT HARASSERS. PICKET. BOYCOTT. DO ANTI-RACISM WORK. FUND WOMEN CANDIDATES...
...GET A SEX CHANGE OPERATION. JOIN THE G.O.P.
LO-IS!
HEY, YOU THOUGHT ABOUT IT FOR A SPLIT SECOND THERE, DIDN'T YOU?

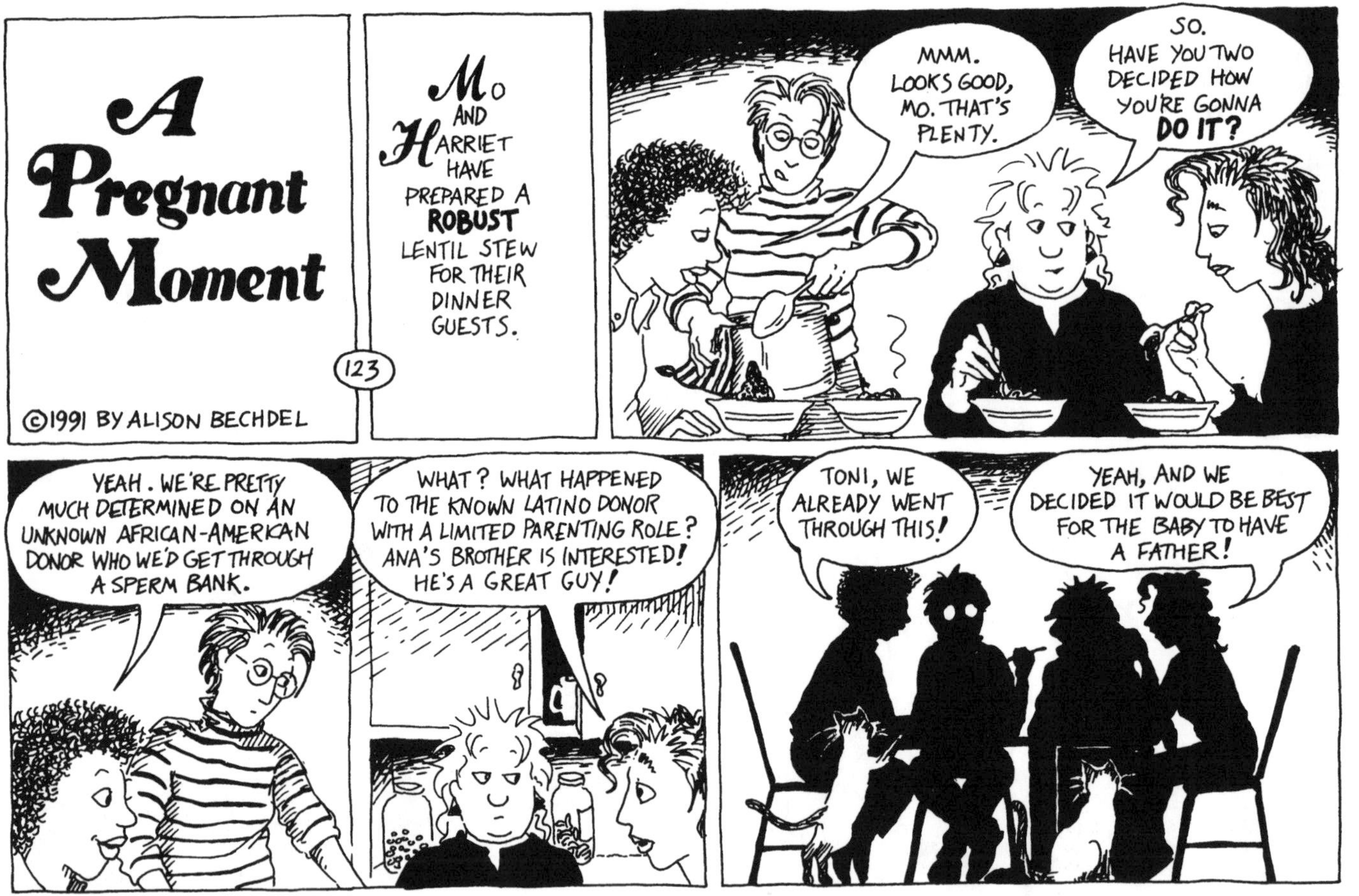
A Pregnant Moment
123
©1991 BY ALISON BECHDEL
MO AND HARRIET HAVE PREPARED A ROBUST LENTIL STEW FOR THEIR DINNER GUESTS.
MMM. LOOKS GOOD, MO. THAT'S PLENTY.
SO. HAVE YOU TWO DECIDED HOW YOU'RE GONNA DO IT?
YEAH. WE'RE PRETTY MUCH DETERMINED ON AN UNKNOWN AFRICAN-AMERICAN DONOR WHO WE'D GET THROUGH A SPERM BANK.
WHAT? WHAT HAPPENED TO THE KNOWN LATINO DONOR WITH A LIMITED PARENTING ROLE? ANA'S BROTHER IS INTERESTED! HE'S A GREAT GUY!
TONI, WE ALREADY WENT THROUGH THIS!
YEAH, AND WE DECIDED IT WOULD BE BEST FOR THE BABY TO HAVE A FATHER!

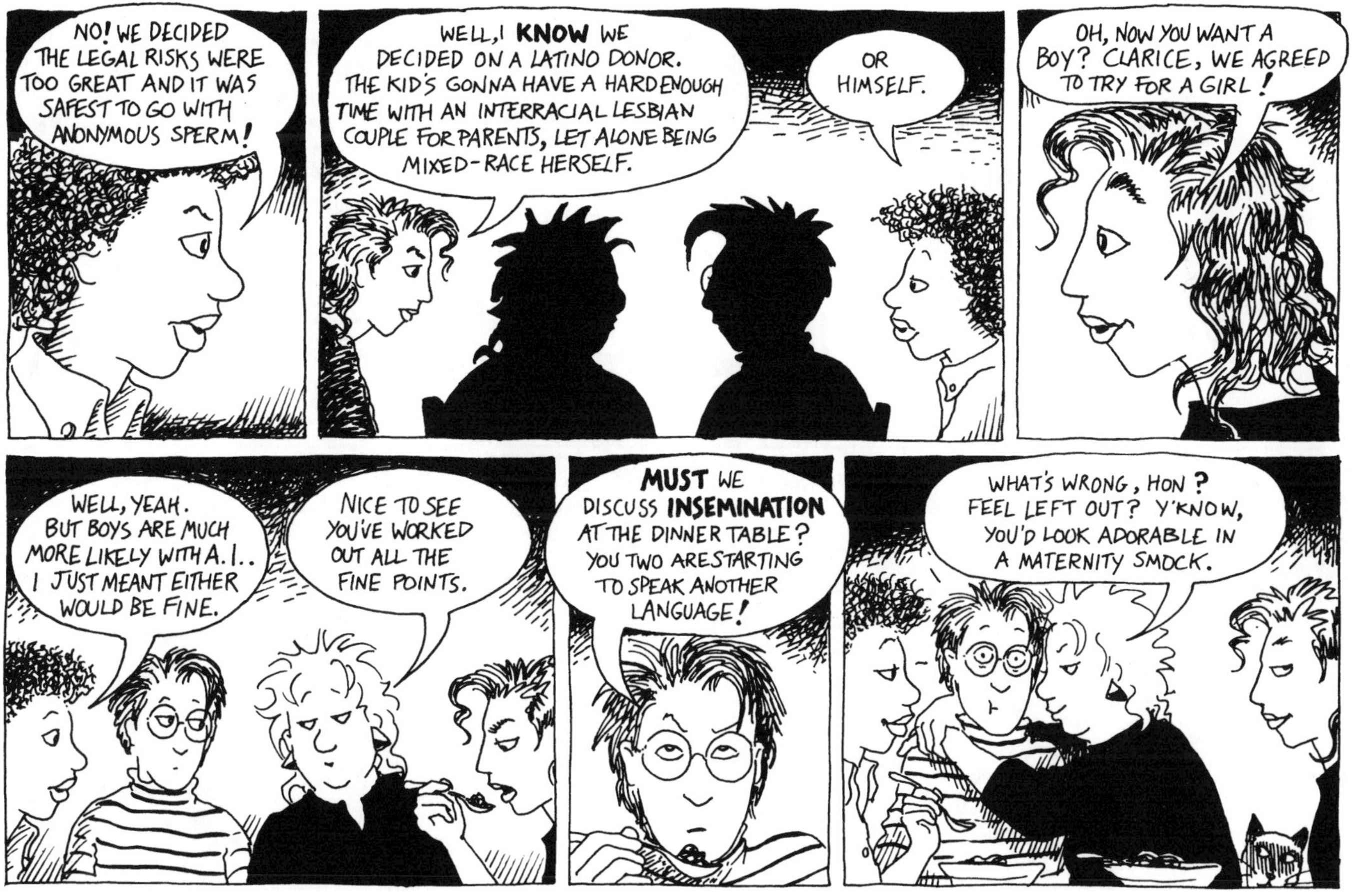

NO! WE DECIDED THE LEGAL RISKS WERE TOO GREAT AND IT WAS SAFEST TO GO WITH ANONYMOUS SPERM!
WELL, I **KNOW** WE DECIDED ON A LATINO DONOR. THE KID'S GONNA HAVE A HARD ENOUGH TIME WITH AN INTERRACIAL LESBIAN COUPLE FOR PARENTS, LET ALONE BEING MIXED-RACE HERSELF.
OR HIMSELF.
OH, NOW YOU WANT A BOY? CLARICE, WE AGREED TO TRY FOR A GIRL!
WELL, YEAH. BUT BOYS ARE MUCH MORE LIKELY WITH A.I.. I JUST MEANT EITHER WOULD BE FINE.
NICE TO SEE YOU'VE WORKED OUT ALL THE FINE POINTS.
MUST WE DISCUSS **INSEMINATION** AT THE DINNER TABLE? YOU TWO ARE STARTING TO SPEAK ANOTHER LANGUAGE!
WHAT'S WRONG, HON? FEEL LEFT OUT? Y'KNOW, YOU'D LOOK ADORABLE IN A MATERNITY SMOCK.

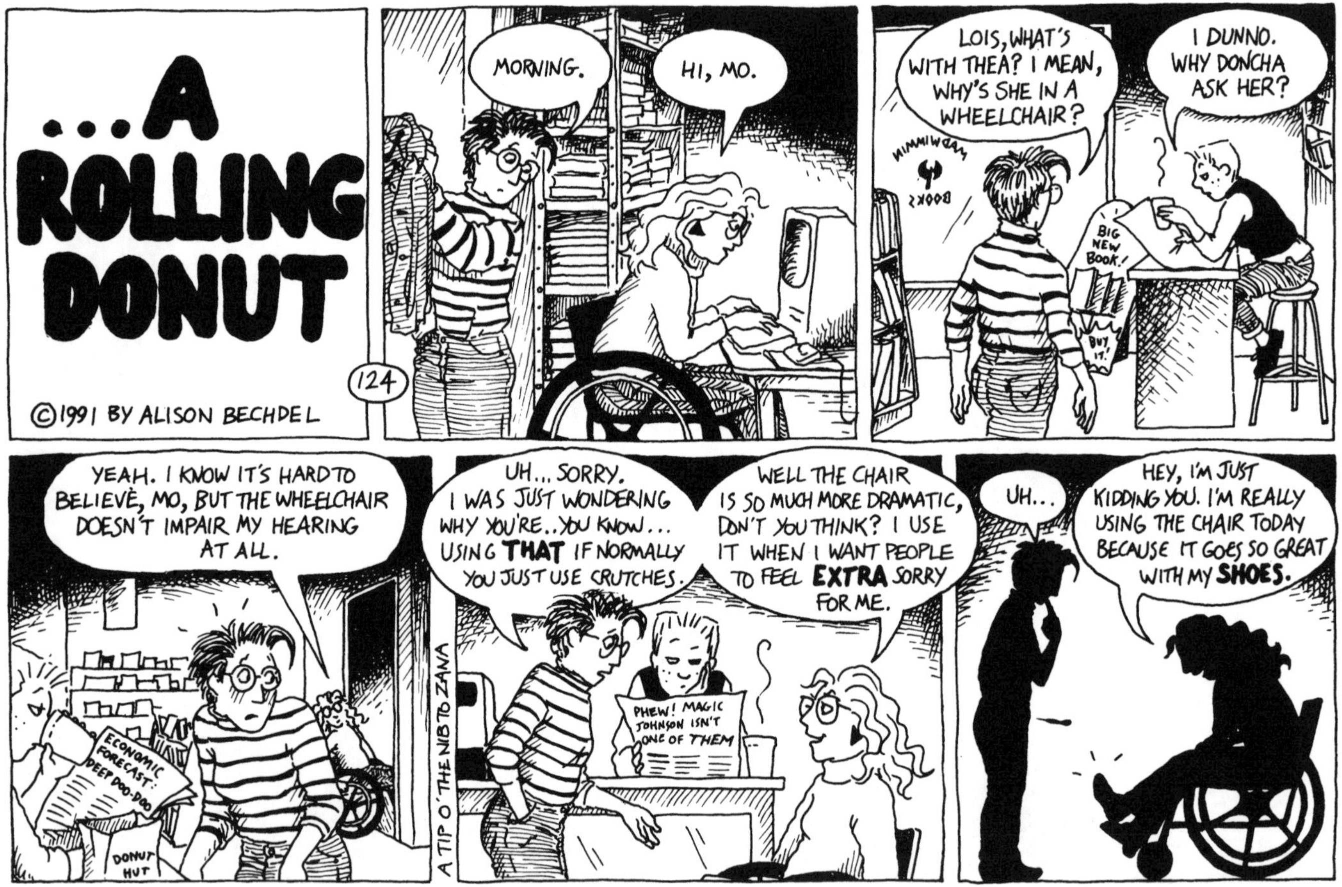
...A ROLLING DONUT
124
©1991 BY ALISON BECHDEL
MORNING.
HI, MO.
LOIS, WHAT'S WITH THEA? I MEAN, WHY'S SHE IN A WHEELCHAIR?
I DUNNO. WHY DONCHA ASK HER?
MADWIMMIN BOOKS
BIG NEW BOOK! BUY IT!
YEAH. I KNOW IT'S HARD TO BELIEVE, MO, BUT THE WHEELCHAIR DOESN'T IMPAIR MY HEARING AT ALL.
ECONOMIC FORECAST: DEEP DOO-DOO
DONUT HUT
A TIP O' THE NIB TO ZANA
UH... SORRY. I WAS JUST WONDERING WHY YOU'RE.. YOU KNOW... USING **THAT** IF NORMALLY YOU JUST USE CRUTCHES.
WELL THE CHAIR IS SO MUCH MORE DRAMATIC, DON'T YOU THINK? I USE IT WHEN I WANT PEOPLE TO FEEL **EXTRA** SORRY FOR ME.
PHEW! MAGIC JOHNSON ISN'T ONE OF THEM
UH...
HEY, I'M JUST KIDDING YOU. I'M REALLY USING THE CHAIR TODAY BECAUSE IT GOES SO GREAT WITH MY **SHOES.**

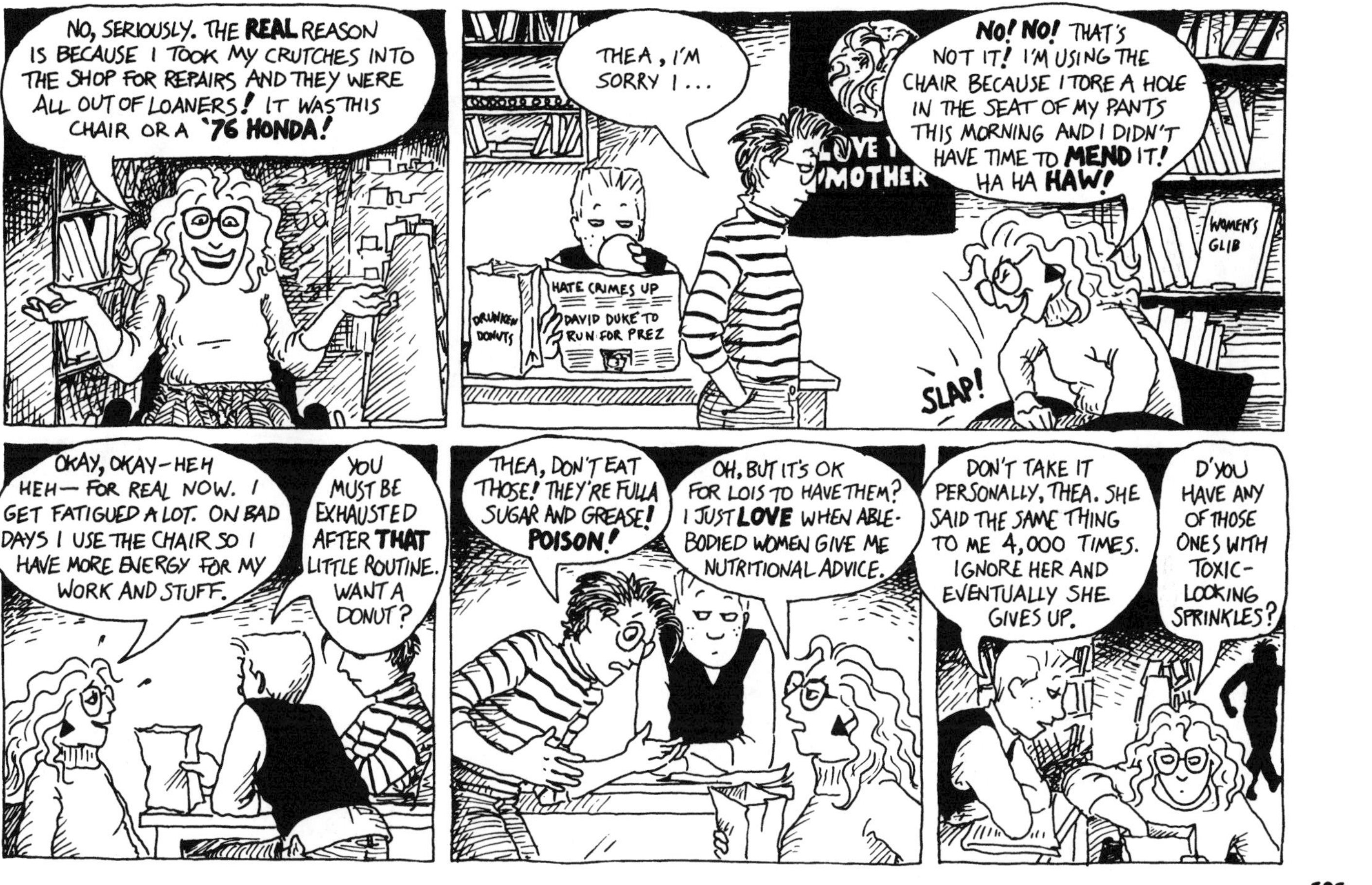
NO, SERIOUSLY. THE **REAL** REASON IS BECAUSE I TOOK MY CRUTCHES INTO THE SHOP FOR REPAIRS AND THEY WERE ALL OUT OF LOANERS! IT WAS THIS CHAIR OR A **'76 HONDA!**
THEA, I'M SORRY I...
DRUNKEN DONUTS
HATE CRIMES UP
DAVID DUKE TO RUN FOR PREZ
NO! NO! THAT'S NOT IT! I'M USING THE CHAIR BECAUSE I TORE A HOLE IN THE SEAT OF MY PANTS THIS MORNING AND I DIDN'T HAVE TIME TO **MEND** IT! HA HA **HAW!**
WOMEN'S GLIB
SLAP!
OKAY, OKAY—HEH HEH—FOR REAL NOW. I GET FATIGUED A LOT. ON BAD DAYS I USE THE CHAIR SO I HAVE MORE ENERGY FOR MY WORK AND STUFF.
YOU MUST BE EXHAUSTED AFTER **THAT** LITTLE ROUTINE. WANT A DONUT?
THEA, DON'T EAT THOSE! THEY'RE FULLA SUGAR AND GREASE! **POISON!**
OH, BUT IT'S OK FOR LOIS TO HAVE THEM? I JUST **LOVE** WHEN ABLE-BODIED WOMEN GIVE ME NUTRITIONAL ADVICE.
DON'T TAKE IT PERSONALLY, THEA. SHE SAID THE SAME THING TO ME 4,000 TIMES. IGNORE HER AND EVENTUALLY SHE GIVES UP.
D'YOU HAVE ANY OF THOSE ONES WITH TOXIC-LOOKING SPRINKLES?

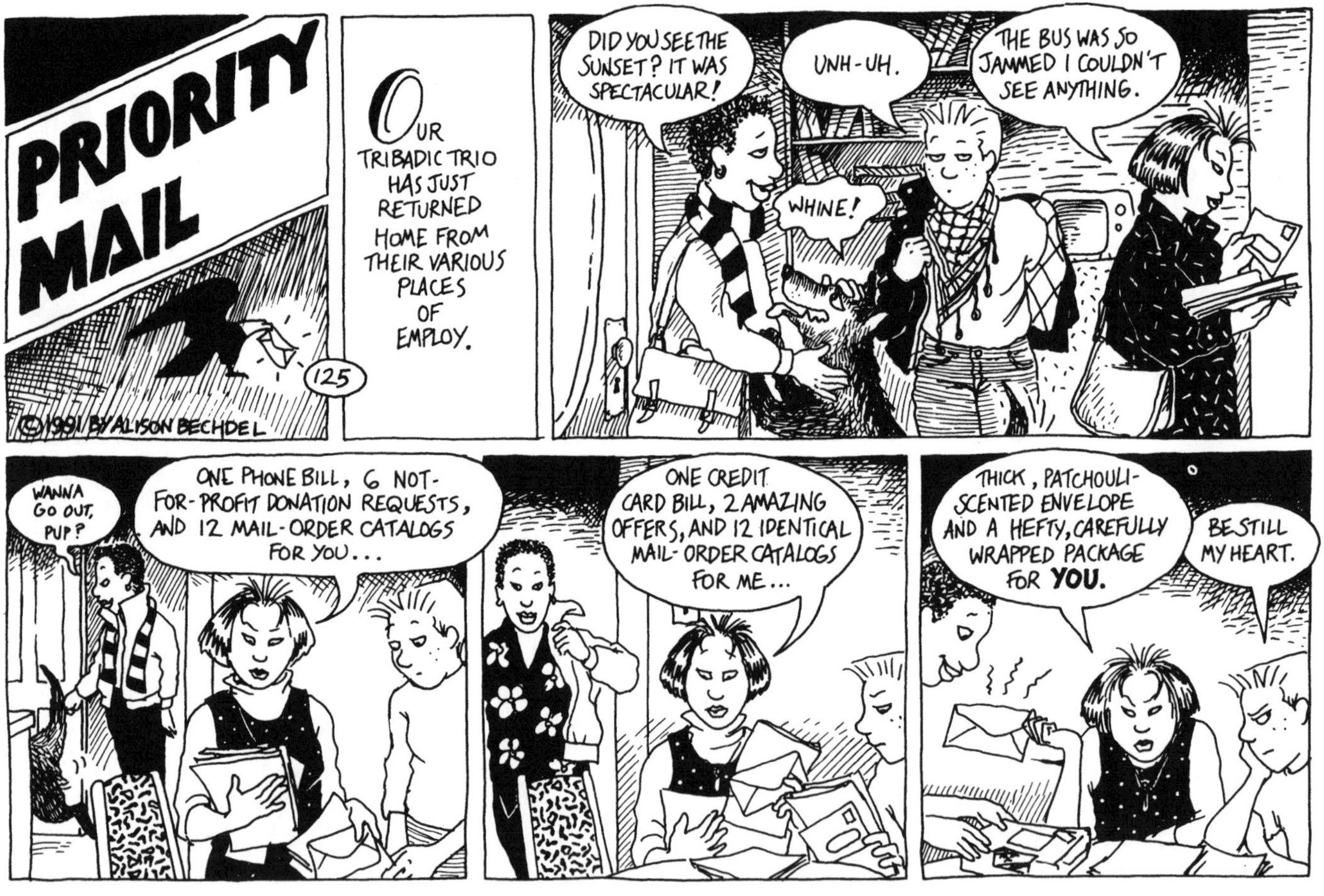
PRIORITY MAIL
125
© 1991 BY ALISON BECHDEL
OUR TRIBADIC TRIO HAS JUST RETURNED HOME FROM THEIR VARIOUS PLACES OF EMPLOY.
DID YOU SEE THE SUNSET? IT WAS SPECTACULAR!
UNH-UH.
THE BUS WAS SO JAMMED I COULDN'T SEE ANYTHING.
WHINE!
WANNA GO OUT, PUP?
ONE PHONE BILL, 6 NOT-FOR-PROFIT DONATION REQUESTS, AND 12 MAIL-ORDER CATALOGS FOR YOU...
ONE CREDIT CARD BILL, 2 AMAZING OFFERS, AND 12 IDENTICAL MAIL-ORDER CATALOGS FOR ME...
THICK, PATCHOULI-SCENTED ENVELOPE AND A HEFTY, CAREFULLY WRAPPED PACKAGE FOR YOU.
BE STILL MY HEART.

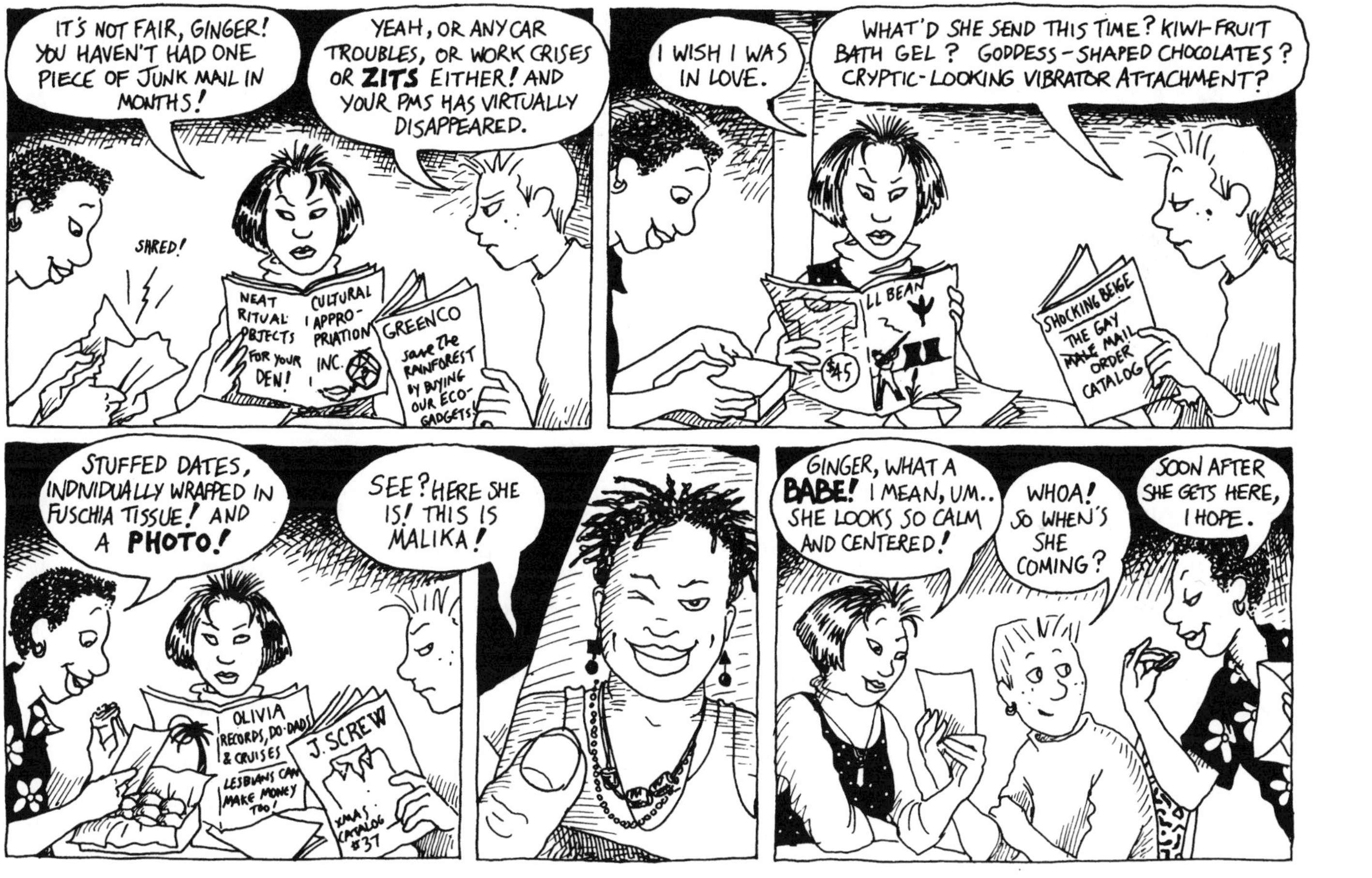
IT'S NOT FAIR, GINGER! YOU HAVEN'T HAD ONE PIECE OF JUNK MAIL IN MONTHS!
YEAH, OR ANY CAR TROUBLES, OR WORK CRISES OR ZITS EITHER! AND YOUR PMS HAS VIRTUALLY DISAPPEARED.
SHRED!
NEAT RITUAL OBJECTS FOR YOUR DEN!
CULTURAL APPROPRIATION INC.
GREENCO
Save the RAINFOREST BY BUYING OUR ECO-GADGETS!
I WISH I WAS IN LOVE.
WHAT'D SHE SEND THIS TIME? KIWI-FRUIT BATH GEL? GODDESS-SHAPED CHOCOLATES? CRYPTIC-LOOKING VIBRATOR ATTACHMENT?
LL BEAN
$45
SHOCKING BEIGE
THE GAY MALE MAIL ORDER CATALOG
STUFFED DATES, INDIVIDUALLY WRAPPED IN FUSCHIA TISSUE! AND A PHOTO!
SEE? HERE SHE IS! THIS IS MALIKA!
OLIVIA RECORDS, DO-DADS & CRUISES
LESBIANS CAN MAKE MONEY TOO!
J. SCREW
XMAS CATALOG #37
GINGER, WHAT A BABE! I MEAN, UM.. SHE LOOKS SO CALM AND CENTERED!
WHOA! SO WHEN'S SHE COMING?
SOON AFTER SHE GETS HERE, I HOPE.

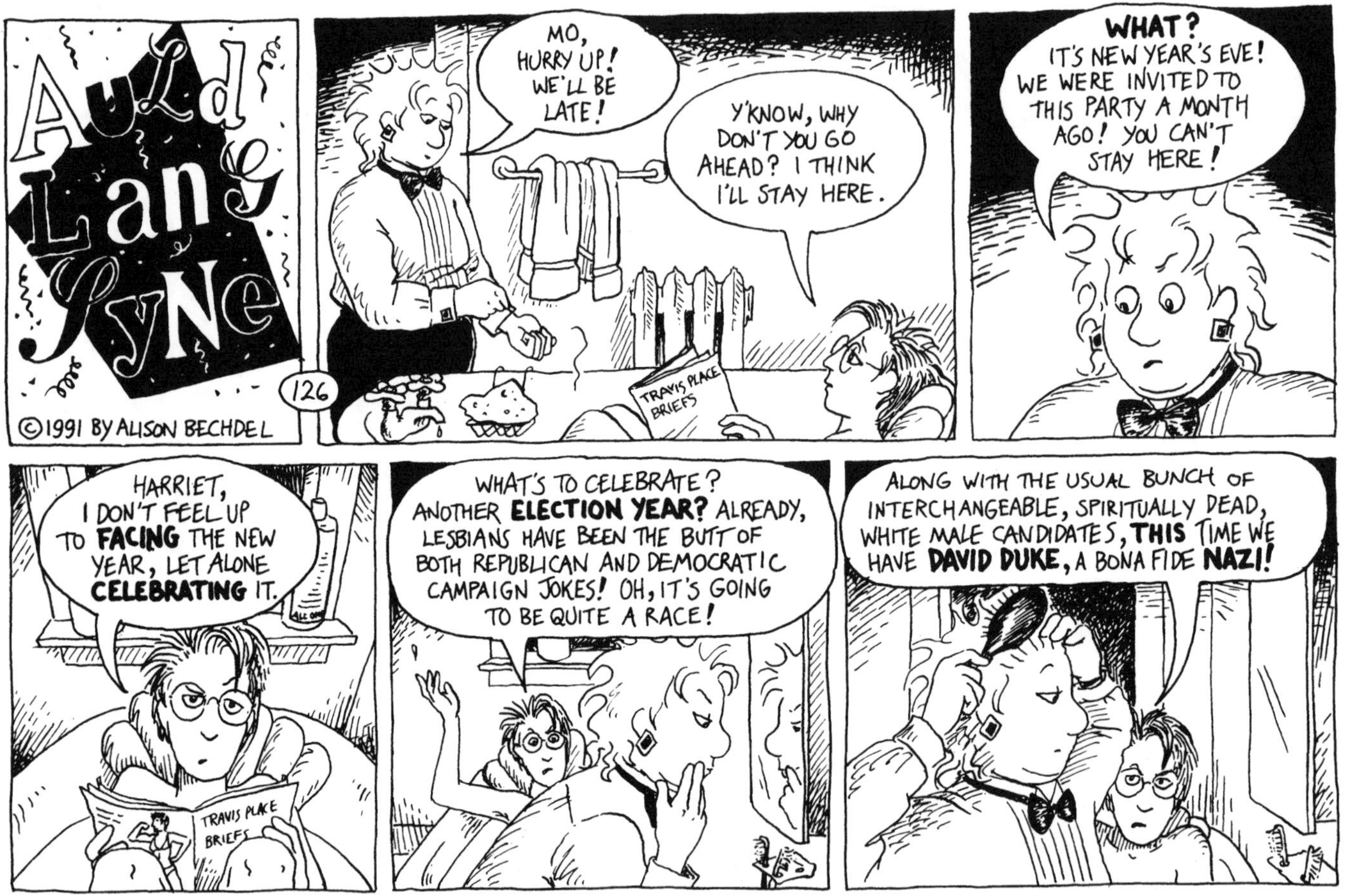
Auld Lang Syne
126
©1991 BY ALISON BECHDEL
MO, HURRY UP! WE'LL BE LATE!
Y'KNOW, WHY DON'T YOU GO AHEAD? I THINK I'LL STAY HERE.
TRAVIS PLACE BRIEFS
WHAT? IT'S NEW YEAR'S EVE! WE WERE INVITED TO THIS PARTY A MONTH AGO! YOU CAN'T STAY HERE!
HARRIET, I DON'T FEEL UP TO FACING THE NEW YEAR, LET ALONE CELEBRATING IT.
TRAVIS PLACE BRIEFS
WHAT'S TO CELEBRATE? ANOTHER ELECTION YEAR? ALREADY, LESBIANS HAVE BEEN THE BUTT OF BOTH REPUBLICAN AND DEMOCRATIC CAMPAIGN JOKES! OH, IT'S GOING TO BE QUITE A RACE!
ALONG WITH THE USUAL BUNCH OF INTERCHANGEABLE, SPIRITUALLY DEAD, WHITE MALE CANDIDATES, THIS TIME WE HAVE DAVID DUKE, A BONA FIDE NAZI!

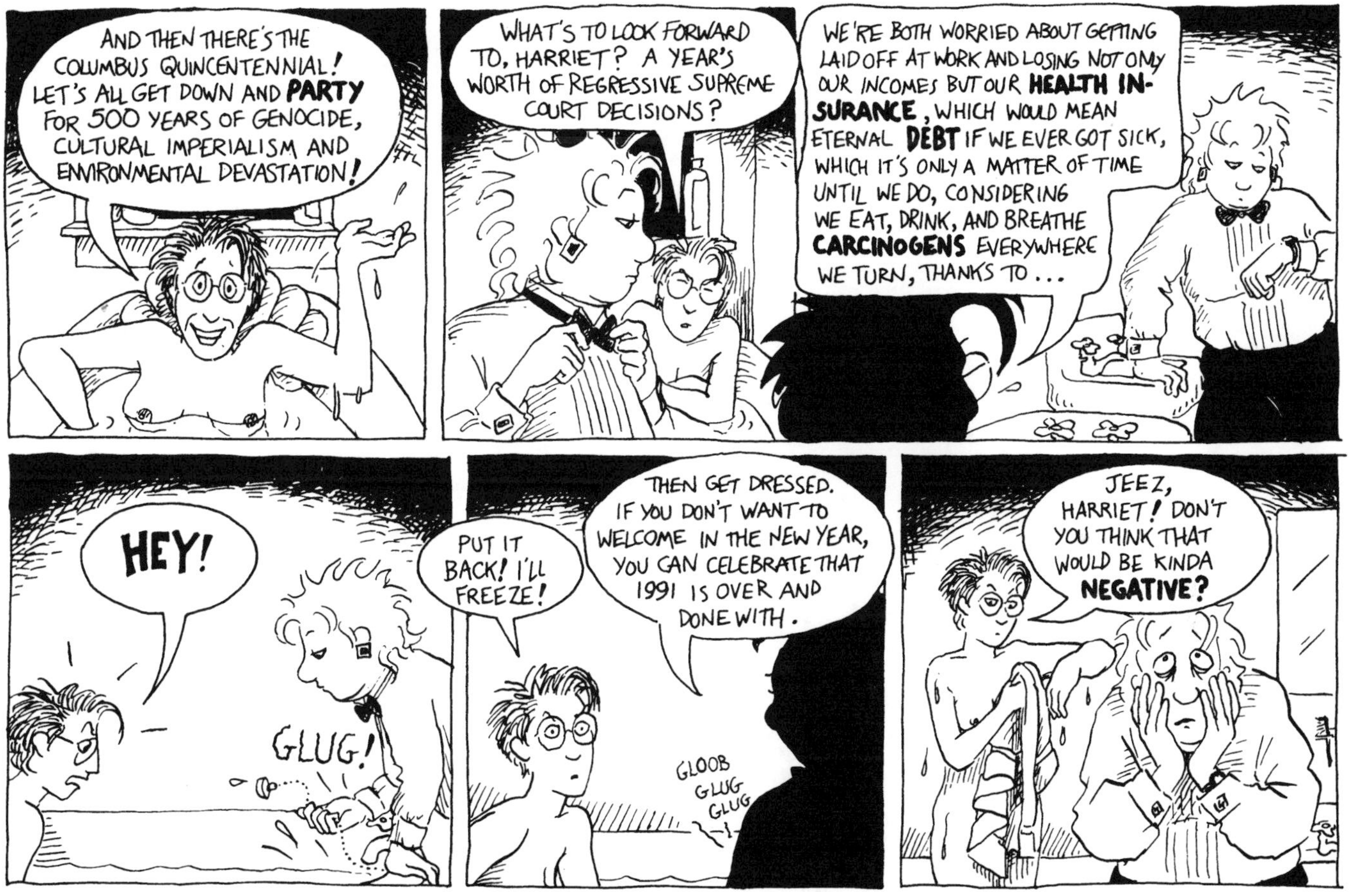

AND THEN THERE'S THE COLUMBUS QUINCENTENNIAL! LET'S ALL GET DOWN AND **PARTY** FOR 500 YEARS OF GENOCIDE, CULTURAL IMPERIALISM AND ENVIRONMENTAL DEVASTATION!
WHAT'S TO LOOK FORWARD TO, HARRIET? A YEAR'S WORTH OF REGRESSIVE SUPREME COURT DECISIONS?
WE'RE BOTH WORRIED ABOUT GETTING LAID OFF AT WORK AND LOSING NOT ONLY OUR INCOMES BUT OUR **HEALTH INSURANCE**, WHICH WOULD MEAN ETERNAL **DEBT** IF WE EVER GOT SICK, WHICH IT'S ONLY A MATTER OF TIME UNTIL WE DO, CONSIDERING WE EAT, DRINK, AND BREATHE **CARCINOGENS** EVERYWHERE WE TURN, THANKS TO...
HEY!
GLUG!
PUT IT BACK! I'LL FREEZE!
THEN GET DRESSED. IF YOU DON'T WANT TO WELCOME IN THE NEW YEAR, YOU CAN CELEBRATE THAT 1991 IS OVER AND DONE WITH.
GLOOB GLUG GLUG
JEEZ, HARRIET! DON'T YOU THINK THAT WOULD BE KINDA **NEGATIVE?**

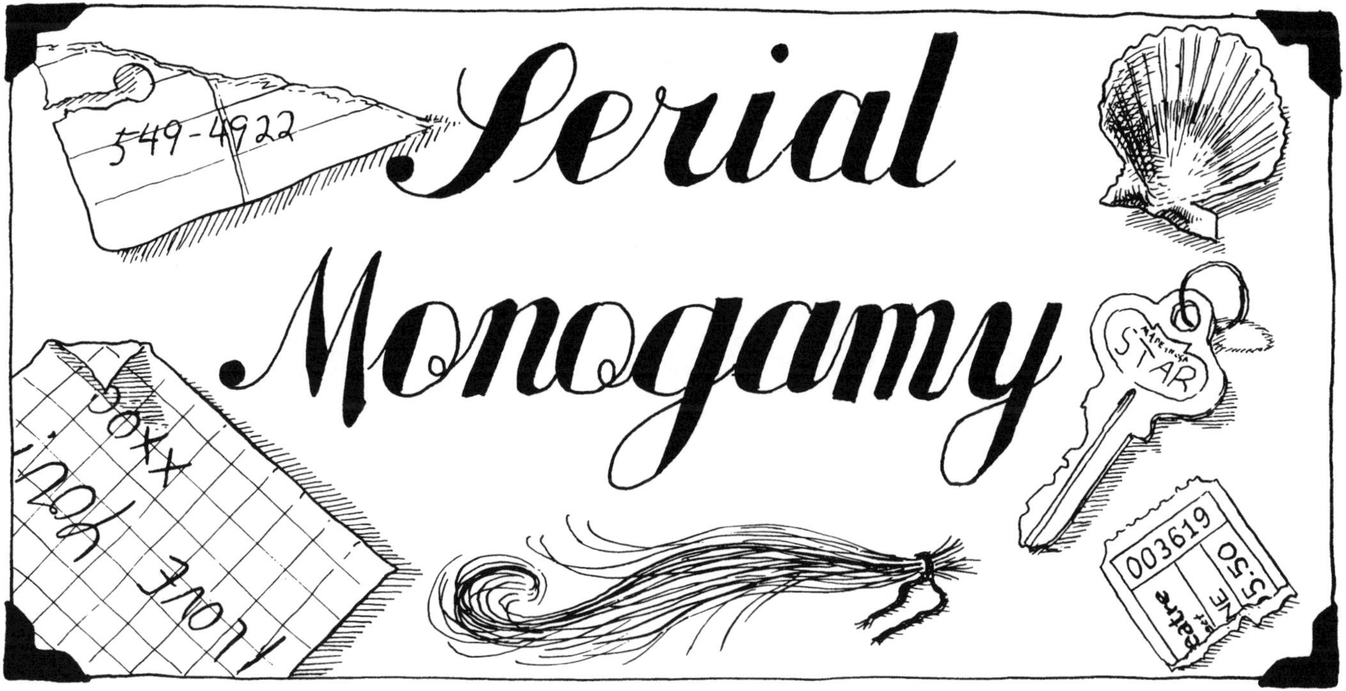
Serial
Monogamy
549-4922
STAR
003619
5.50

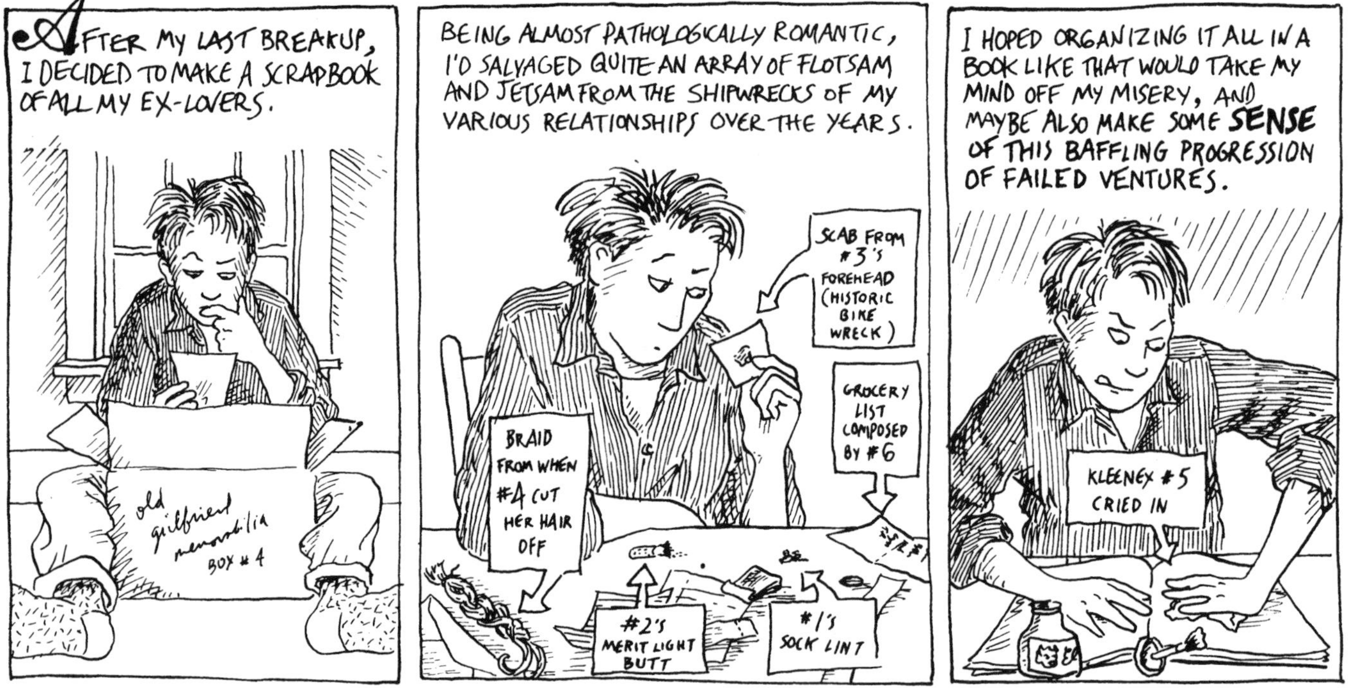
AFTER MY LAST BREAKUP, I DECIDED TO MAKE A SCRAPBOOK OF ALL MY EX-LOVERS.
old girlfriend memorabilia BOX #4
BEING ALMOST PATHOLOGICALLY ROMANTIC, I'D SALVAGED QUITE AN ARRAY OF FLOTSAM AND JETSAM FROM THE SHIPWRECKS OF MY VARIOUS RELATIONSHIPS OVER THE YEARS.
SCAB FROM #3'S FOREHEAD (HISTORIC BIKE WRECK)
GROCERY LIST COMPOSED BY #6
BRAID FROM WHEN #4 CUT HER HAIR OFF
#2'S MERIT LIGHT BUTT
#1'S SOCK LINT
I HOPED ORGANIZING IT ALL IN A BOOK LIKE THAT WOULD TAKE MY MIND OFF MY MISERY, AND MAYBE ALSO MAKE SOME **SENSE** OF THIS BAFFLING PROGRESSION OF FAILED VENTURES.
KLEENEX #5 CRIED IN

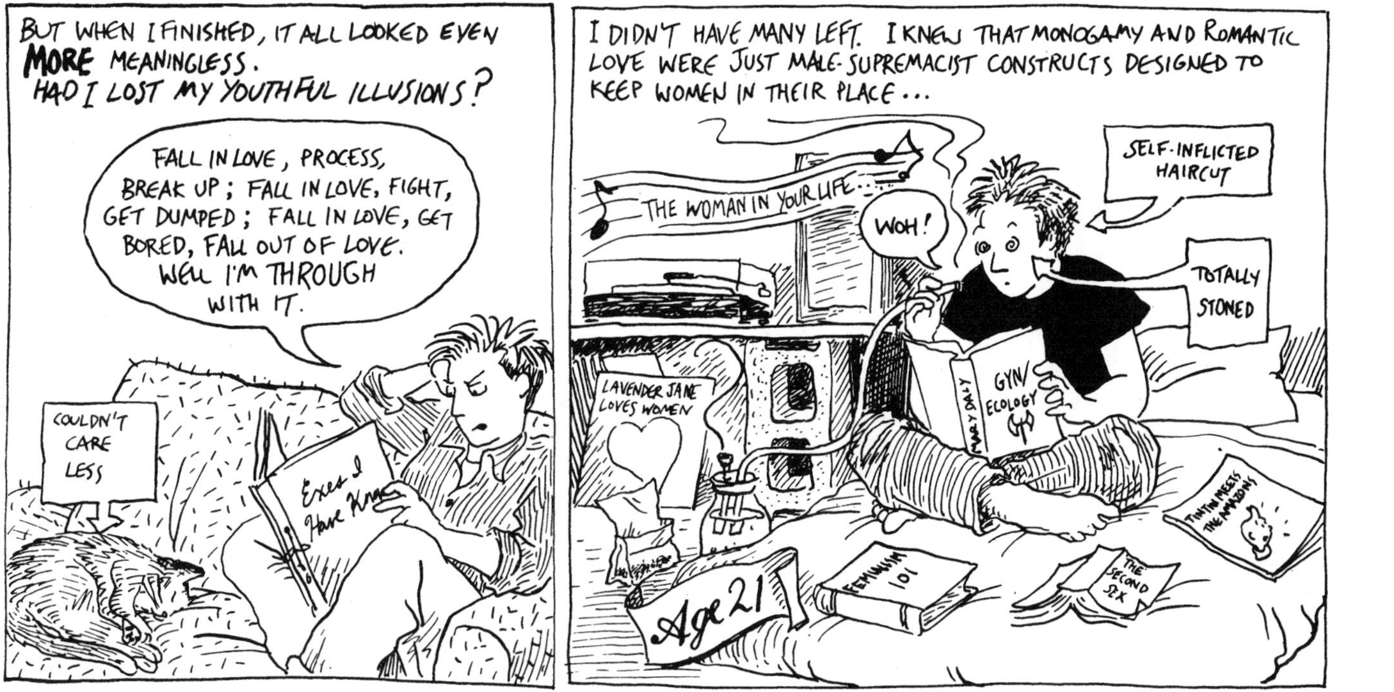
BUT WHEN I FINISHED, IT ALL LOOKED EVEN **MORE** MEANINGLESS.
HAD I LOST MY YOUTHFUL ILLUSIONS?
FALL IN LOVE, PROCESS, BREAK UP; FALL IN LOVE, FIGHT, GET DUMPED; FALL IN LOVE, GET BORED, FALL OUT OF LOVE. WELL I'M THROUGH WITH IT.
COULDN'T CARE LESS
I DIDN'T HAVE MANY LEFT. I KNEW THAT MONOGAMY AND ROMANTIC LOVE WERE JUST MALE-SUPREMACIST CONSTRUCTS DESIGNED TO KEEP WOMEN IN THEIR PLACE...
THE WOMAN IN YOUR LIFE
WOH!
SELF-INFLICTED HAIRCUT
TOTALLY STONED
LAVENDER JANE LOVES WOMEN
MARY DALY
GYN/ECOLOGY
TINTIN MEETS THE AMAZONS
FEMINISM 101
THE SECOND SEX
Age 21

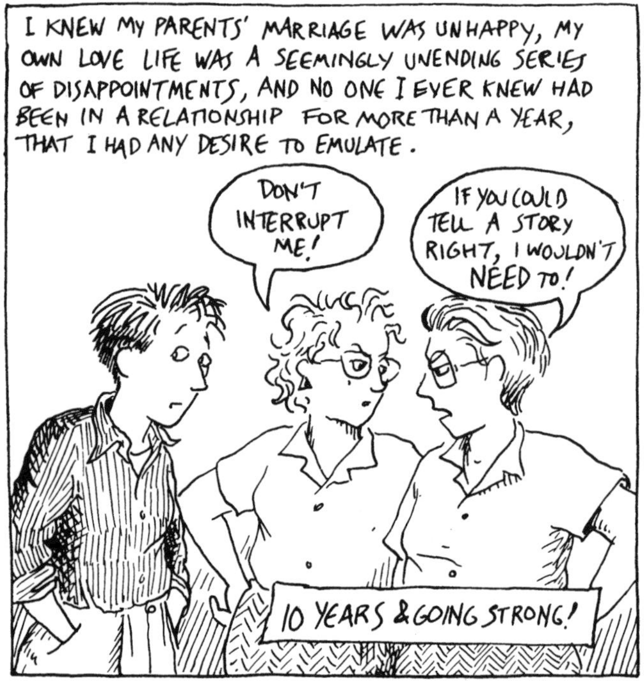
I KNEW MY PARENTS' MARRIAGE WAS UNHAPPY, MY OWN LOVE LIFE WAS A SEEMINGLY UNENDING SERIES OF DISAPPOINTMENTS, AND NO ONE I EVER KNEW HAD BEEN IN A RELATIONSHIP FOR MORE THAN A YEAR, THAT I HAD ANY DESIRE TO EMULATE.
DON'T INTERRUPT ME!
IF YOU COULD TELL A STORY RIGHT, I WOULDN'T NEED TO!
10 YEARS & GOING STRONG!

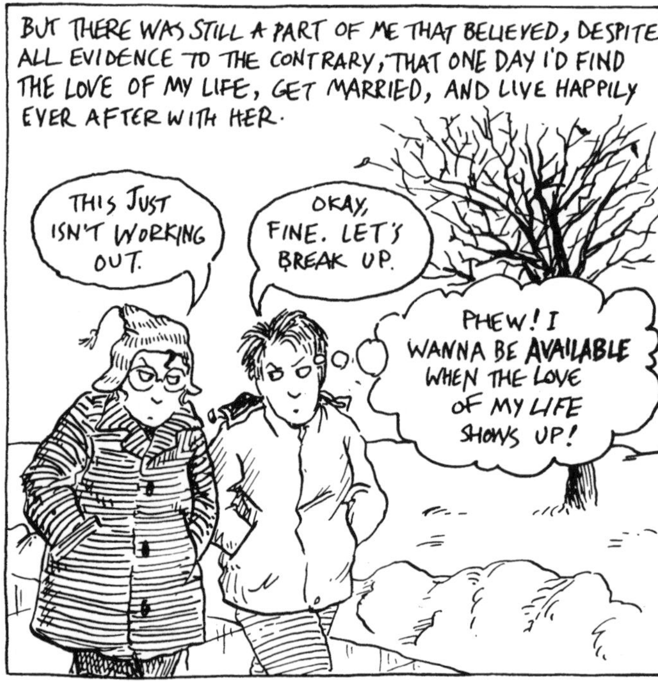
BUT THERE WAS STILL A PART OF ME THAT BELIEVED, DESPITE ALL EVIDENCE TO THE CONTRARY, THAT ONE DAY I'D FIND THE LOVE OF MY LIFE, GET MARRIED, AND LIVE HAPPILY EVER AFTER WITH HER.
THIS JUST ISN'T WORKING OUT.
OKAY, FINE. LET'S BREAK UP.
PHEW! I WANNA BE AVAILABLE WHEN THE LOVE OF MY LIFE SHOWS UP!

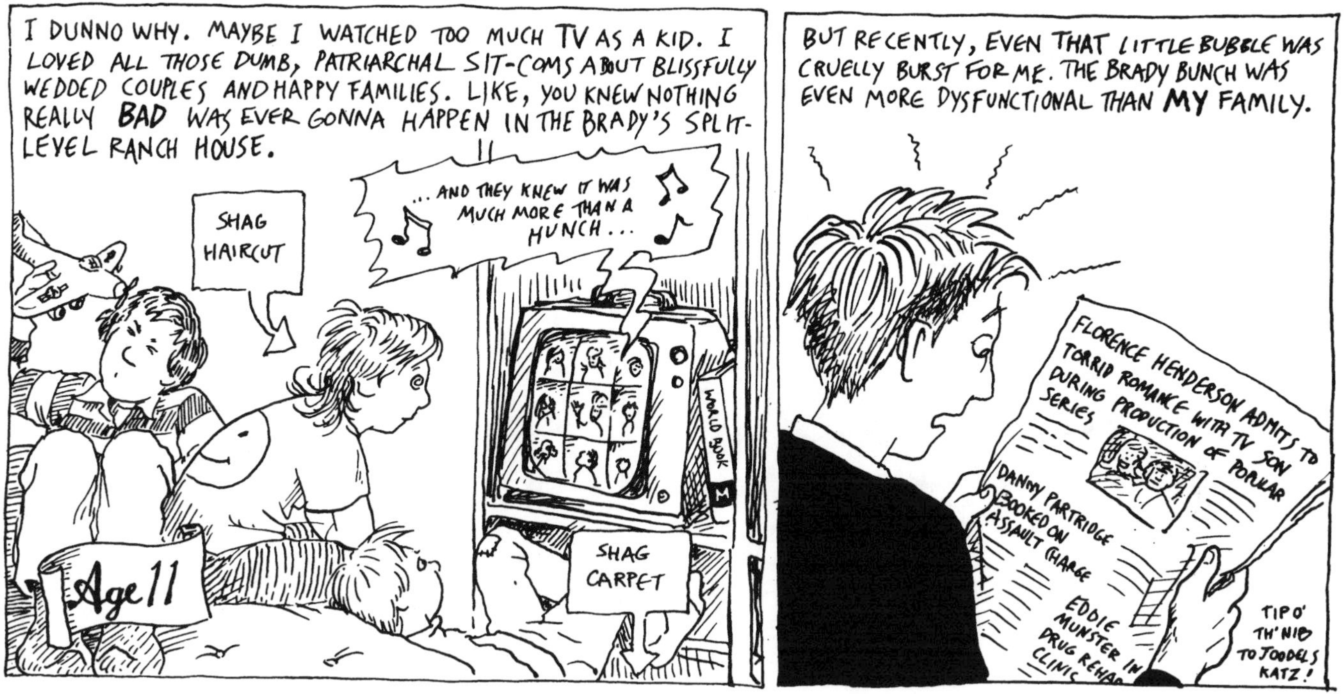
I DUNNO WHY. MAYBE I WATCHED TOO MUCH TV AS A KID. I LOVED ALL THOSE DUMB, PATRIARCHAL SIT-COMS ABOUT BLISSFULLY WEDDED COUPLES AND HAPPY FAMILIES. LIKE, YOU KNEW NOTHING REALLY BAD WAS EVER GONNA HAPPEN IN THE BRADY'S SPLIT-LEVEL RANCH HOUSE.
SHAG HAIRCUT
...AND THEY KNEW IT WAS MUCH MORE THAN A HUNCH...
WORLD BOOK
M
Age 11
SHAG CARPET
BUT RECENTLY, EVEN THAT LITTLE BUBBLE WAS CRUELLY BURST FOR ME. THE BRADY BUNCH WAS EVEN MORE DYSFUNCTIONAL THAN MY FAMILY.
FLORENCE HENDERSON ADMITS TO TORRID ROMANCE WITH TV SON DURING PRODUCTION OF POPULAR SERIES
DANNY PARTRIDGE BOOKED ON ASSAULT CHARGE
EDDIE MUNSTER IN DRUG REHAB CLINIC
TIP O' TH' NIB TO JOODELS KATZ!

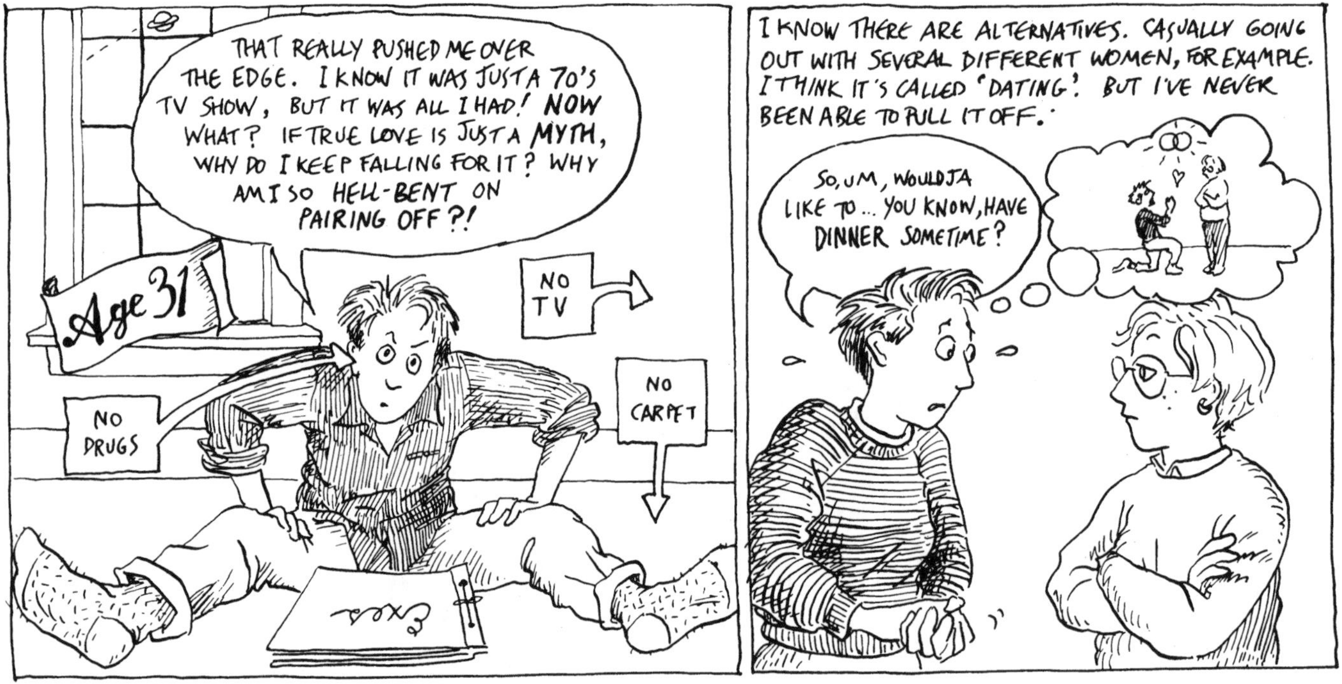
THAT REALLY PUSHED ME OVER THE EDGE. I KNOW IT WAS JUST A 70'S TV SHOW, BUT IT WAS ALL I HAD! NOW WHAT? IF TRUE LOVE IS JUST A MYTH, WHY DO I KEEP FALLING FOR IT? WHY AM I SO HELL-BENT ON PAIRING OFF?!
Age 31
NO TV
NO DRUGS
NO CARPET
I KNOW THERE ARE ALTERNATIVES. CASUALLY GOING OUT WITH SEVERAL DIFFERENT WOMEN, FOR EXAMPLE. I THINK IT'S CALLED 'DATING'. BUT I'VE NEVER BEEN ABLE TO PULL IT OFF.
SO, UM, WOULDJA LIKE TO... YOU KNOW, HAVE DINNER SOMETIME?

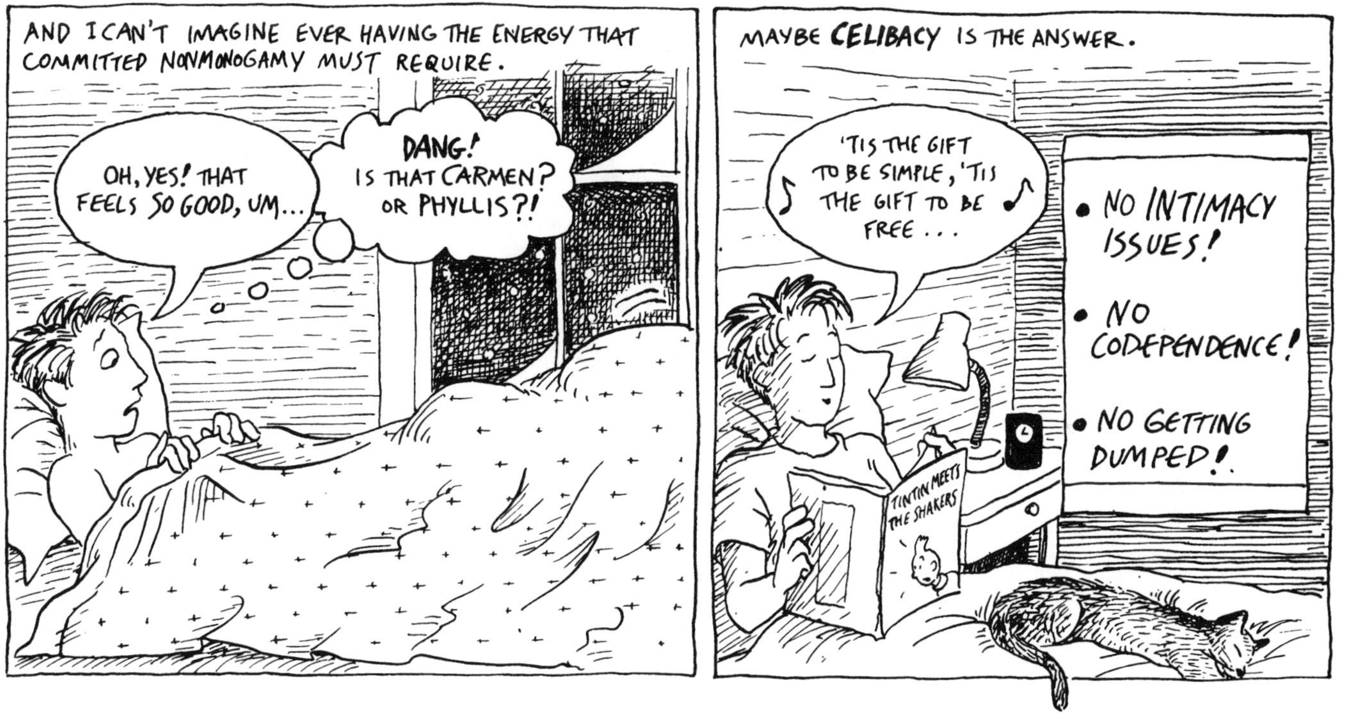
AND I CAN'T IMAGINE EVER HAVING THE ENERGY THAT COMMITTED NONMONOGAMY MUST REQUIRE.
OH, YES! THAT FEELS SO GOOD, UM...
DANG! IS THAT CARMEN? OR PHYLLIS?!
MAYBE CELIBACY IS THE ANSWER.
'TIS THE GIFT TO BE SIMPLE, 'TIS THE GIFT TO BE FREE . . .
TINTIN MEETS THE SHAKERS
• NO INTIMACY ISSUES!
• NO CODEPENDENCE!
• NO GETTING DUMPED!

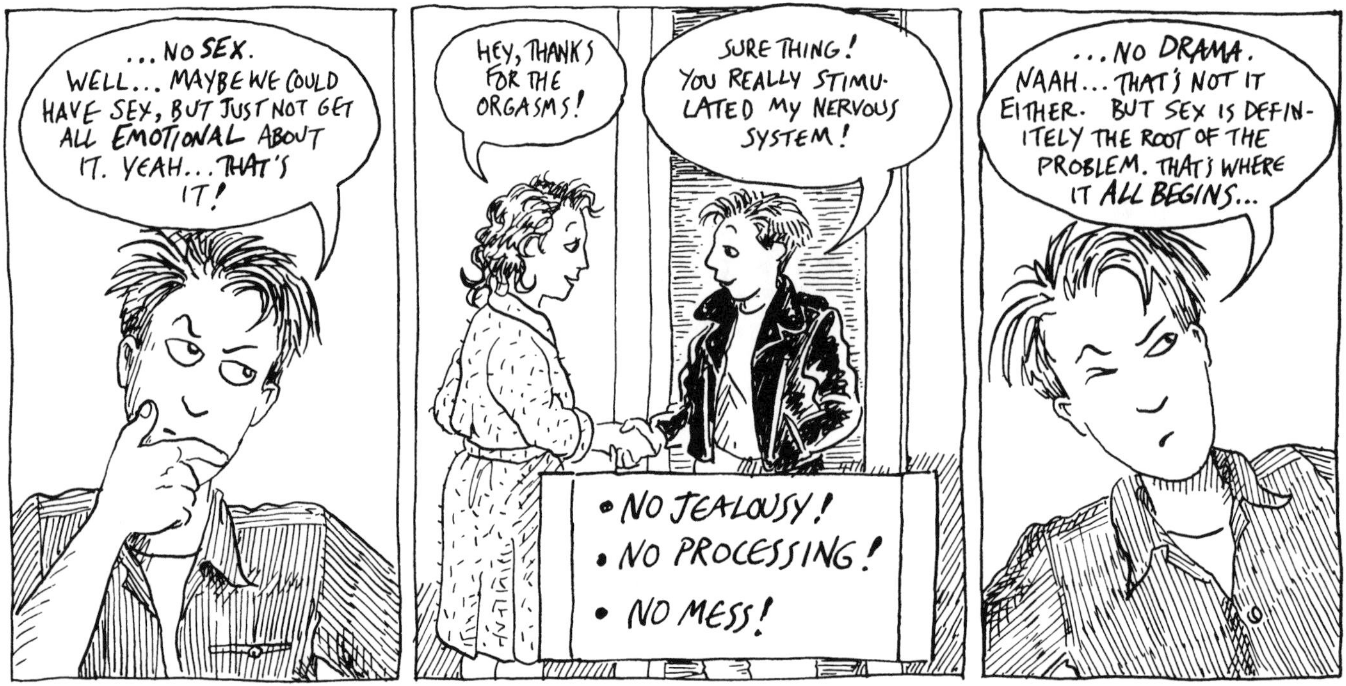
...NO SEX. WELL... MAYBE WE COULD HAVE SEX, BUT JUST NOT GET ALL EMOTIONAL ABOUT IT. YEAH... THAT'S IT!
HEY, THANKS FOR THE ORGASMS!
SURE THING! YOU REALLY STIMULATED MY NERVOUS SYSTEM!
• NO JEALOUSY!
• NO PROCESSING!
• NO MESS!
...NO DRAMA. NAAH... THAT'S NOT IT EITHER. BUT SEX IS DEFINITELY THE ROOT OF THE PROBLEM. THAT'S WHERE IT ALL BEGINS...

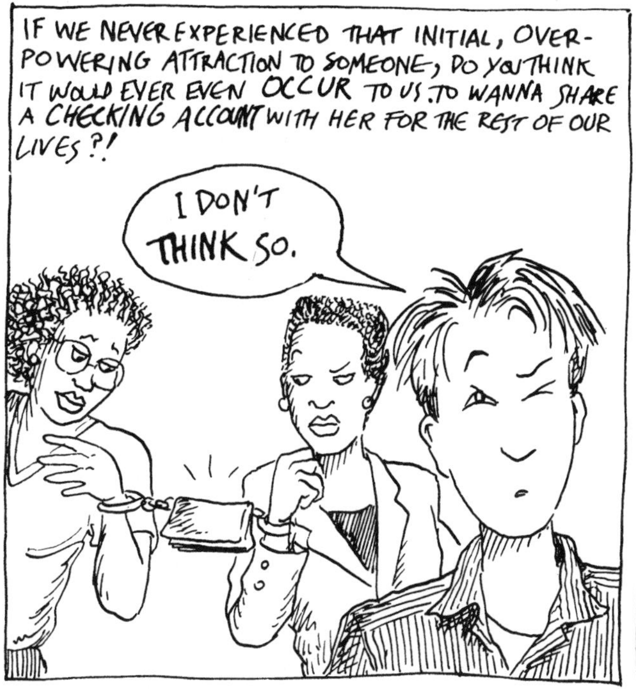
IF WE NEVER EXPERIENCED THAT INITIAL, OVERPOWERING ATTRACTION TO SOMEONE, DO YOU THINK IT WOULD EVER EVEN OCCUR TO US TO WANNA SHARE A CHECKING ACCOUNT WITH HER FOR THE REST OF OUR LIVES?!
I DON'T THINK SO.

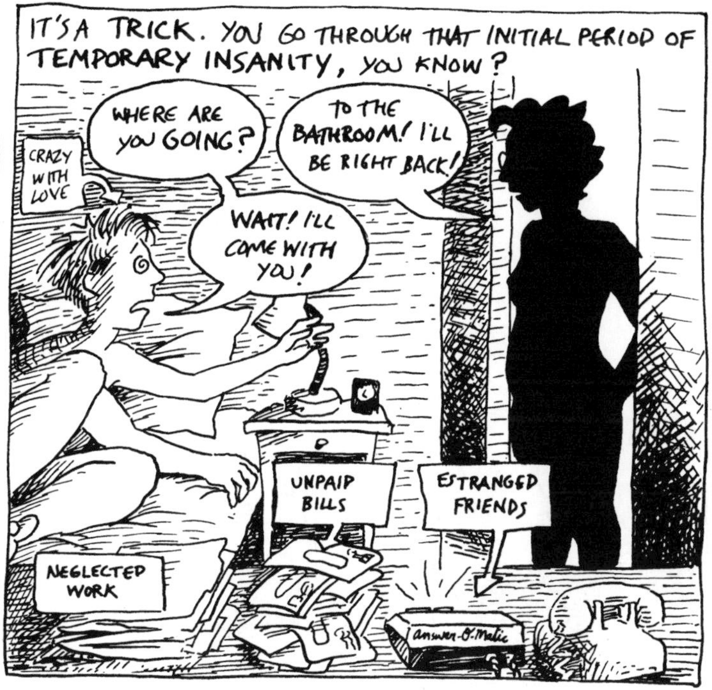
IT'S A TRICK. YOU GO THROUGH THAT INITIAL PERIOD OF TEMPORARY INSANITY, YOU KNOW?
CRAZY WITH LOVE
WHERE ARE YOU GOING?
TO THE BATHROOM! I'LL BE RIGHT BACK!
WAIT! I'LL COME WITH YOU!
UNPAID BILLS
ESTRANGED FRIENDS
NEGLECTED WORK
Answer-O-Matic

THEN YOU WAKE UP 6 MONTHS LATER . . . AND FIND THAT THE TWO OF YOU ARE JOINED AT THE FRONTAL LOBE.

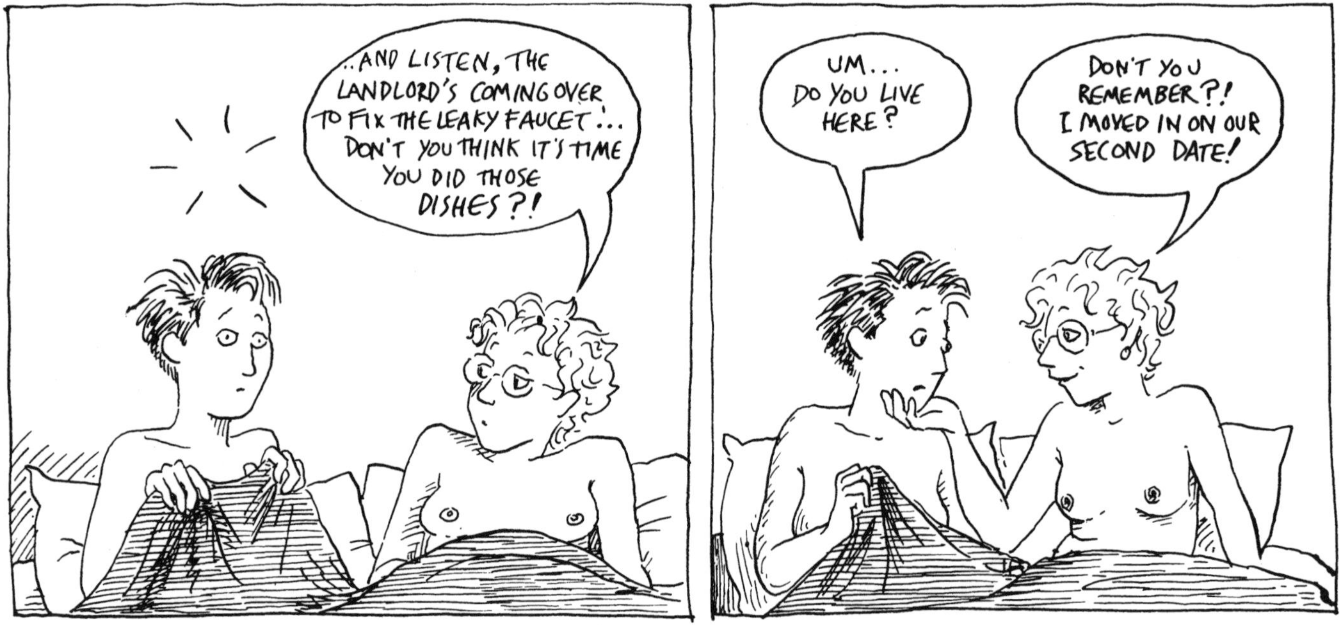
..AND LISTEN, THE LANDLORD'S COMING OVER TO FIX THE LEAKY FAUCET!.. DON'T YOU THINK IT'S TIME YOU DID THOSE DISHES?!
UM... DO YOU LIVE HERE?
DON'T YOU REMEMBER?! I MOVED IN ON OUR SECOND DATE!

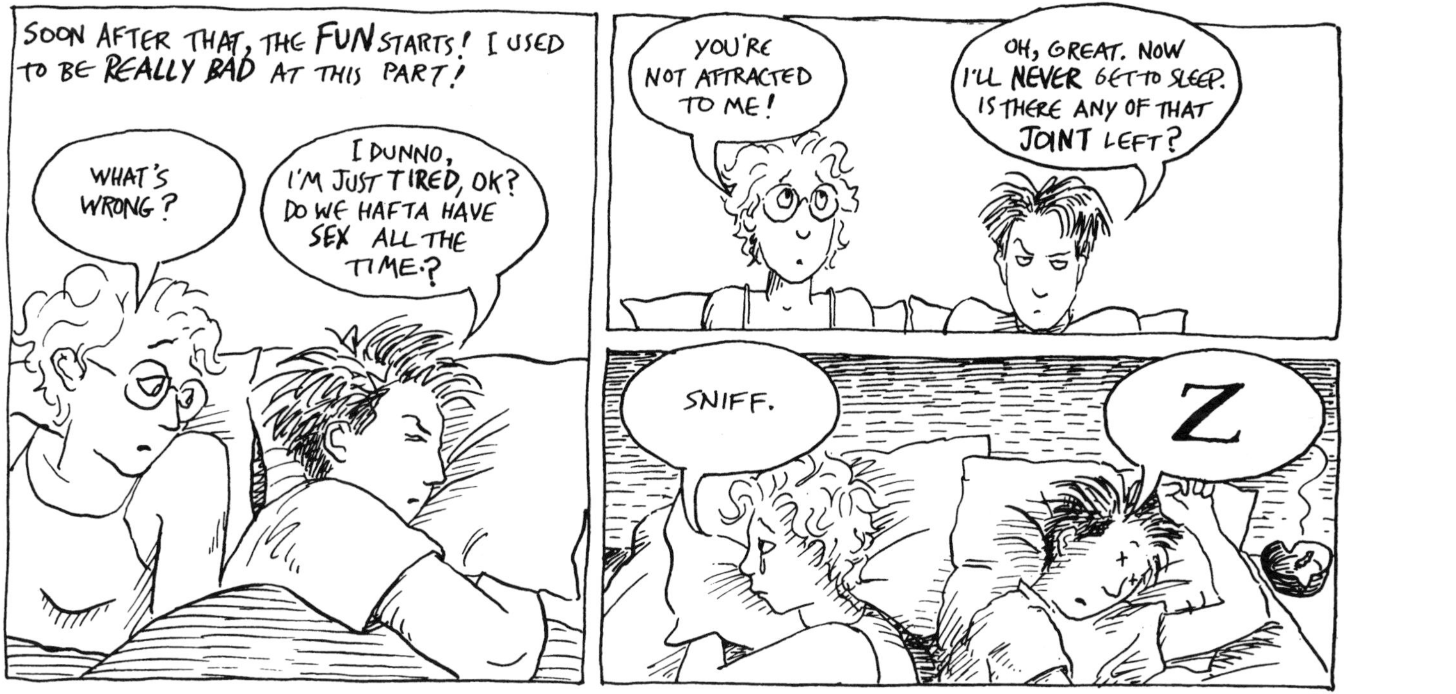
SOON AFTER THAT, THE FUN STARTS! I USED TO BE REALLY BAD AT THIS PART!
WHAT'S WRONG?
I DUNNO, I'M JUST TIRED, OK? DO WE HAFTA HAVE SEX ALL THE TIME?
YOU'RE NOT ATTRACTED TO ME!
OH, GREAT. NOW I'LL NEVER GET TO SLEEP. IS THERE ANY OF THAT JOINT LEFT?
SNIFF.
Z

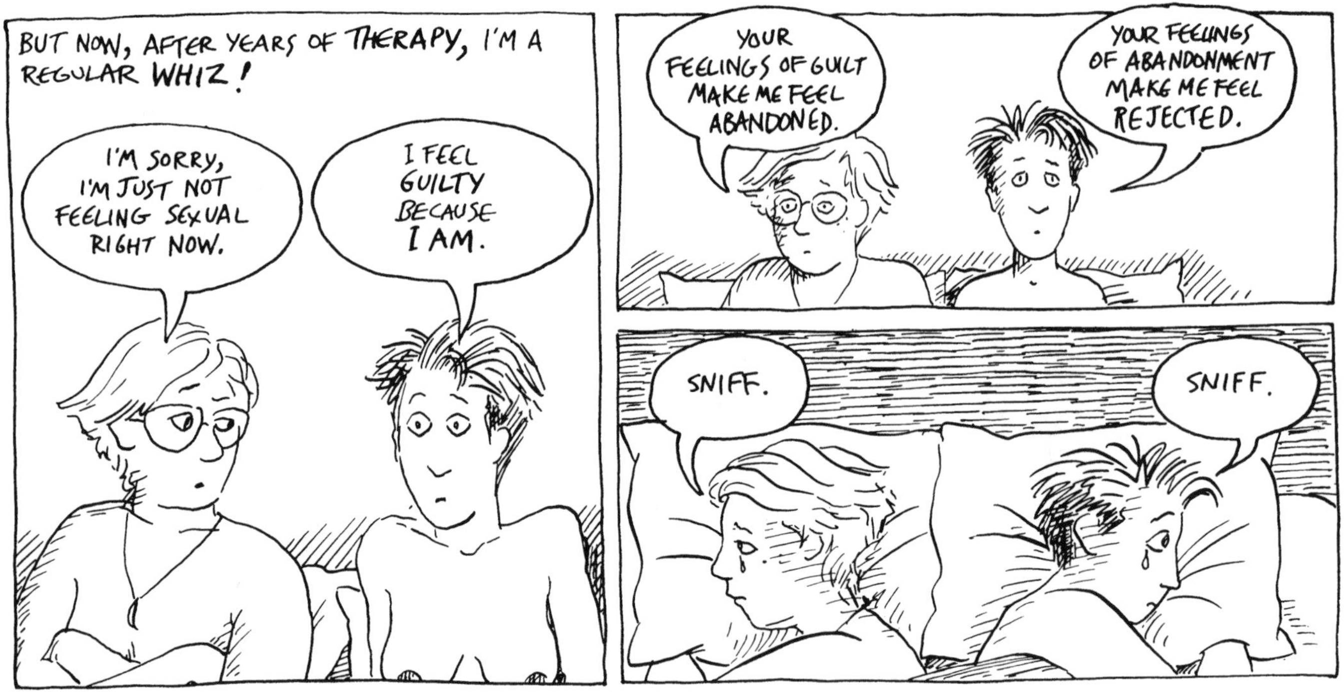
BUT NOW, AFTER YEARS OF THERAPY, I'M A REGULAR WHIZ!
I'M SORRY, I'M JUST NOT FEELING SEXUAL RIGHT NOW.
I FEEL GUILTY BECAUSE I AM.
YOUR FEELINGS OF GUILT MAKE ME FEEL ABANDONED.
YOUR FEELINGS OF ABANDONMENT MAKE ME FEEL REJECTED.
SNIFF.
SNIFF.

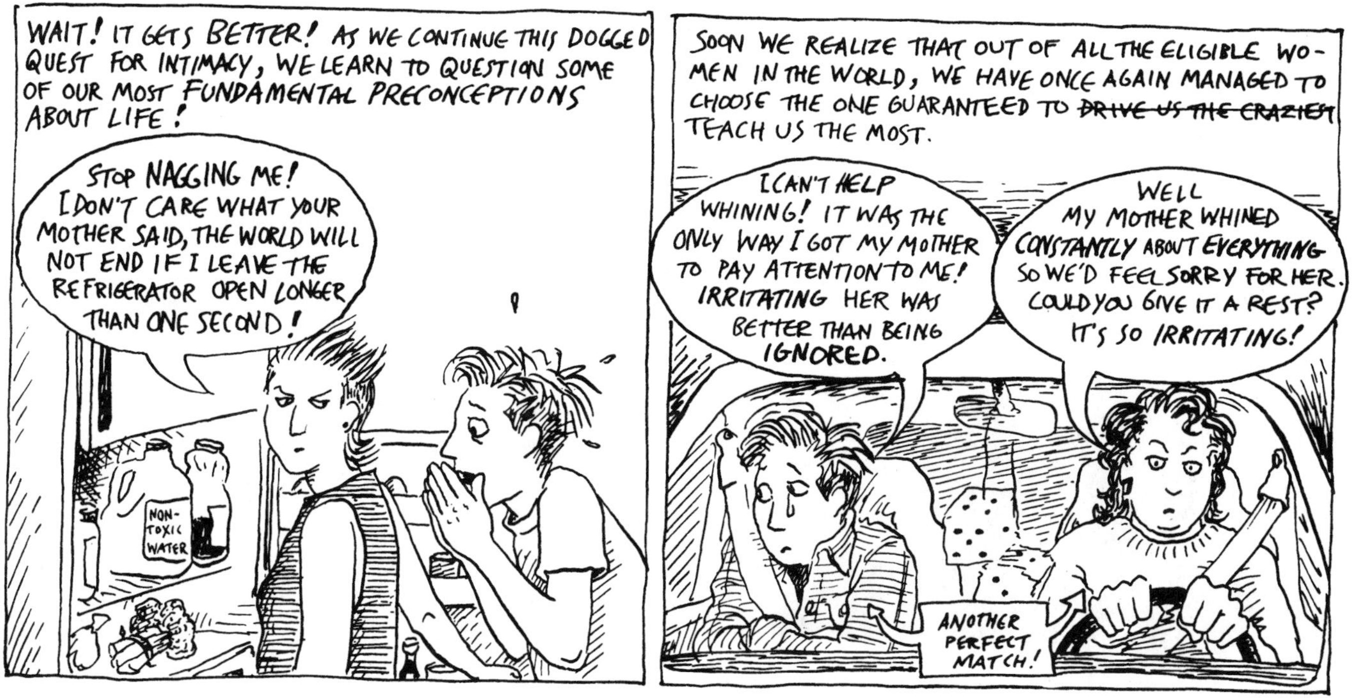
WAIT! IT GETS BETTER! AS WE CONTINUE THIS DOGGED QUEST FOR INTIMACY, WE LEARN TO QUESTION SOME OF OUR MOST FUNDAMENTAL PRECONCEPTIONS ABOUT LIFE!
STOP NAGGING ME! I DON'T CARE WHAT YOUR MOTHER SAID, THE WORLD WILL NOT END IF I LEAVE THE REFRIGERATOR OPEN LONGER THAN ONE SECOND!
NON-TOXIC WATER
SOON WE REALIZE THAT OUT OF ALL THE ELIGIBLE WOMEN IN THE WORLD, WE HAVE ONCE AGAIN MANAGED TO CHOOSE THE ONE GUARANTEED TO ~~DRIVE US THE CRAZIEST~~ TEACH US THE MOST.
I CAN'T HELP WHINING! IT WAS THE ONLY WAY I GOT MY MOTHER TO PAY ATTENTION TO ME! IRRITATING HER WAS BETTER THAN BEING IGNORED.
WELL MY MOTHER WHINED CONSTANTLY ABOUT EVERYTHING SO WE'D FEEL SORRY FOR HER. COULD YOU GIVE IT A REST? IT'S SO IRRITATING!
ANOTHER PERFECT MATCH!

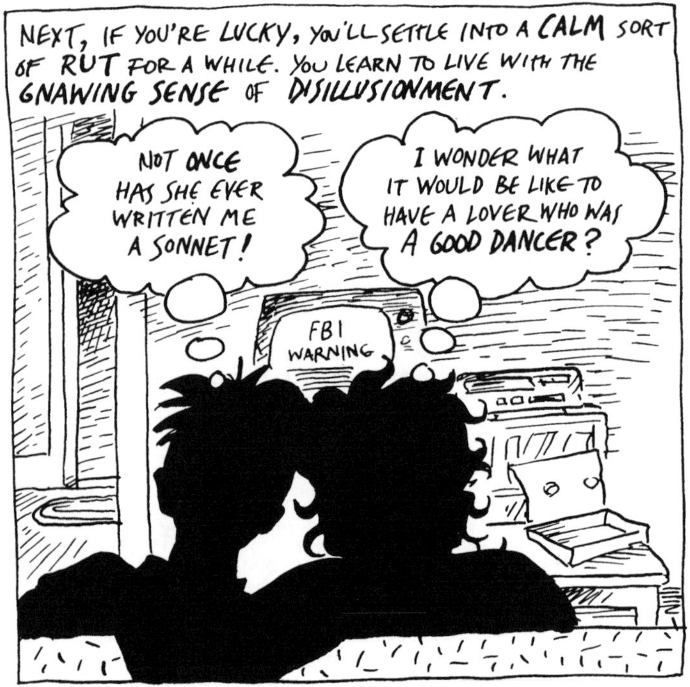
NEXT, IF YOU'RE LUCKY, YOU'LL SETTLE INTO A CALM SORT OF RUT FOR A WHILE. YOU LEARN TO LIVE WITH THE GNAWING SENSE OF DISILLUSIONMENT.
NOT ONCE HAS SHE EVER WRITTEN ME A SONNET!
I WONDER WHAT IT WOULD BE LIKE TO HAVE A LOVER WHO WAS A GOOD DANCER?
FBI WARNING

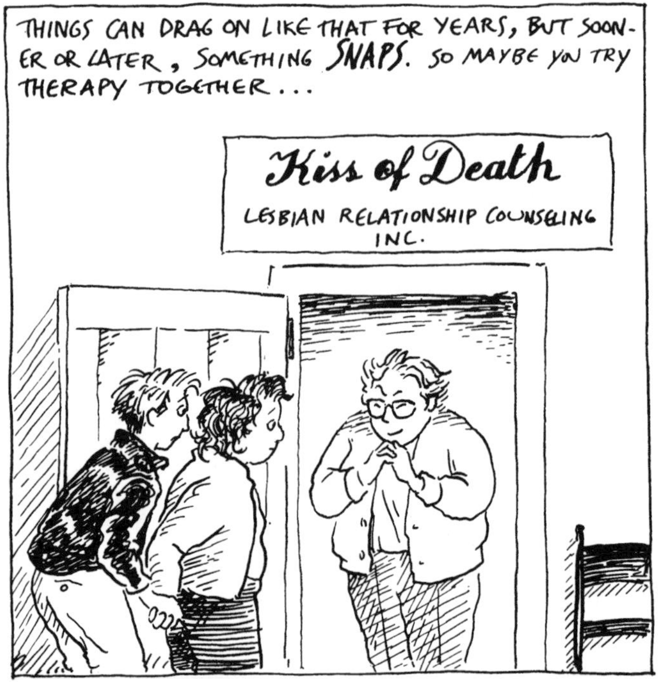
THINGS CAN DRAG ON LIKE THAT FOR YEARS, BUT SOONER OR LATER, SOMETHING SNAPS. SO MAYBE YOU TRY THERAPY TOGETHER...
Kiss of Death
LESBIAN RELATIONSHIP COUNSELING INC.

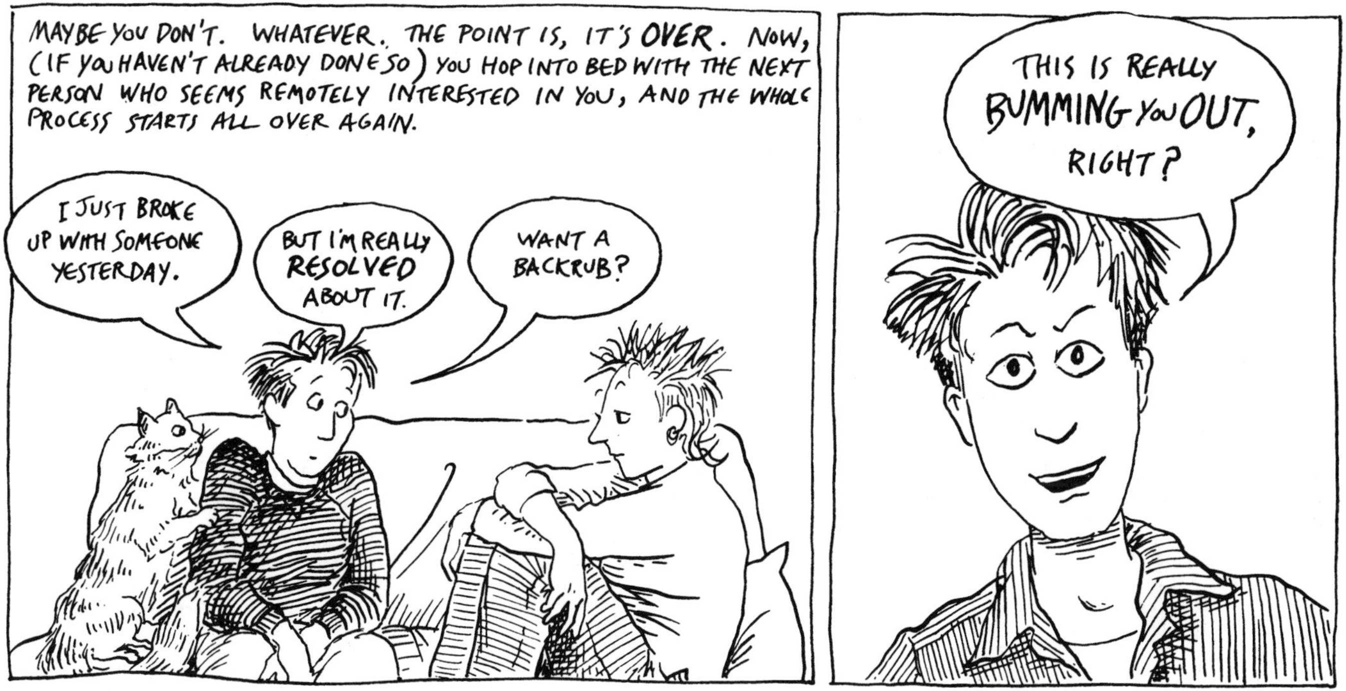
MAYBE YOU DON'T. WHATEVER. THE POINT IS, IT'S **OVER**. NOW, (IF YOU HAVEN'T ALREADY DONE SO) YOU HOP INTO BED WITH THE NEXT PERSON WHO SEEMS REMOTELY INTERESTED IN YOU, AND THE WHOLE PROCESS STARTS ALL OVER AGAIN.
I JUST BROKE UP WITH SOMEONE YESTERDAY.
BUT I'M REALLY **RESOLVED** ABOUT IT.
WANT A BACKRUB?
THIS IS REALLY **BUMMING** YOU **OUT**, RIGHT?

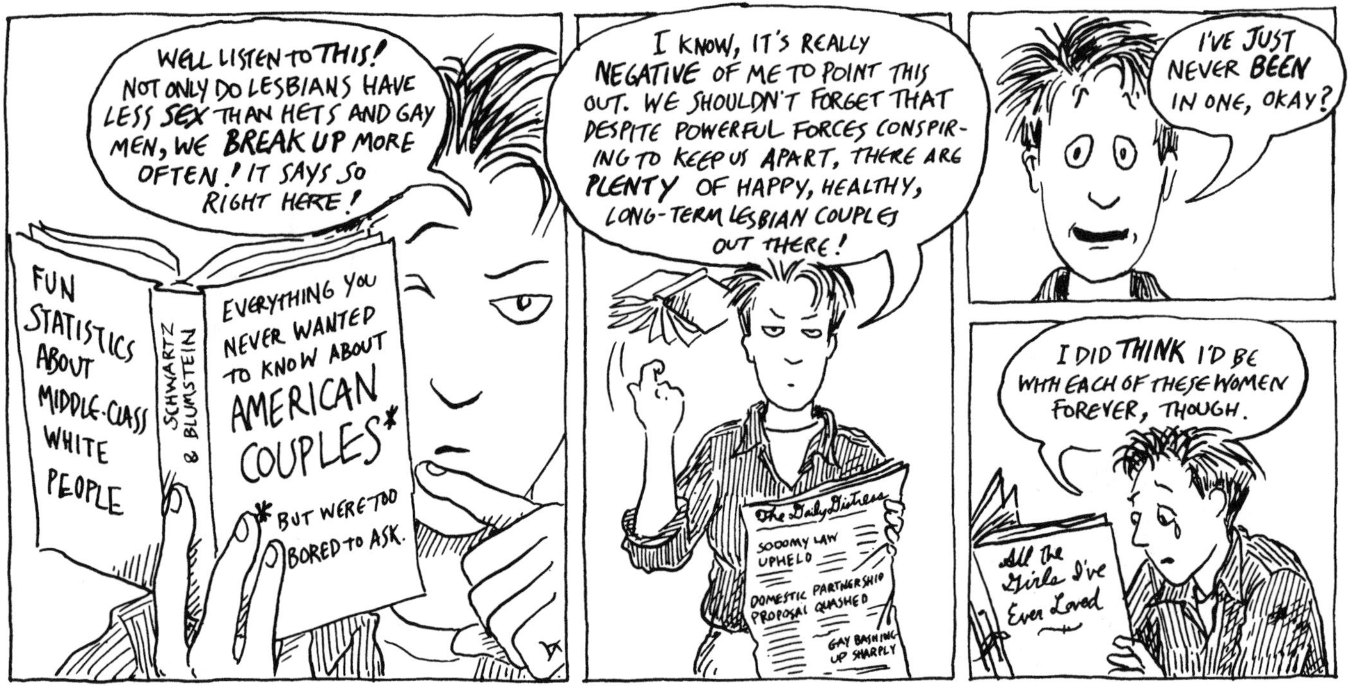
WELL LISTEN TO THIS! NOT ONLY DO LESBIANS HAVE LESS SEX THAN HETS AND GAY MEN, WE BREAK UP MORE OFTEN! IT SAYS SO RIGHT HERE!
FUN STATISTICS ABOUT MIDDLE-CLASS WHITE PEOPLE
SCHWARTZ & BLUMSTEIN
EVERYTHING YOU NEVER WANTED TO KNOW ABOUT AMERICAN COUPLES*
* BUT WERE TOO BORED TO ASK.
I KNOW, IT'S REALLY NEGATIVE OF ME TO POINT THIS OUT. WE SHOULDN'T FORGET THAT DESPITE POWERFUL FORCES CONSPIRING TO KEEP US APART, THERE ARE PLENTY OF HAPPY, HEALTHY, LONG-TERM LESBIAN COUPLES OUT THERE!
The Daily Distress
SODOMY LAW UPHELD
DOMESTIC PARTNERSHIP PROPOSAL QUASHED
GAY BASHING UP SHARPLY
I'VE JUST NEVER BEEN IN ONE, OKAY?
I DID THINK I'D BE WITH EACH OF THESE WOMEN FOREVER, THOUGH.
All the Girls I've Ever Loved

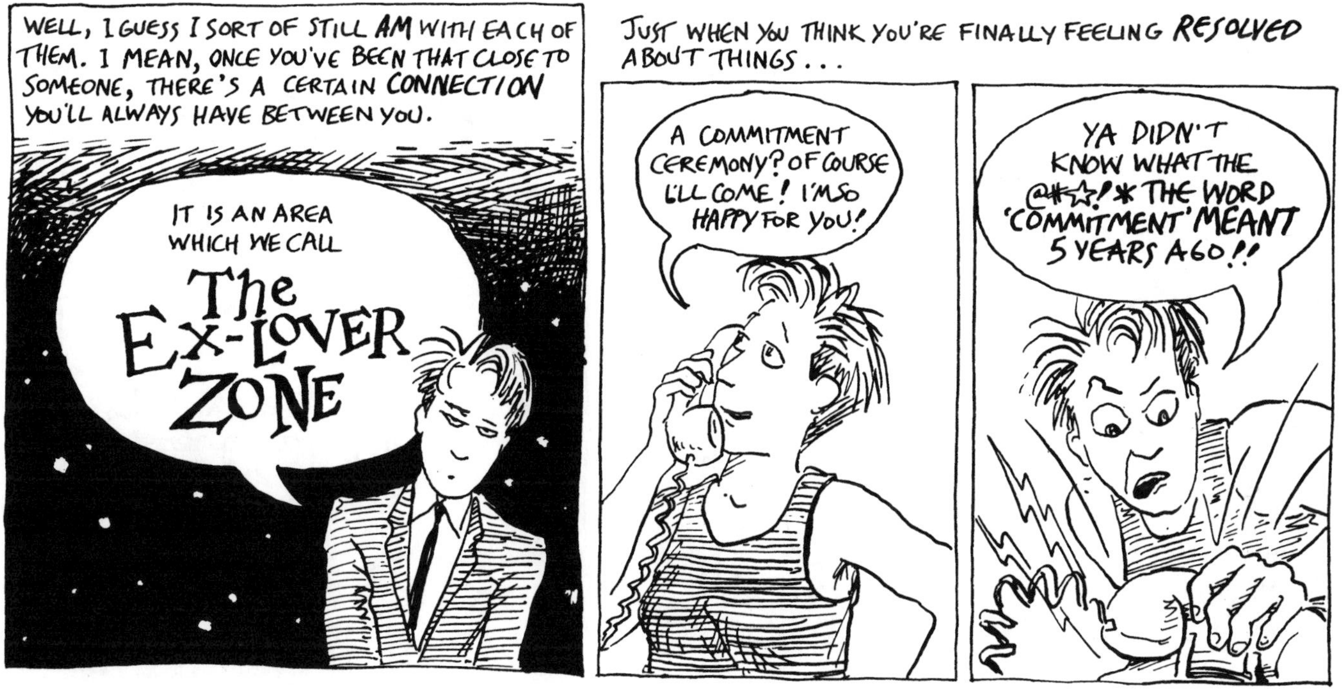
WELL, I GUESS I SORT OF STILL AM WITH EACH OF THEM. I MEAN, ONCE YOU'VE BEEN THAT CLOSE TO SOMEONE, THERE'S A CERTAIN CONNECTION YOU'LL ALWAYS HAVE BETWEEN YOU.
IT IS AN AREA WHICH WE CALL The EX-LOVER ZONE
JUST WHEN YOU THINK YOU'RE FINALLY FEELING RESOLVED ABOUT THINGS . . .
A COMMITMENT CEREMONY? OF COURSE I'LL COME! I'M SO HAPPY FOR YOU!
YA DIDN'T KNOW WHAT THE @#☆!* THE WORD 'COMMITMENT' MEANT 5 YEARS AGO!!

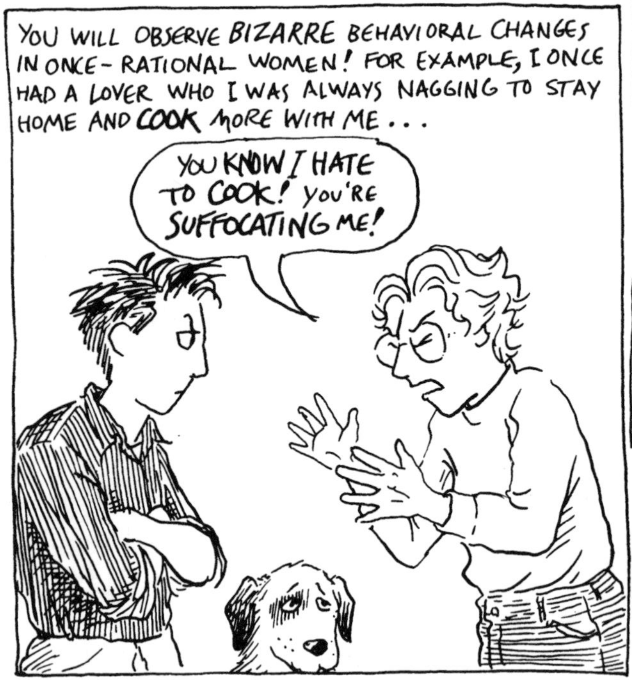
YOU WILL OBSERVE BIZARRE BEHAVIORAL CHANGES IN ONCE-RATIONAL WOMEN! FOR EXAMPLE, I ONCE HAD A LOVER WHO I WAS ALWAYS NAGGING TO STAY HOME AND COOK MORE WITH ME . . .
YOU KNOW I HATE TO COOK! YOU'RE SUFFOCATING ME!

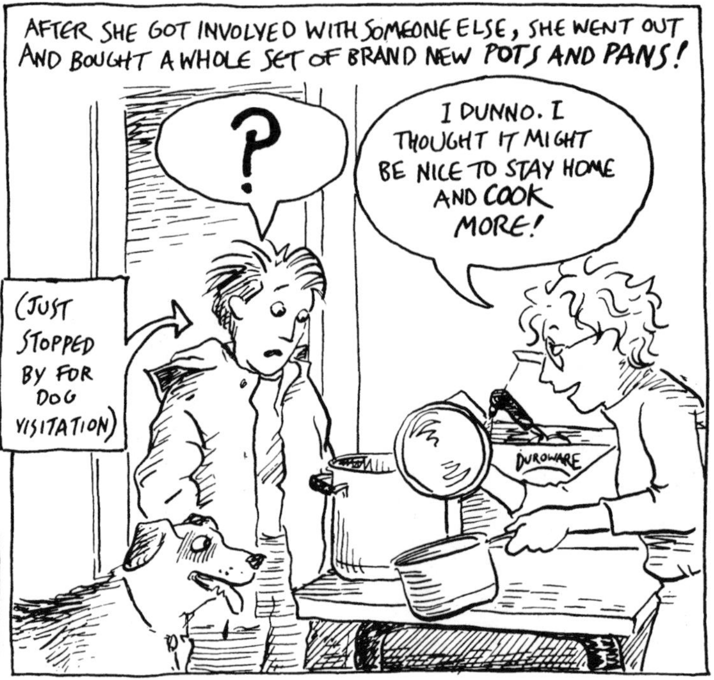
AFTER SHE GOT INVOLVED WITH SOMEONE ELSE, SHE WENT OUT AND BOUGHT A WHOLE SET OF BRAND NEW POTS AND PANS!
(JUST STOPPED BY FOR DOG VISITATION)
?
I DUNNO. I THOUGHT IT MIGHT BE NICE TO STAY HOME AND COOK MORE!
DUROWARE

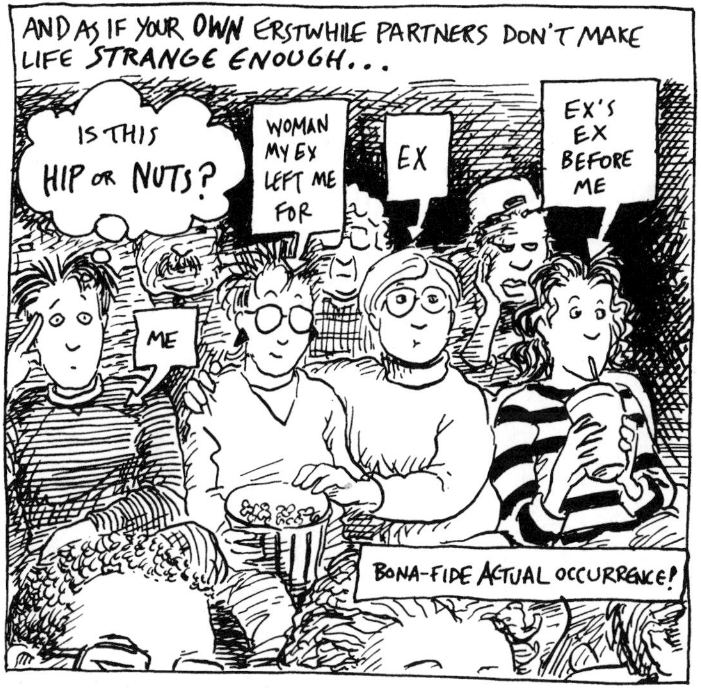
AND AS IF YOUR OWN ERSTWHILE PARTNERS DON'T MAKE LIFE STRANGE ENOUGH...
IS THIS HIP OR NUTS?
ME
WOMAN MY EX LEFT ME FOR
EX
EX'S EX BEFORE ME
BONA-FIDE ACTUAL OCCURRENCE!

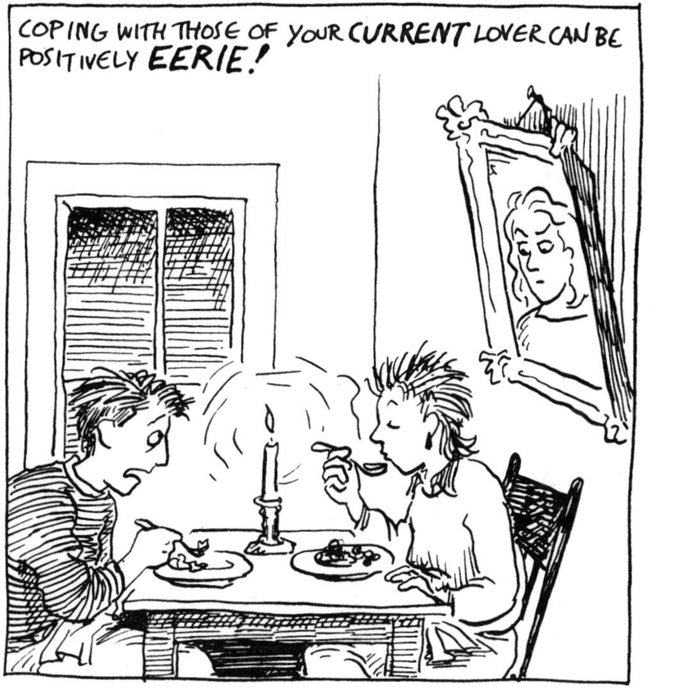
COPING WITH THOSE OF YOUR CURRENT LOVER CAN BE POSITIVELY EERIE!

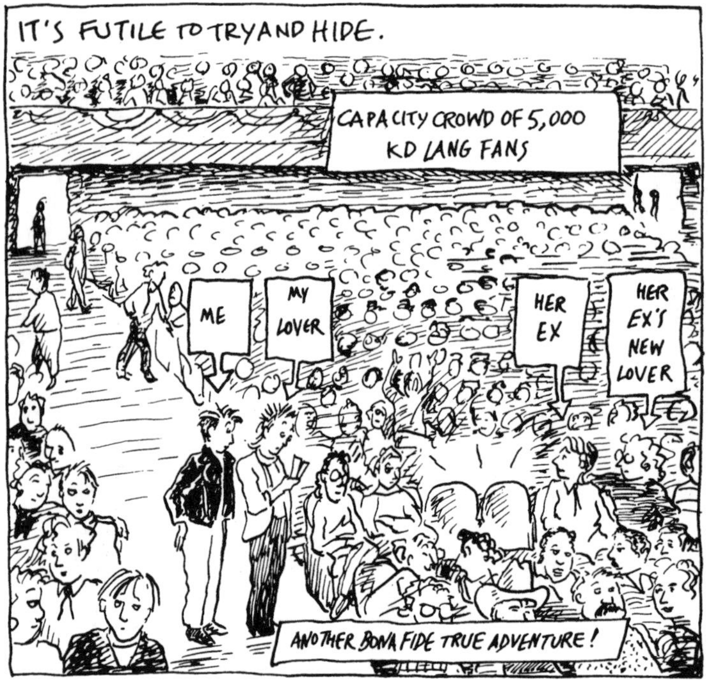

IT'S FUTILE TO TRY AND HIDE.
CAPACITY CROWD OF 5,000 KD LANG FANS
ME
MY LOVER
HER EX
HER EX'S NEW LOVER
ANOTHER BONA FIDE TRUE ADVENTURE!

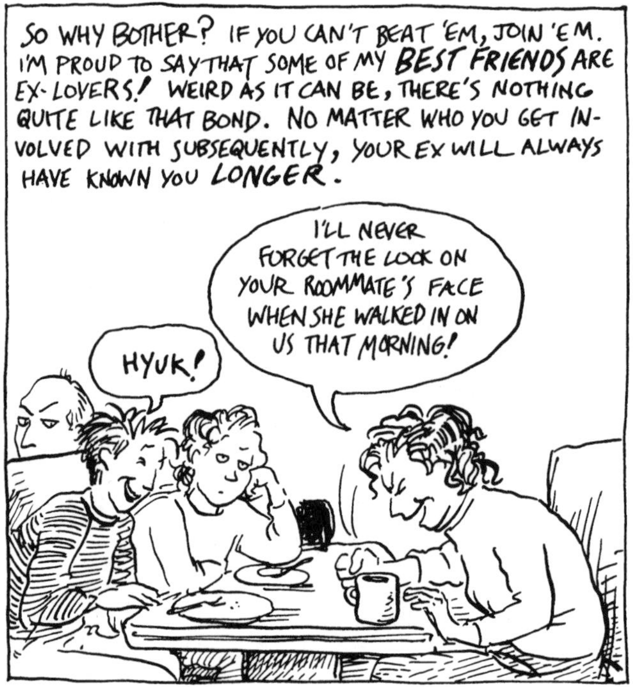

SO WHY BOTHER? IF YOU CAN'T BEAT 'EM, JOIN 'EM. I'M PROUD TO SAY THAT SOME OF MY BEST FRIENDS ARE EX-LOVERS! WEIRD AS IT CAN BE, THERE'S NOTHING QUITE LIKE THAT BOND. NO MATTER WHO YOU GET INVOLVED WITH SUBSEQUENTLY, YOUR EX WILL ALWAYS HAVE KNOWN YOU LONGER.
HYUK!
I'LL NEVER FORGET THE LOOK ON YOUR ROOMMATE'S FACE WHEN SHE WALKED IN ON US THAT MORNING!

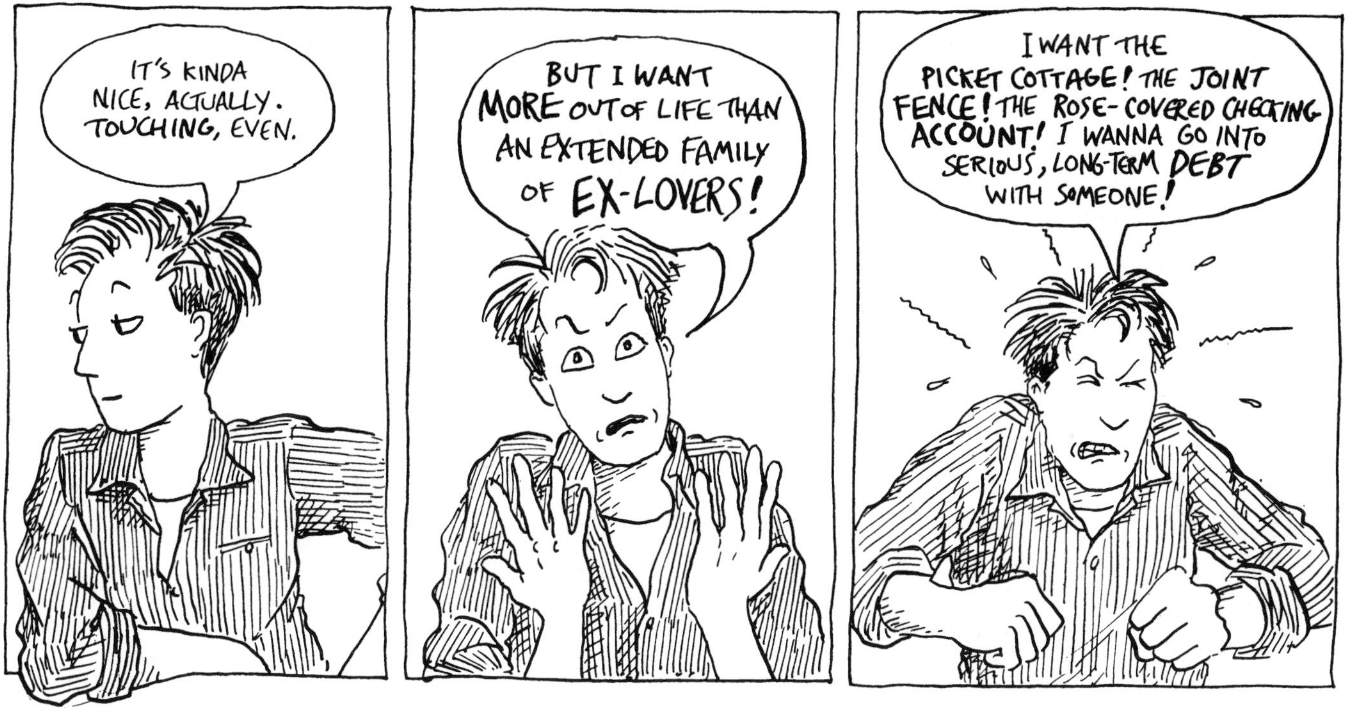
IT'S KINDA NICE, ACTUALLY. TOUCHING, EVEN.
BUT I WANT MORE OUT OF LIFE THAN AN EXTENDED FAMILY OF EX-LOVERS!
I WANT THE PICKET COTTAGE! THE JOINT FENCE! THE ROSE-COVERED CHECKING ACCOUNT! I WANNA GO INTO SERIOUS, LONG-TERM DEBT WITH SOMEONE!

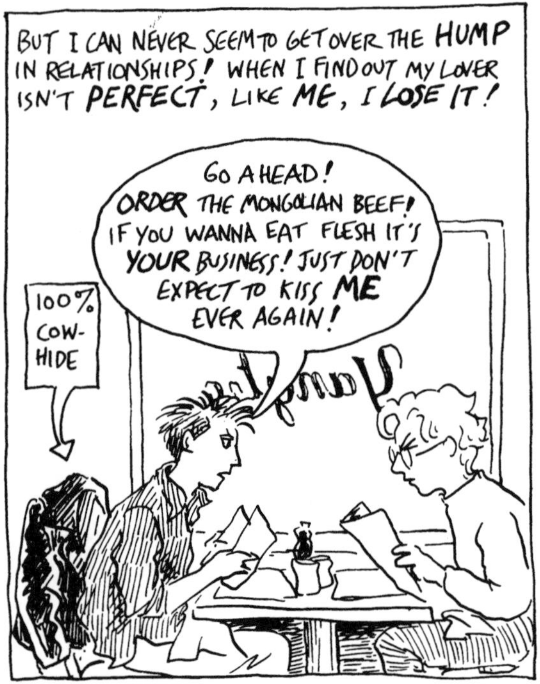
BUT I CAN NEVER SEEM TO GET OVER THE HUMP IN RELATIONSHIPS! WHEN I FIND OUT MY LOVER ISN'T PERFECT, LIKE ME, I LOSE IT!
GO AHEAD! ORDER THE MONGOLIAN BEEF! IF YOU WANNA EAT FLESH IT'S YOUR BUSINESS! JUST DON'T EXPECT TO KISS ME EVER AGAIN!
100% COW-HIDE

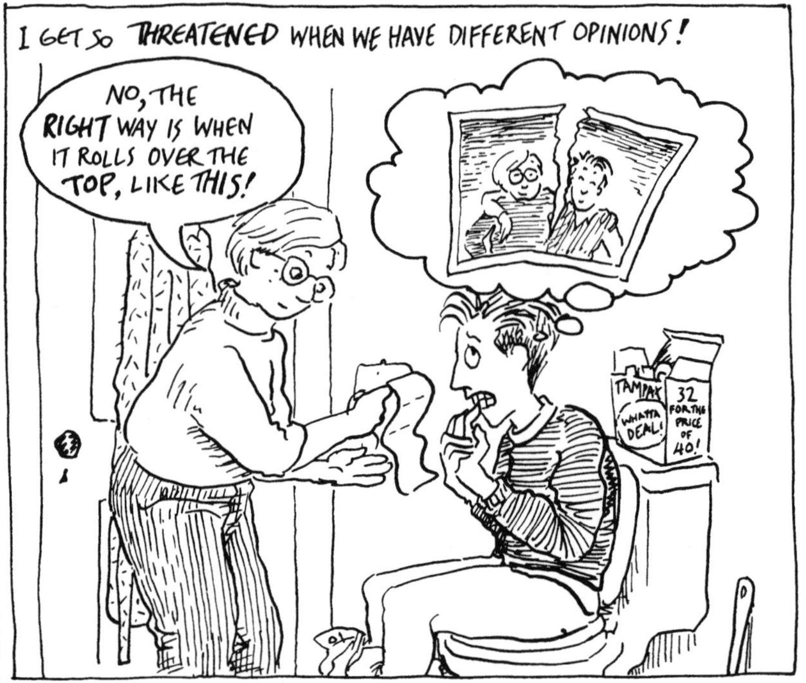
I GET SO THREATENED WHEN WE HAVE DIFFERENT OPINIONS!
NO, THE RIGHT WAY IS WHEN IT ROLLS OVER THE TOP, LIKE THIS!
TAMPAX
WHATTA DEAL!
32 FOR THE PRICE OF 40!

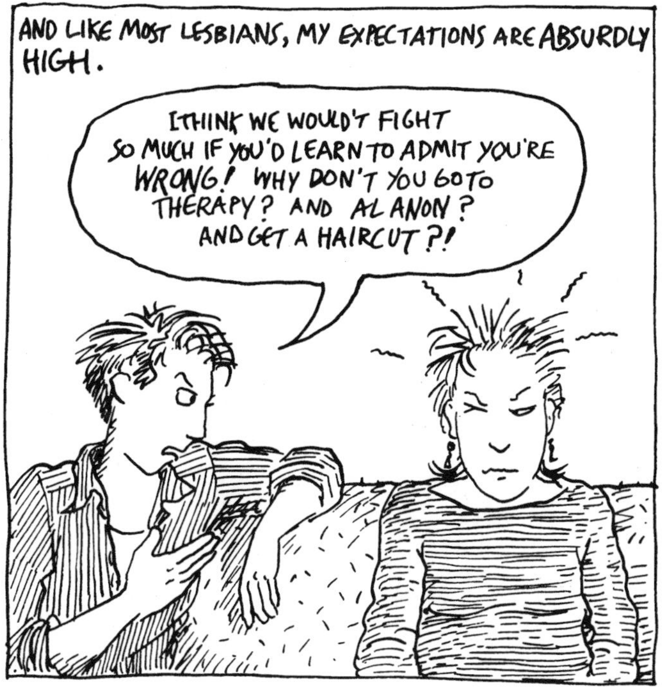
AND LIKE MOST LESBIANS, MY EXPECTATIONS ARE ABSURDLY HIGH.
I THINK WE WOULD'T FIGHT SO MUCH IF YOU'D LEARN TO ADMIT YOU'RE WRONG! WHY DON'T YOU GO TO THERAPY? AND AL ANON? AND GET A HAIRCUT?!

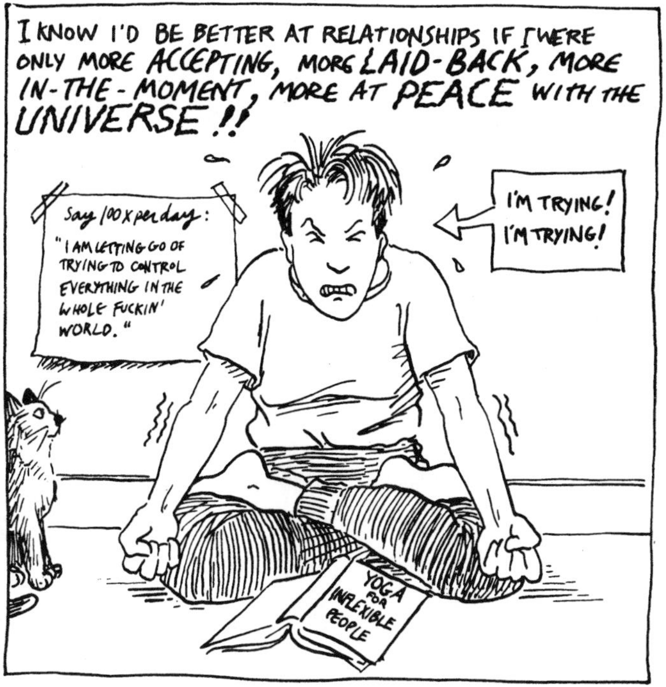
I KNOW I'D BE BETTER AT RELATIONSHIPS IF I WERE ONLY MORE ACCEPTING, MORE LAID-BACK, MORE IN-THE-MOMENT, MORE AT PEACE WITH THE UNIVERSE!!
Say 100 x per day: "I AM LETTING GO OF TRYING TO CONTROL EVERYTHING IN THE WHOLE FUCKIN' WORLD."
I'M TRYING! I'M TRYING!
YOGA FOR INFLEXIBLE PEOPLE

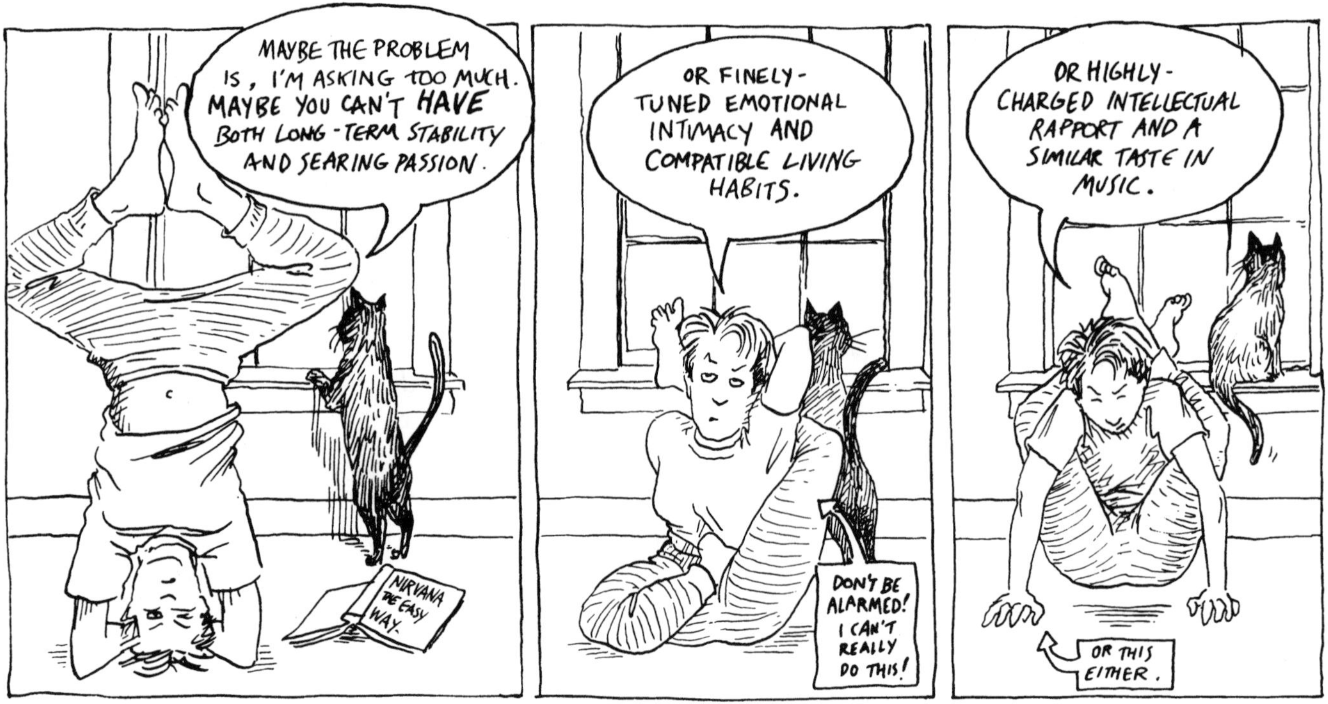
MAYBE THE PROBLEM IS, I'M ASKING TOO MUCH. MAYBE YOU CAN'T HAVE BOTH LONG-TERM STABILITY AND SEARING PASSION.
NIRVANA THE EASY WAY.
OR FINELY-TUNED EMOTIONAL INTIMACY AND COMPATIBLE LIVING HABITS.
DON'T BE ALARMED! I CAN'T REALLY DO THIS!
OR HIGHLY-CHARGED INTELLECTUAL RAPPORT AND A SIMILAR TASTE IN MUSIC.
OR THIS EITHER.

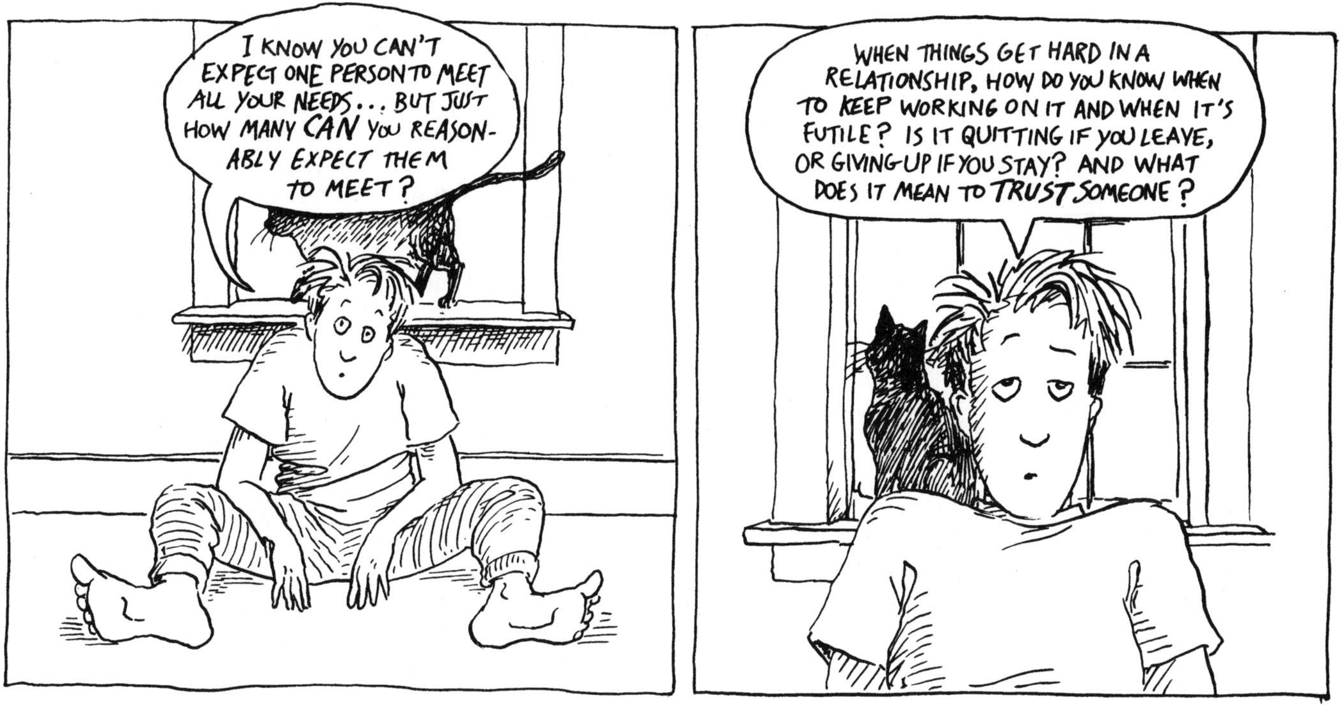
I KNOW YOU CAN'T EXPECT ONE PERSON TO MEET ALL YOUR NEEDS... BUT JUST HOW MANY CAN YOU REASONABLY EXPECT THEM TO MEET?
WHEN THINGS GET HARD IN A RELATIONSHIP, HOW DO YOU KNOW WHEN TO KEEP WORKING ON IT AND WHEN IT'S FUTILE? IS IT QUITTING IF YOU LEAVE, OR GIVING UP IF YOU STAY? AND WHAT DOES IT MEAN TO TRUST SOMEONE?

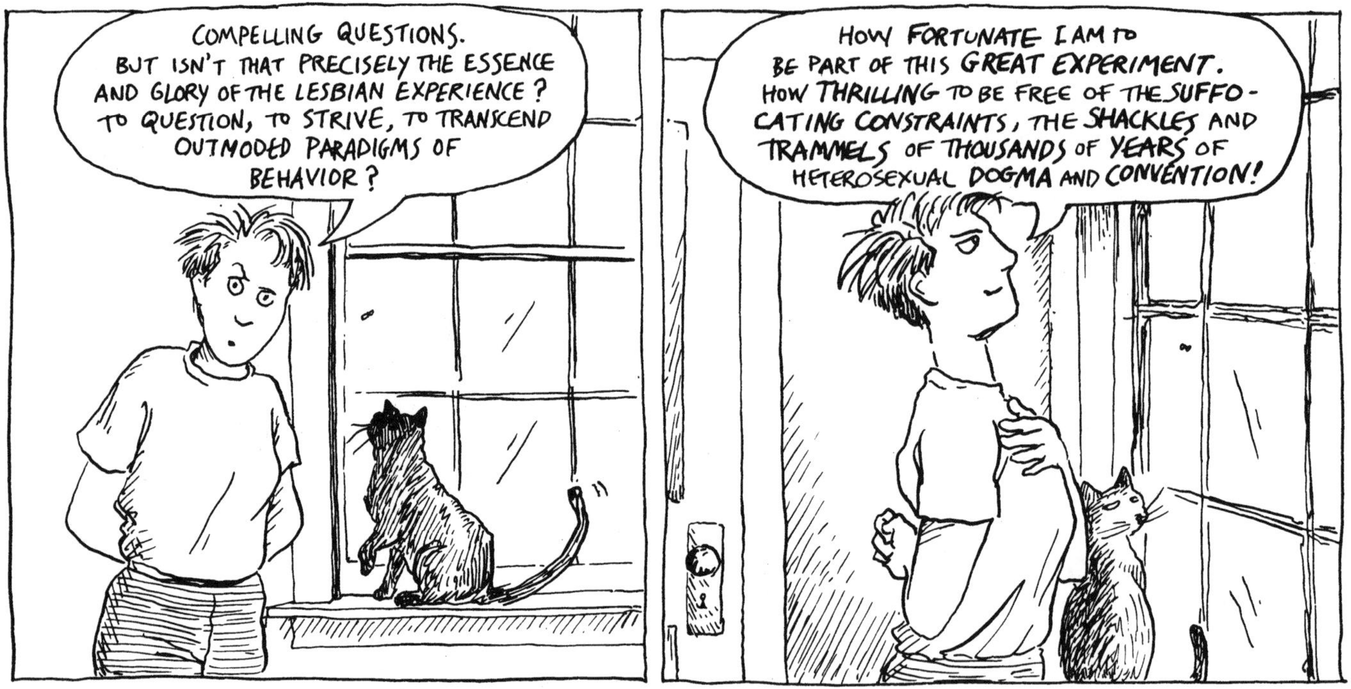
COMPELLING QUESTIONS. BUT ISN'T THAT PRECISELY THE ESSENCE AND GLORY OF THE LESBIAN EXPERIENCE? TO QUESTION, TO STRIVE, TO TRANSCEND OUTMODED PARADIGMS OF BEHAVIOR?
HOW FORTUNATE I AM TO BE PART OF THIS GREAT EXPERIMENT. HOW THRILLING TO BE FREE OF THE SUFFOCATING CONSTRAINTS, THE SHACKLES AND TRAMMELS OF THOUSANDS OF YEARS OF HETEROSEXUAL DOGMA AND CONVENTION!

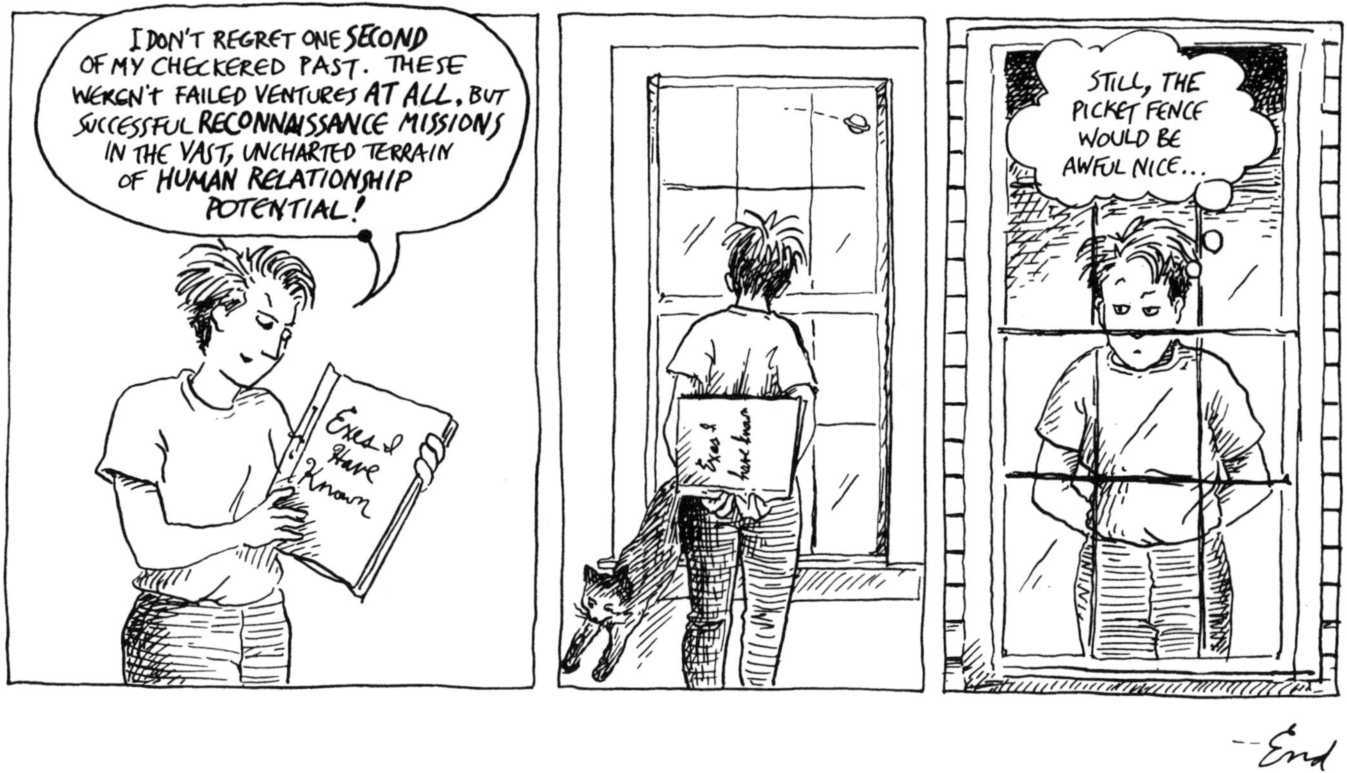
I DON'T REGRET ONE SECOND OF MY CHECKERED PAST. THESE WEREN'T FAILED VENTURES AT ALL, BUT SUCCESSFUL RECONNAISSANCE MISSIONS IN THE VAST, UNCHARTED TERRAIN OF HUMAN RELATIONSHIP POTENTIAL!
Exes I Have Known
Exes I have known
STILL, THE PICKET FENCE WOULD BE AWFUL NICE...
--End